WALKING THE WORLD

Memories and Adventures

By

Alan Cook

ISBN: 1-4140-2041-4 (e-book)
ISBN: 1-4140-2040-6 (Paperback)

Library of Congress Control Number: 2003097669

This book is printed on acid free paper.

Printed in the United States of America
Bloomington, IN

1stBooks — rev. 10/27/03

BOOKS BY ALAN COOK

The Saga of Bill the Hermit
Freedom's Light: Quotations from History's Champions of Freedom
Walking to Denver
Lillian Morgan mysteries:
Thirteen Diamonds
Catch a Falling Knife

ACKNOWLEDGMENTS

Sincere thanks to Ethan Loewenthal, Robert Sweetgall, Noel Blackham and Wendy Bumgardner, walkers all, who contributed in many ways to this book. And to all the other walkers whose quotes and stories I've used.

DEDICATION

To Bonny, who has walked beside me for 39 years.

TABLE OF CONTENTS

PREFACE

MORNING WALK

Step, step, step, step,
left, right, left, right,

rhythm, rhythm, rhythm, rhythm,
chin up, shoulders back,
arms swinging, muscles singing,
blood is coursing through the body,
breathing, breathing, breathing, breathing.
Payoff for this undertaking?
Dawn is breaking, world is waking.

Flowers open, greet the morning,
waft aromas through the air.
Rabbits hopping shyly, scorning
safety of a hidden lair.

Hear the harmonizing voices,
small and mighty join in chorus;
bass, soprano, alto—choices
of cricket, frog and brontosaurus.

Faces kissed by baby breezes,
clouds play tag with newborn sun.
Hummingbird darts, hovers, teases,
Mother Nature's having fun.

Step, step, step, step,
left, right, left, right,
walking, walking, walking, walking,
muscles tensing, senses sensing.

Walking is the world's oldest physical activity for human beings. People have walked since long before bicycles were invented. Walking also became the world's first sporting event, predating the first marathon run by Phidipides to announce the victory of the Greeks over the Persians. Maybe if he had walked to Athens he wouldn't have dropped dead at the finish. Walking requires less equipment than other sports. Anyone can become a walker who has two operational legs with attached feet—real or artificial.

Our ancestors did a lot of walking when they hunted and gathered. (Sometimes they also did some running, by necessity, when what they hunted decided to hunt them.) Husbands and wives would walk to visit their neighbors in other caves, to check out the animal skins their friends sat on and the pictograph murals on their walls, and determine whether they needed to remodel their own caves based on the current fads.

More recently, our ancestors walked because it was the only way to get from point A to point B. There weren't enough horses or camels to go around. The working stiffs who were fortunate enough to have horses or camels found them more valuable as farm animals or beasts of burden than for personal transportation. In addition, many of the roads weren't paved, which made it difficult to ride bicycles and skateboards.

Then along came the internal combustion engine and eventually everybody stopped walking. Well, not everybody. A few intrepid souls still went out on the roads, the sidewalks, the paths and the trails and put one foot in front of the other. Other people stared at them and wondered whether they were executing a new dance step. What the non-walkers didn't realize was that the walkers were happier and healthier (both physically and mentally) than they were and also looked better in short shorts.

Some people say that walking is boring. Since boredom is a state of mind, we can make up our minds to abolish boredom and turn walking into an exciting adventure, if we are open to the possibilities.

For example, as I said, walking is healthy. I suppose good health may be boring to those who have never known the contrast of poor health, but since most of us have had health problems at one time or another, the feeling of being healthy shouldn't be boring. So doing something to improve one's health shouldn't be boring, either. We've all read the studies that demonstrate the salubrious effects of walking on cardiovascular systems, weight, cholesterol, bone density, mental health—and on and on. The wonderful thing about the benefits of walking is that almost everybody can enjoy them.

Walking is social. Many people walk in pairs. Two is probably the ideal number for walking and talking at the same time. When I take my morning walk I often meet two people walking together. How much they talk depends on the sexual mix of the couple. A male and a female or two males talk intermittently; two females walking together usually chatter incessantly, as if they hadn't seen each other for a month, rather than a day. Sometime I'm going to do research on what it is they find to talk about.

Walking is sensual. Why do children run and jump, just for the fun of it? Because it feels good. Because body movement is sensual. And we are sensual beings. Sorry, but there is nothing sensual about driving a Lexus Sport Utility Vehicle. All right, we use our eyes and ears, but the rest of our bodies don't participate. They vegetate while the healthiness drains out of our health globules.

Walking is a great way to see the country. You can see a lot more at three or four miles-per-hour than you can at 50 or 60—or 500. Every tree, every fencepost, every cow, comes into complete focus and isn't gone before you can blink. You become part of the place where you are walking. You can interact with your surroundings when you emerge from your artificial shell. You are no longer just a spectator watching the landscape whiz by faster than scenes in a movie on fast-forward.

Walking is a time for fantasy. Don't tell me you don't have fantasies. Everybody has fantasies. Everybody needs to take time to fantasize. Some people call it daydreaming. If we do our daydreaming while we walk we will be more productive when we are working. We can scale Mt. Everest as we labor up a hill. We can run a marathon and live to tell about it. We can walk across the country instead of around the block.

Or we can step completely outside our bodies and do something unrelated to walking. Take a trip, hit a homerun, become a movie star or the lord-high executioner. Daydreams are good for us. They get us away from our humdrum lives and clean out our psyches. And when we are walking we don't feel guilty about taking the time to daydream.

Walking is a stimulus to creativity. It gives us time to think. Many a poem has been born during a walk, and many a painting, book and musical composition. Inventions have been invented; problems have been solved. The world is a better place because of walkers.

This book is partly a memoir, but it also includes quotations from other walkers. It is partly my observations about walking (and life) and partly a compendium of interesting places to walk in various parts of the world. Included are four long walks for the really adventurous, three that were taken by me and one by Ethan Loewenthal.

It is my contention that walking will make anybody a healthier and happier person (it has certainly made me one) and that if we are going to walk we should do so as much as possible in captivating surroundings, even if we have to imagine them.

Part I Memories and Observations

Let's start with the basics. First comes learning to walk. We take walking for granted and forget about the agony we went through before we took those first important steps. However, relearning to walk after a stroke or other medical problem may be even harder. Many of us have fond memories of walking with family and fond or not so fond memories of walking to school. And what about walking in college or even walking for love? Two important reasons to walk. Don't forget that even though walking is one of the safest sports, it has its hazards. We take a light look at fashions observed while walking on the beach and something every walker has encountered: the befuddled motorist asking for directions. And why do we walk? A number of walkers give their reasons.

Alan Cook

CHAPTER 1 Learning to Walk

WANDERER—Mason's Report at Age One

I'm a free-range baby;
that's what my daddy said,
because I'm free to roam about,
except when I'm in bed.
Many things call out to me
and have a great attraction.
I scamper to investigate
wherever there is action.
I want to be where my brother is,
whatever he is doing;
he has puzzles, books and animals,
neat shapes and cattle mooing.
I'm endlessly persistent,
even if my path is blocked;
I'll head right for a cupboard
the one time it's unlocked.
I'll scramble up the stairs
if you leave the door cracked open.
I haven't been outdoors yet,
but I'm watchin' and I'm hopin'.

My grandsons are curious by nature. Matthew, the older one, was already feeling his blanket with his fingers at the ripe old age of two days, trying to figure out why it had a different texture than the uterus he was accustomed to.

With the innate drive of all babies, Matthew and Mason started exploring as soon as they realized that the world was larger than a small sack of water. First crawling, and later walking, became high priorities for them.

I've read that the reason animals (as opposed to plants) need brains is because movement is so complicated. If you have ever watched a baby develop you realize how true this is. Just rolling over requires the coordination of multiple muscles, flexing in the correct sequence, moving in the right direction, with just the right amount of force. What a problem for the brain. And you thought calculus was tough. Fortunately, once babies repeat the proper movements a few thousand times the sequences get stored away in their mental databases and become habitual.

Babies often roll before they crawl, but rolling is an unsatisfactory form of locomotion because they get dizzy and for half of each roll they can't see where they're going. So they bump into things. As soon as the boys were able to lie on their bellies and hold their heads up they decided that they needed to learn to crawl. They practiced for hours, trying to get the proper coordination between arms and legs.

Bellies turned out to be a major problem. As long as they couldn't get their bellies off the ground they were unable to move very far. Parents and grandparents placed hands where M & M could use them to push off against with their feet, and they might propel themselves a few inches in this manner, but it was only a short-term and short-distance solution. However, as they grew bigger and practiced their movements, their arms and legs became stronger and they were able to lift their bellies off the ground.

Fortunately for my grandsons, my son and daughter-in-law, Andy and Melissa, declared them to be free-range babies, which meant that they were never going to be incarcerated in a playpen. The world was theirs to explore. Well, at their parents' home at least the family room was theirs to explore. The step between the family room and the kitchen turned out to be their Mt. Everest—an almost insurmountable height to be conquered.

They rose to the challenge. Both Matthew and Mason, in turn, worked on that step as if they were attempting to break out of jail. First, place hands on the step. Next, lift one leg onto it. Fall back. How many hundreds of times did their attempts end in failure? Finally, the day came for Matthew when he lifted a leg onto the step and it stuck. Then, after a great deal of effort he was able to lift the second leg and it stuck. He had reached the kitchen—and the world. Two years later Mason followed in his brother's crawlsteps.

The boys now had a wonderful outlet for their curiosity. They were fascinated with the kitchen cupboards. They would open the ones that weren't secured with baby locks and go through their contents. Although Matthew couldn't open the refrigerator by himself, when Melissa opened it he would sort through the jars of baby food to find the one he wanted to eat. When Mason tried to open a cupboard that had once been unlocked but was suddenly locked, he squealed like a stuck pig.

Melissa's mother, Loajean, babysat the boys when they were young, at her house. One day, not long after Matthew had learned to crawl, she realized that he was not in sight. She raced to the front of the house and found him halfway up the stairs and grinning. Mason also became an escape artist at a very young age. He had special radar that sensed when someone left the kitchen doors open at his house. He would be through the doorway in a flash, heading for the stairs.

Walking was next on their agendas. Walking took months of practice. Practice standing while holding on to objects or the hands of a parent or grandparent. Practice standing without support, which is a necessary prerequisite to walking. Practice walking, holding on to a table or anything that was handy. At last the great day came when they took their first steps by themselves. How proud they were. How proud their parents and grandparents were.

I don't know of anybody who took his first steps with a better flair for showmanship than my grandnephew, Adam. He was seven months old at the time, attending the wedding of his cousin Amy. A number of celebrants had gathered at the home of his Great Great

Great Aunt Minnie. Adam took his first steps in the presence of five generations of family members, all applauding.

Walking for Matthew and Mason not only made houses easier to navigate, it now made the outdoors accessible to them. Matthew was more inclined to push a stroller than ride in it. In a shopping mall, amid crowds of people, we had to either hold his hand or keep a very sharp eye on him because he could disappear in the time it took to inhale. We became very sympathetic to parents who keep their children on leashes.

When he was four, Matthew walked with Andy and me for several miles on a circuit of his neighborhood, which included crossing a wooden bridge, crossing an earthen dam and visiting his future elementary school and its playground equipment. Those interesting destinations kept him going.

Mason is another story. It was necessary to have somebody watch him fulltime, with the job of chaser. When he was two and a half, Andy and Melissa brought Matthew and Mason to visit their California grandparents—Bonny and me. It was their first trip to California, so in addition to taking them to Disneyland we had a party for them.

Mason quickly figured out that our front door was easy to open from the inside, even when the deadbolt was in place, because a single handle operated the lock and the latch. Whenever an opportunity presented itself he was out the door and down the street—running. One of the adults had to chase him and steer him back to the house. Fortunately, it is possible to go quite a distance in our neighborhood without crossing a street and Mason's parents had trained him to stay on the sidewalk.

On one of his excursions a neighbor drove alongside him, probably wondering what deadbeat relative of his wasn't watching him. I was the relative in question and after telling Matthew to stay in the driveway I ran after Mason and apologized to the neighbor.

We held the party in our backyard. In order to restrain Mason, Andy set large flowerpots on the walk leading to the front of the house. Mason watched with amused contempt, and as soon as Andy was finished he went over and demonstrated how strong he was by muscling one of the pots out of the way. Then he took off.

After bringing him back, Andy placed the pots several deep on the walk so that Mason couldn't move them, although he tried. He yelled, "I'm stuck, I'm stuck," but received no sympathy from the adults. This arrangement kept him in check for the duration of the party.

After the party was over we were cleaning up and the front door was left open, without anybody watching it. Mason saw his opportunity and took off again, barefoot, in the uphill direction from our house (where we live you either have to go uphill or downhill— there ain't no level). I followed, perhaps thinking that the lateness of the hour or the fact that he was barefoot would limit his excursion.

But nothing slowed him down. He ran/walked almost half a mile without crossing any streets, oblivious to the impact of the concrete sidewalk on his bare feet, talking and singing the song from Bob the Builder, a cartoon character. Periodically, he shouted, "Let's go!" Finally, I told him that he had to turn around. He did so, reluctantly. Several times he tried to reverse direction and duck past me. He stopped and hugged trees to prolong his walk. When he reached our driveway he would have kept going, had I not blocked his path.

More recently, I was walking with Matthew in his neighborhood. He told me that we had to look for cars coming down each driveway that we crossed. I agreed with him and asked him whether he had learned that at his preschool. He said no, he had known that as soon as he was born.

It appears that my grandsons have followed in my footsteps, so to speak.

CHAPTER 2 Relearning to Walk

THE SOUL OF LIBERTY

I walk the streets, the lanes, the paths,
the trails, the avenues and byways.
I reflect the color wheel of seasons, from green
to brown to red to white, then round again.
I sniff the pine-rich air on mountainsides
that loom along life's highways,
and listen to the curious owls
ask "Who?" I answer then:
I am the ghosts of pioneers
who blazed these trails with sweat
and blood; I am the voice of those to come
who'll cry out to be free.
I am the key to the chains of those who have
not seen the sunrise yet;
I am the hope of all who yearn—
the soul of liberty.

On July 6, 2002, my mother had what the doctors diagnosed as a "hard stroke." It almost paralyzed the left side of her body. She was 91 years old.

She had always been a very active person. After my father died in November 1993 she continued to live on the 54-acre farm in Clarence, New York, near Buffalo, that my parents had purchased in 1950. She lived alone except for Cristy, her part collie and party husky dog. She continued to participate in community affairs, just as she always had.

Winters can get very cold in Buffalo. She slipped on the ice and fell when the wind chill was in the neighborhood of minus 50 degrees F. Since the farmhouse is isolated and she was in the backyard at the time, my brothers and I wondered what would have happened if she had broken her leg and hadn't been able to get up. Fortunately, she escaped with only frostbite on her ankle.

Despite the fact that she hated to leave the farm, Mother finally agreed to move to the Carol Woods Retirement Community in Chapel Hill, North Carolina, in September 1995. My brother, Phil, and his wife, Judy, live nearby.

Each morning she walked Cristy a mile around the Carol Woods ring road. She taught English as a second language to Chinese and Japanese people temporarily in the United States and took a Spanish class from another resident. She led the poetry group and became a member of several Carol Woods committees. She traveled to visit her sons and other relatives.

Mother is a very cheerful person. Her brother, Jim, said that as a girl she was always sunny and smiling. She looked on the bright side of life, despite having lived through a depression, two world wars and a handful of others, and having raised four boys.

Immediately after her stroke she became depressed. At one point she told Judy and me that she wanted to die, but she didn't know how to stop breathing. Her sons all came to see her after her stroke and kept coming back. She told somebody else that her sons wouldn't let her die.

Mother's condition improved and she was transferred to the rehabilitation center of the University of North Carolina medical complex, but before she could achieve very much there she suffered a blood clot in her leg, which traveled to her lungs and affected her breathing. The reduced blood flow resulted in a minor heart attack. She was placed in the cardiac care unit of the hospital.

Again she improved and returned to rehabilitation. She had three kinds of therapists: physical therapists, occupational therapists and speech therapists. The stroke had affected her speech as well as her strength and movement. The therapists loved her because she worked hard and was determined to recover the abilities she had before the stroke so that she could go back to Carol Woods.

But she had a lot to relearn. Like a baby, she had to learn some basic movements such as how to roll over and how to sit up while maintaining her balance. She had to learn how to transfer from her bed to a wheelchair and back. Her left arm was almost useless. She did basic exercises to learn how to move her hand and how to pick up things. It was the same with her left leg. First she had to learn how to move her foot. She practiced standing between two parallel bars in the physical therapy room, with a therapist steadying her. Since she couldn't put any weight on her left arm and not much on her left foot she had to depend on her right arm to help with her balance.

Mother kept insisting that she wanted to return to Carol Woods. She did so, on August 29, after almost two months in the hospital and rehabilitation center. The Skilled Nursing facility at Carol Woods is excellent, as are the therapists. She had therapy as many as to six days a week. Here, as at the hospital, the therapists loved her because she worked so hard and was so eager to improve.

In many ways, learning how to walk a second time is harder than learning how to walk the first time. Babies have a lot to learn, but their bodies and brains are working for them. About the only thing Mother had going for her was persistence similar to that of young people. Part of her brain that dealt with walking had been affected by the stroke and it had to rewire itself and relearn the motor sequences. Her left leg and arm were weak and hard for her to control. She only gained strength and coordination by working continuously. She had to learn how to balance again.

A couple of days a week her therapy session took place in the Carol Woods pool. Here the buoyancy of the water helped to hold her up so that her legs didn't have to carry as much weight. She found that she could walk much easier in the water than on dry land. It made her think that people with walking problems might be better off if they could live like amphibians, spending most of their time in the water.

She could do leg lifts and other strengthening exercises, with the water both holding her up and providing resistance that made the exercises more valuable. She also practiced balancing. The therapist made waves so that she had to make the minute adjustments that everyone constantly has to make when standing.

On dry land, Mother practiced walking between parallel bars, and by November she was able to walk some with a walker. She walked slowly and carefully, with a therapist holding onto her waist strap so that she could be confident that she would be caught if she started to fall. She walked for a while with the walker and then sat and rested for a while.

If you asked Mother how she was doing she would say that her progress was very slow. And of course that was true for a person who was used to an active lifestyle. But the fact that she lived an active life undoubtedly helped give her the incentive to get back as much of it as possible. Her basic fitness also speeded up the process.

She had difficulty talking to the other patients in Skilled Nursing. Some were senile and some were deaf. And Mother, herself, had worn hearing aids for a number of years. Her friends came to visit her, but she wanted to be in a place where she could converse with the other residents. So her next goal was to transfer from Skilled Nursing to the Assisted Living area of Carol Woods.

Because of her determination she was able to convince the staff that she could handle Assisted Living, even though she couldn't walk much by herself, even with a walker. She enjoyed living in the new building (she was the first occupant of her room) and taught members of the staff how to play Scrabble. She purchased an electric wheelchair to use for much of her transportation, but continued to practice her walking.

Several happy months went by. Then one night she fell while attempting to get to the bathroom and broke several bones in her foot. This put her walking temporarily on hold, but she was able to stay in her Assisted Living room. Unfortunately, she then suffered a further setback, requiring an operation. She went back to the hospital for a few days and then to the Skilled Nursing facility again. This cancelled out most of the walking gains she had made.

Mother celebrated her 92nd birthday while in Skilled Nursing. But she amazed the physical therapists by attempting to make another comeback. By then her foot had healed so she was able to practice standing and walking again, first with parallel bars and then with a walker. Her progress reached a plateau and the staff thought she would never be able to return to Assisted Living, but still she didn't give up. And I'm convinced that she never will.

CHAPTER 3 Walking with Family

NIGHT WALK

The dark envelops us with its black cloak,
but we are one with nighttime spirits here
and kinsmen to the owl in yonder oak;
our companion is elation and not fear.
A beam of moonlight reveals our hilly path;
the gentle sounds of night are heard when cease
the cacophonies of daytime's noisy wrath.
Activity slows down; we welcome peace.
Our hungry strides eat up delicious miles;
our concentration acts to banish time,
replacing it with honest talk and smiles,
so we will not be punished for this crime.
The trees are layered grays in moon's pale light,
and so are we as we merge into the night.

When my father was an undergraduate at the University of Michigan, he lived in the home of a professor. It took him half an hour to walk to and from the campus each day. After he entered graduate school he took long walks with his friends.

My parents met in 1933 while on a hike sponsored by the Graduate Outing Club of the University. This was serendipity because my mother wasn't really a hiker. In fact, she rode in a car on the return trip. My parents were married in 1935 and I was born in 1938.

According to my mother, I took my first steps at the age of nine months and promptly fell down. I didn't attempt to walk again for another six months. This was not a very auspicious start for a person who would someday write a book about walking, but I want to show all the obstacles I overcame to get where I am today (wherever that is).

I got involved in sports at an early age. My family lived in the town of Amherst, New York, near Buffalo, at 246 Roycroft Boulevard. Roycroft was a divided street, with a parkway in the middle, covered with grass, bushes and trees. One day Mother marched me out to the parkway, where children were playing baseball, and demanded that they let me play. That was the beginning of my athletic career. We used the parkway for many games, including hide-and-go-seek and football. When the quarterback faded to pass, he could duck behind a tree and use it as a blocker.

I am the oldest of four boys. My father would walk with us to Saratoga, the first cross street to the south, or sometimes even to Kensington, the second street. When I was old enough to go by myself I walked around the corner on Saratoga to a small store and spent all my money on candy and comic books.

I walked to school, starting in kindergarten. The route was north to Kings Highway, west one block and north one block. Sometimes I even walked home for lunch. I was home eating lunch one day when Mother was listening to the radio broadcast of the inauguration of President Truman. The only time I can remember getting a ride home was the day it started snowing in the morning. By noon the snow was a foot deep. Mother came and picked my brothers and me up and the school closed for the rest of the day. We loved snow days, when we didn't have to go to school. Mother didn't.

Dad was a walker, or rather, a hiker. He enjoyed hiking in the Adirondack Mountains of New York, the Green Mountains of Vermont and the White Mountains of New Hampshire. He read books that described their trails in excruciating detail, down to the red pebble at the bend, seven-tenths of a mile from the trailhead. The authors of those books would push a bicycle wheel attached to an odometer the length of the trail, so they knew exact distances. Dad ate this stuff up.

When I was about five we stayed for a week in a primitive cabin at Allegheny State Park. The park is in southwestern New York, on the Pennsylvania border. Dad took me on a hike of several miles, from the cabin to the Thunder Rocks, an impressive collection of big rocks in the park. I remember that we climbed a tree-covered slope, looking for markers for the trail that ran along the ridge. I didn't know what a trail marker looked like. I had a new pocketknife and was more interested in sitting and whittling on twigs than I was in walking. Mother drove to the Thunder Rocks to pick us up. The next year we returned to Allegheny. Dad and I walked the round trip to the Thunder Rocks and back to the cabin.

I wasn't exactly an intrepid hiker in those days. One day I was walking home on a weekend when I got stuck in the mud at the corner of Kings Highway and Roycroft. I was still standing, but I couldn't lift my feet out of the gook. Instead of trying to find a logical solution to my problem I panicked and started screaming for my father. I don't how I expected him to hear me from across the street and seven houses down the block, but somebody must have told him about my predicament. He eventually showed up and freed me.

As my brothers and I grew older, Dad and Mother took us on more and more elaborate vacations. Dad took the older boys hiking while Mother stayed at the campsite or cabin with the boys too young to go. Mother suffered from a rapid heartbeat when she was young and didn't think of herself as a hiker, even though she had hiked with Dad a few times. It is interesting to note that as she grew older her heart problem abated and she was able to hike some fairly rugged trails.

My first official mountain climb was Blue Mountain, in the Adirondacks. Many of the trails in the Adirondacks go through forests so thick that there are few viewpoints. However, the best thing about Blue Mountain was that it had a fire tower on the peak. Our prize for making it to the top was the privilege of climbing the fire tower and talking to the firewatcher. He had a spectacular view of the surrounding mountains.

Firewatchers are sturdy people. My father told the story of one firewatcher who was working on the roof of the hut where he slept. He slipped and slid down the roof. A ring he was wearing caught on a nail and ripped off his finger. He radioed what had happened and then he managed to hike down the trail and get help.

Hiking in New York can be a wet experience, with rain and muddy trails. The trails often cross a series of brooks. I can remember coming down one trail where the brook crossings seemed to be infinite in number. At each brook I plaintively asked whether it was the last one. This didn't win me any points with Dad, who didn't like whiners.

We graduated to the highest peaks in the Adirondacks, the 4,000 footers as they are called. Although not high by western standards, the total climbs can be significant. One year, Dad, my brother Steve and I rowed a rented boat across Lake Placid, a winter Olympics site, and climbed Mt. Whiteface. At the top we felt superior to the flabby tourists who had driven up the auto road. On the row back across the lake a breeze came up, along with some undistinguished waves. I felt a little nervous, but Dad, who was an experienced canoeist, remained in complete control of the situation.

Early on, we boys started to outdo Dad. One year Dad, Steve and I climbed Giant, one of the 4,000 footers. We still felt frisky when we were finished, so Steve and I climbed a smaller peak called Noonmark by ourselves. My legs had lead weights attached to them as we neared the top, but we made it.

Mt. McIntyre, Mt. Colden and Mt. Marcy are located in a line, and their impressive bulks are clearly visible from the road. Mt. McIntyre, which actually has four peaks, including the second highest peak in New York, is the easiest to climb because it is closest to the road. That is, unless you do all four peaks. When we became old enough, we boys did climb all four peaks of McIntyre in one day.

We climbed Mt. Colden one year and Mt. Marcy another year. Mt. Marcy, the highest peak in the Adirondacks (5,344 feet), is a boring 15-mile roundtrip, but it is a necessary peak for the complete Adirondack hiker to conquer.

In 1965, the year after we got married, I took Bonny to the Adirondacks where we met Dad and Mother (who was now hiking) for several days of mountain climbing. Bonny and I climbed Mt. McIntyre on a rainy day, when the trail was more river than trail. She slipped and hurt her knee, which did not increase her love for the mountain. On the following days we made some relatively easy climbs with Dad and Mother.

We stayed at Johns Brook Lodge, which was only reachable on foot. There were two bunkrooms, one for men and one for women. Bonny complained long and loudly about the sleeping arrangements because she didn't want to be separated from me. I felt the same way, but I didn't have the guts to complain.

We met many interesting people on our hikes. On this trip, there was an older man named Oliver who was staying at Johns Brook Lodge. An Englishman, he hiked by himself. One evening he didn't return to the lodge. He returned the next morning and said he had gotten lost. He had spent the night in the cool woods by himself, but survived, none the worse for wear, with a hearty appetite. He became good friends with my parents and visited them at their farm.

While on that trip, Bonny and I climbed a mountain called the Gothics, unique in the Adirondacks, because much of the trail is very exposed and there are cables to help hikers make it up the rocks. Bonny was very exposed, also, because she had torn the seat of her pants, but she gamely made it to the top.

We spent most of our hiking time with Dad in the White Mountains of New Hampshire. The Appalachian Mountain Club maintained (and still maintains) a series of huts at strategic locations along the trails. The bunkrooms contain beds, stacked three and four high, with odors of sweat and dirty underwear. The bunkrooms were segregated by sex in the 1950s, but now they are coed.

The meals, prepared by high school and college-age hut boys (and now girls) are basic, but nourishing. The hikers help to set the tables, wash dishes and prepare trail lunches. We loved the camaraderie of the huts and admired the hut boys, who packed 100-pound loads of food and supplies up the trails, or—in the case of the Lakes of the Clouds Hut—down the trail from the top of Mt. Washington. They often ran down the trails to the food trucks, wearing, it was rumored, sometimes only jockstraps, until the wife of the chief hutmaster put a stop to it. They would also run over the rocky trails at night and play tricks on the boys who worked in the other huts.

The Pemigewasset Wilderness is within walking distance of several of the huts and is surrounded by peaks. One year we heard that an 80-year-old man had been lost in the Pemi, as it was called, for three days—with a cucumber. Shortly after that we passed a man on the trail who could have been 80 and I wondered whether he was the one. I looked in vain for his cucumber.

Our favorite hut was the Lakes of the Clouds Hut, named after two very small lakes, not suitable for swimming or even wading, and located on the shoulder of Mt. Washington, the highest peak in New England (6,288 feet). Mt. Washington's supporters proudly claim that it has the world's worst weather. In April 1934 the wind was clocked on top at 231 miles-per-hour and we have been there in 70 mile-per-hour winds. Non-hikers can drive the auto road or ride the cog railroad to the top of the mountain.

The hike over the Gulfside Trail from Mt. Washington to the hut on the shoulder of Mt. Madison is above timberline and completely exposed to the weather. When the mountains were socked in with clouds we had to walk from one cairn to another, always keeping at least one in sight, to make sure we stayed on the trail. The cairns, piles of rock built as high as 15 or 20 feet in some cases, are located along all the trails that are above timberline.

One year a storm threatened as we started out on the Gulfside Trail from Mt. Washington. Dad gave my youngest brother, Phil, and me permission to go ahead, while poor Steve had to stay with Dad. Phil and I made it to Madison in family record time, before the rain started and hours before Steve and Dad, who got thoroughly soaked.

Mt. Monroe is a small peak beside the Lakes of the Clouds Hut. Our tradition was to climb it in the afternoon after hiking up to the hut. One time I offered Phil all the change in my pocket if he would climb Mt. Monroe barefoot, over the rocks. He did so, which impressed the heck out of me.

Although I moved to Los Angeles, I couldn't stay away from the White Mountains. I took Bonny there in 1969 to hike the Gulfside Trail in the rain. We were returning to civilization on another trail that goes from Mt. Madison down to Pinkham Notch, called the

Valley Way. The rain continued to fall hard and unceasingly and when we came to a rushing and overflowing creek we didn't know how to cross it at first. Finally, we threw our packs over to the other side and skipped quickly across on some partially submerged stones, while Bonny quaked in her hiking boots. Farther down the trail we met a group of boys going up. We warned their leaders about the creek, but they blithely assured us that they were experienced and would have no problem. Since we didn't read about any mass drowning we assumed they made it safely across.

We repeated the Gulfside Trail hike in 1980, this time with our son, Andy, who was 12. In 1991 I climbed Mt. Washington alone in sneakers (not recommended) and then hiked across the rocky Gulfside Trail to the Madison Huts. To top off the day, I hiked the Gulfside back the other way and then descended to my starting point, near the base station of the cog railroad, a rugged 19 miles in all. At that age I should have at least been smart enough to wear lug soles. I never tried that again, but I have climbed Mt. Washington as recently as 1998.

I was living, alone and unmarried, in Los Angeles in 1962, when Dad came out on business (he was a Chemist and worked for Union Carbide). The first weekend he was there I took him hiking in the San Gabriel Mountains north of Los Angeles. I asked him what he would like to do the second weekend and he said he would like nothing better than to go hiking again, so we did.

Dad also took me to a strip show while he was visiting, something he had never done back home. Perhaps he was trying to check my sexual orientation since I was still single. In any case he sat stone-faced throughout the show, which featured some foxy girls. This put somewhat of a damper on my own enjoyment.

During the summer of 1962, Dad, Mother and Phil drove out to California. Steve, who was working there for the summer, and I joined them in Yosemite National Park, which is more beautiful than anybody's artistic impression of paradise, with its waterfalls falling from and its cliffs rising to heaven, especially Halfdome and El Capitan. We hiked up a trail to the top of Eagle Peak by way of Yosemite Falls.

Steve and I slept in sleeping bags on the floor of Yosemite Valley, without a tent. All night long I watched for bears. When I finally saw one walk by some distance away it was no big deal, but that didn't restore my lost sleep.

About 10 years later, Phil and I climbed Halfdome, starting at Glacier Point. Since Glacier Point is the high point above Yosemite Valley from where the rangers used to drop the fire fall each evening, the route we took went first down and then up. The last stretch to the top of Halfdome is on bare granite, with cables for hikers to cling to, much like those on the Gothics, in the Adirondacks. On the return, Phil backed down this stretch, so that he wouldn't have to look straight down the exposed surface of the mountain. Not as exposed as the vertical face on the side that appears in all the pictures of Halfdome, however, which is the province of rock climbers who don't mind sleeping in slings, suspended over nothing.

In 1984, Bonny, Andy and I camped in the high country of Yosemite for several nights. During the day we hiked on trails among the pristine rocks, so clean that they look as if an army of maintenance people scrubbed them every night. A deer silhouetted against these shining rocks looked too perfect to be real, like an animated cartoon.

In his sixties, Dad had several small strokes, which ended his hiking days. After his strokes he walked down the lane of the family farm, using a cane and sometimes carrying a collapsible seat so he could sit down and rest before he made the return trip. The family dog often went with him.

Over a period of years he developed dementia, and Mother finally couldn't trust him to walk outdoors alone. But his love of hiking lives on in his sons, his grandchildren and his great grandchildren.

CHAPTER 4 Walking to School

When my son, Andy, started sixth grade at Malaga Cove School on the Palos Verdes Peninsula, we had to figure out how he was going to get to and from school. The Palos Verdes School District does not provide transportation for its pupils. This left the following choices: car pooling, public or private bus transportation, bicycling, hang gliding or walking.

We couldn't join a car pool because Bonny and I both worked. The private bus company contracted to serve a number of pupils in a given area, but it was rather expensive. We didn't consider bicycling because the route to the school by road was a winding three miles long and too steep for a sixth grader riding a bike, both the downhill going to school and the uphill returning. Hang gliding was fine for going to school because it was downhill, but were there enough updrafts for the return glide? Public transportation seemed like the most practical alternative, even though the routes served by the Los Angeles bus system did not come very close to our house.

I knew it was possible to walk to Malaga Cove from our house on a route considerably shorter than the road. I talked Andy into trying it with me. From our house, at an altitude of 700 feet, we first walked to an undeveloped park nearby. This involved about a 50-foot gain in altitude. Nothing in Palos Verdes is flat. From the park we went down the hill on a dirt path until we came to a residential area with paved roads. Here the going got easier as we went past a golf course,

21

over a bridge, through architecturally elegant Malaga Cove Plaza with its Neptune fountain (four members of Neptune's coterie are mermaids squirting water from their nipples) and then on down to the school, which is on a cliff overlooking the ocean.

Andy agreed that going downhill was fine. However, after we reversed the route and went back up the hill he had serious doubts about this being a viable alternative to taking the bus. Andy was not a stranger to hiking. He had already climbed Mt. Mitchell in North Carolina, and hiked through Haleakala Crater on Maui (see chapter 12 for more on these feats).

However, doing a tough climb every day was something else again. Bonny also doubted that her son was ready for this. After all, it hadn't been many years since Andy had fallen down whenever he tried to kick a soccer ball. Although his athletic prowess had increased greatly since then, he was small for his age and below average in strength.

I thought he could do it and that it would be good for him. So I took a direct approach. I bribed him. I told him he could keep the bus fare every day that he walked home. Being a financially astute individual, he pictured all the baseball cards he could buy with this loot. So he started walking to school. He talked one friend and then another into walking with him. Soon several boys walked to school on a regular basis. They walked in groups of two or three. Occasionally, a girl would walk with them.

They quickly found shortcuts, such as an easement that allowed them to go between some houses instead of around them. Bored with the basic route, they explored the hill and found variations, involving such activities as acrobatic walking across a pipe over a gully and sliding down the nearly vertical sides of the canyon that winds its way up the hill. They took these routes at top speed, chasing each other through the brambles to see how fast they could get down the hill.

When they went past the golf course they collected golf balls that duffers had hit out of bounds, and sometimes rolled them down the street. One of the balls hit the underside of a moving car. In the spring, when mustard flowers painted the hillsides yellow, the plants grew taller than they were and they walked blindly, trying to avoid the cliffs. They found a board, tied to a long rope. The other end was tied to a branch high in a eucalyptus tree. On this crude swing they swung out over the almost-vertical canyon wall. Andy reports that only one boy ever fell off the swing and he didn't get hurt.

One morning, Andy and some other boys came across a skunk going to school. The boys were going to school, that is; it isn't recorded where the skunk was headed. One of the boys taunted it and it did what skunks do—it sprayed. Andy caught the brunt of the stink on his jacket. He continued on to school and put the odoriferous jacket in his locker. Why he didn't get sent home we were never told.

The boys built forts in the park out of brush and had rock fights with other boys. Sometimes the older boys chased them. Older students had parties on the hill and left cans and bottles behind. This was great for Andy because he had begun to collect beer cans, and the hill was a gold mine for a beer can collector. A couple of his friends collected bottles. One time they were stopped by an employee of the California State Department of Transportation (CALTRANS) with armloads of bottles, but were able to convince him that they were not going to break them on the road.

The boys also learned about nature on their walks. They collected spiders to feed to a tarantula owned by one of them. During the spring, if it rained enough, a pond materialized in the park. They collected tadpoles from the pond and watched them grow into frogs. They saw an occasional water snake. There were also rattlesnakes on the hill, but, fortunately, the kids rarely saw them. We told them to always watch for snakes and we hope they did.

There are a number of wild peacocks living in Palos Verdes. They are protected from predatory humans. This is good if you enjoy their beauty or bad if you dislike the messes they make and their eardrum-piercing call that sounds like the howl of a sick cat. They have been known to chase little old ladies and upon occasion a resident circulates a recipe for peacock stew. The kids observed them first hand as they rested on the roofs of houses or arrogantly strutted across the streets, looking neither to the right nor to the left, with their chicks marching behind them.

The boys crossed over the bridge on the road beside the golf course. Or sometimes under it. They would walk across a steel pipe, suspended beneath the roadbed. There were two wooden handrails they could hang onto when walking on the pipe, but most of the boys weren't tall enough to reach both rails at the same time. So they had to slide sideways along the pipe, holding onto one rail with both hands.

They had races that involved going across the pipe to a wooden trellis with diagonal slats that went down to the rocky bottom of the canyon spanned by the bridge. They climbed down one trellis and then up another trellis and across the rest of the pipe to the other side. After school they would sit on the pipe and eat snacks. Or in a secret room with concrete walls that were part of the bridge supports, containing the skeleton of a dog.

One time, Andy and a friend took a flashlight and some tape and entered a large sewer pipe. They marked their route by putting tape at intersections in the pipes and reached a spot that was just below a street, with an opening into the sewer. They heard a conversation taking place on the street above, unbeknownst to the speakers. Spy kids. Fortunately, they were smarter than Hansel and Gretel, whose trail markers of breadcrumbs were eaten by birds. Andy and his friend successfully followed their tape markings out of the sewer.

Andy walked to school practically every day for three years. Each day was a new adventure, a new learning experience. Boys being boys, it wasn't until years later that he told us about some of his adventures. It's probably just as well. Do you really want your children to level with you all the time?

He counted the times he took the bus home on his fingers. Occasionally, when it was very rainy and muddy he hitched a ride with friends. But for the most part he walked. His legs grew strong and muscular and he developed the wind of a runner. This helped him with his sporting activities: soccer, baseball and cross-country. Nowadays, this conditioning helps him keep up with his two boys.

CHAPTER 5 Walking in College

TUCK-IN SERVICE

(Written for Andy when he told us about Tuck-in Service at his coed
dorm)

When I was young and went to college
I did accumulate some knowledge.
The problem was, I'd like to say,
The coeds lived a mile away.

I'd stumble through a winter storm
And wish that I were someplace warm.
The problem was, I'd like to state,
'Twas difficult to have a date.

When my girl and I were having fun
We'd watch the clock, we had to run.
The problem was, I'd like to tell,
When it got late we ran like hell,

For curfew always rang at night
For girls in dorms—that was our plight.
The problem was, I'd like to cry,
Is that too soon we said goodbye.

And now, my son, you are in college;
We hope you're soaking up some knowledge.
But coed dorms do make us nervous,
And what's this thing called Tuck-in Service!!?

I attended the University of Michigan, in Ann Arbor, Michigan, starting in September 1955. The university was big even then, with more students that it was possible to count, and the campus was extensive. I lived in Huber House, on the eighth floor of South Quad, the newest men's dormitory.

The elevators stopped only at the odd-numbered floors, so just to get to my room I had to climb a flight of stairs. The architects had the fitness of the guys who lived on the even-numbered floors in mind. I don't know whether a study was done to determine whether they were fitter than those who lived on the odd-numbered floors.

I had to walk everywhere I went. Almost no undergraduates had cars (there was no place to park, anyway) and I didn't have a bicycle on campus. Everyday the swarming hordes walked to classes, along the sidewalks and diagonals. We got used to this. Well, we almost got used to this.

When I returned to Michigan from my sojourn on the west coast (a year at UCLA, half a year at Stanford) it was February. For the first two weeks after I was back on campus I don't think the temperature rose above single digits, Fahrenheit. We shoe-skated to class on icy sidewalks—and sometimes fell. If I hadn't been convinced that I wanted to live in California before that time, those two weeks did it for me.

Anyway, we also had to get used to the fact that most of the women's dorms were on the other side of the campus (there were no coed dorms in those days). In order to have a date I had to walk across campus to pick up the girl, then walk back (most of the activities were on our side of the campus) then walk her back to her dorm, then return to South Quad.

On one of my first days at the university as a freshman a bunch of the brothers from Huber House were designated to walk to Victor Vaughan House and escort some coeds back to South Quad for a mixer. I'm not sure exactly how far it was, but it seemed like more than a mile. On the way back I found myself walking beside a coed named Mary Beth, who was a sophomore and a year and a half older than I was (I started college at 17).

I had worked that summer as a copyboy for the Buffalo Evening News and Mary Beth, somewhat to my surprise, expressed an interest in the newspaper business. So during the walk back to South Quad I expounded at great length on how a daily newspaper was written, type-set (in the days before computers) and printed. During this dissertation Mary Beth pretended to be enthralled.

The upshot of this was that I dated her on and off for months of my freshman year. We walked many miles together, holding hands (and never did much more than that). I even took her to the J-Hop, one of the big dances, featuring Les Brown and his band of renown. My roommate, Warren, brought a car on campus for this event, so we actually had wheels and didn't have to walk while wearing our formal clothes.

I finally decided that Mary Beth was not for me. In the spring a carnival was held, during which various campus organizations had booths and raised money using more or less creative ideas. For example, in one sorority the women dyed their bras and wore them to perform what was for that time a lascivious dance.

Mary Beth told me she was going to be a cancan dancer for her dorm. This sounded like a more exciting side of her than I had yet seen so I said I would catch her performance. For reasons I didn't understand she tried to dissuade me. Nevertheless, after I finished working the dinner shift at South Quad as a busboy I hightailed it down to the building where the carnival was in progress.

I arrived too late to watch her perform, but not too late to see her walking away from the booth in her fancy costume, complete with plumed hat, arm and arm with a male student. We had never promised we would be faithful to each other, but I guess this sight made me realize that there were other birds in the forest.

Flash forward to the second semester of my senior year, in the fall of 1959. I had lost a semester's credit, due to an ill-advised foray into law school, so I was graduating from the University of Michigan at the end of the semester. On my first day back on campus I walked

27

across campus to a women's dorm for a mixer (does this sound familiar?), only the dorm was Mary Markley and the mixer was there so I didn't have to walk all the way back to South Quad to attend it.

I was standing around surveying the scene when a small girl with long brown hair containing red highlights (as she would have said) walked past me toward the refreshments. Her hair attracted my attention because most girls wore their hair short at that time. I caught up to her after she left the refreshment table and asked her to dance. She pointed out that her hands were full of food, but she said she would talk to me.

Ann was different from any girl I had ever known. A first-semester freshman, cute and petite, she was also a blunt-spoken New Yorker with enormous intelligence, and as she classified herself, "a little girl with big ideas." I fell for her. I set a personal record for walking that semester. Walking to her dorm to pick her up, walking all over campus and Ann Arbor with her, returning her, hopefully, before curfew (at least once we returned to her dorm late and she was grounded) and then walking back to South Quad.

To demonstrate her bluntness, at the end of that first evening we were sitting and chatting. She pointed out that the button had come off the top of her skirt. I said something inane like, won't it fall down? She said, "The zipper holds it up. Don't you know anything about girls' clothes?" When we said goodbye, she said, "Am I going to see you again?" I had been planning to go to another mixer the following night, but all at once my plans changed. I took Ann to the mixer and didn't date anybody else that semester.

While we were dancing the next night I regaled her with the local legend that said, in order to become an official coed a female student had to be kissed underneath the Engineering Arch at midnight. We left the mixer and walked a good distance to the arch. Ann was impatient but I insisted on waiting for the stroke of midnight before we kissed. (At least that's my side of the story.) Then we had to walk back to her dorm. As I recall, she told me not to kiss her there, amidst a sea of newly met couples saying goodnight, because it would make her appear to be too forward.

We walked to dances, we walked to movies, we walked to the Arboretum (which, for you Latin-challenged is a campus park area devoted to trees). We walked to football games. It was so cold at one game that we left at halftime, after walking all the way to Michigan Stadium, a good long trek. Michigan's football team wasn't great that year, anyway.

Ann liked to eat ice cream cones so we feasted on strawberry and vanilla as we walked. As the days grew colder this made less and less sense, but her love of ice cream was greater than her dislike of being cold. She also smoked a handful of cigarettes a day—but I refused to buy her cigarettes.

Over Christmas vacation I went to visit Ann at her parents' Manhattan apartment in the east eighties. I stayed with Mickey, a high school friend who was at Columbia University, which is on the west side of Manhattan. We walked to museums and movies in the snow when we weren't able to borrow her father's Opel. (She ill advisedly told her father that I was a better driver than he was.) It must have been 3 a.m. one morning when I was returning to Columbia from her apartment on the subway. I got off at the wrong stop and found myself in Harlem. Instead of going back into the subway I walked from there to the Columbia campus, keeping a wary lookout for bad guys. It wasn't the smartest thing I've ever done.

So, what happened to that romance? I graduated from Michigan in January. Ann had just turned 18 and wasn't ready for a commitment. I was anxious to get back to California. I hopped on an airplane and never saw her again.

CHAPTER 6 Walking for Love

WALK WITH ME

Come walk the lane with me, the sun is high,
and lazy clouds bedeck the summer sky.
The corn stalks stand erect and fat with grain.
They bow to unseen breezes drifting by
and hear the promise of an evening rain.

We'll walk this close together, hand in hand,
and talk and laugh and say the world is grand;
and if you accidentally brush my thigh
you'll know that even though it was unplanned,
caresses from you teach my heart to fly.

Unseen, well hidden by the corn's green rows,
we'll shed our inhibitions and our clothes.
I'll be your Adam and you'll be my Eve.
A secret that the blackbird only knows
is once you walk in Eden you can't leave.

Long years from now when we are far apart
you'll still be walking with me in my heart.
Our naked bodies tingle when they touch,

but I blink back the welling tears that start
because you are the girl I loved too much.

The first date my wife, Bonny, and I had was a walking date. We went to the San Diego Zoo and walked with the animals. What a wonderful way to get to know somebody.

Actually, we already knew each other quite well because we met through a computer match organization and had corresponded anonymously for several weeks prior to our first date. Those of you who were present in 1964 may be skeptical as to whether computers were actually involved, as I was (I worked for IBM at the time) but whatever method the company used worked.

At the zoo a flock of pink flamingos welcomed us just inside the entrance. We were holding hands by the time we got to the sea lions. We saw the apes, the mountain mammals in the enclosures on the rocky hillsides, and the big cats, paying special attention to the tigers because Bonny's students called her Miss Tiger (she was a teacher at the time). We avoided the snake building because she had a fear of snakes, dating back to her childhood. We encountered a light rain, which was actually beneficial because mild adversity tends to bring people together. After we finished touring the zoo we stopped in La Jolla and strolled along the shore near the rocks. Many times since then we have gone to the San Diego Zoo on the anniversary of our first date.

Not long after that we rode the Palm Springs tram, which goes up to the 8,500-foot level on Mt. San Jacinto. The tram had opened only a few months before. We were feeling our oats and decided to hike to the top of Mt. San Jacinto. The only problem was that soon after we started up the trail we ran into three feet of snow. We became bogged down in the snow banks, which matched Bonny's white sweater, and never got anywhere near the top, but that didn't stop us from enjoying ourselves. (See chapter 28 for more on Mt. San Jacinto.)

Bonny's primary walking influence was from her grandfather, Frank Robinson. Frank was a founding member of the Young Men's Athletic Club, started about 1900. On weekends the group would walk from one Connecticut town to another and back. There are pictures of them sitting on improbable structures, wearing their hats and looking stern, which was necessitated by the state of photography at that time. Frank continued to be a member of this club for many years and lived to be almost 95. He worked for International Silver in Meriden for 59 years as a dye cutter. He continued to ride the train to California to visit Bonny and me into the 1970s, when he was approaching 90. I took him to baseball games, which he loved.

Bonny and I had more successful walking and hiking trips during our courtship. When Frank heard that she was dating a hiker, he sent her $10 to help her buy a pair of hiking shoes. She had lived with him and her grandmother when she was young and she respected his opinion. I was the first one of her boyfriends he had shown support for.

My brother, Steve, was working in Los Angeles during the summer of 1964, on a break from Harvard. The three of us climbed Mt. Baldy, the 10,000-foot peak that dominates the skyline northeast of Los Angeles. As Bonny describes it, the top is a pile of rocks. You go up two feet and slide down one. But she made it. On the hike down the mountain I picked up a piece of wood she admired and carried it the rest of the way, which impressed her. It impressed me too since I had never done that for anyone else. After we were married we made a lamp using that wood as a base.

One Sunday, Bonny and I drove to Santa Barbara, and after visiting with her uncle and aunt, who lived there, we went on to Nojoqui Falls Park to take a nature hike and fool around. Within 24 hours of that hike I realized that I had a case of poison oak. By this time I knew the symptoms of poison oak well. I had been introduced to it in a way I wouldn't forget during my year at UCLA (see chapter 11) and had suffered from it several times since.

The poison travels through the bloodstream and I developed itchy red bumps over more than 50 percent of my body. The urge to scratch was so intense that I had to tie my hands together at night to prevent me from scratching in my sleep. By the time I saw Bonny the following Friday I looked like some sort of monster. Fortunately, she hadn't caught the poison oak. But she treated me very gently until it went away.

We also drove to the Big Sur and climbed a peak known as Mt. Manuel. As we hiked along the edge of a canyon a rattlesnake skittered across the trail in front of us. Bonny almost jumped off the cliff and it took her a while to calm down, but she showed her spunk by continuing the hike. As we neared the top the heat got to her. She sank down in a sweaty heap and announced that she couldn't go any farther.

Certain that the top was close I struggled on and found it. I returned and persuaded her to continue a few hundred more feet. On the top she took off her shirt and basked in the glory of her achievement while I decided not to let her get away. Our only companions were a herd of wild pigs. I ended up getting the worst of the hike because I developed blisters, which hobbled me for several days thereafter.

We eloped to Reno in August 1964 and spent our honeymoon in the northwest. In Glacier National Park, Montana, we took a hike that I will let Bonny describe in her own words from a log she kept: "Arrived at McDonald Lake, Glacier National Park, shortly after noon. Made lunch and ate in car while parked in meadow with bees. Set off on foot to spend the night at Sperry Chalet, six miles up the mountainside (only reached by foot and horse trails). Hiked through mud, light sprinkles near top and in the middle of streamlets. Made it in three hours. Had meals in a small lodge near sleeping lodge. Girls and older ladies there are all studying to be teachers. Met a la-di-dah family from Princeton, N.J. Two members had just taken a swim in a nearby pond. Brrr!

"After supper, A and B played dominoes. A kept getting cockier and cockier as B let him win again and again and again. (B must really learn how to play dominoes one of these days. Ha-ha.) Spent the night under five blankets in a room at the chalet. Could see the stars through the windows."

We also walked a lot in Yellowstone National Park and hiked up Mt. Washburn to the fire lookout tower. On the trail we stalked the mountain sheep and took pictures of them. Throughout the park the bears stalked us. One walked through our campsite while we were preparing dinner. I banged on pots and it finally went away without eating anything. It must have liked quiet meals. Over a period of several days of walking and exploring we saw moose, antelope and various other fauna.

Alan Cook

After we got married, Bonny discovered a thick callus on the bottom of my left foot, which I had had for some time and which hurt when I stepped directly on it. She treated that callus for months with acid until it finally disappeared. I understood then that I needed her to take care of me, for walking and for everything else, and she has done that ever since.

CHAPTER 7 Walking Safely

One morning in the spring of 2003, while I was writing this book, I took my usual walk. Warmer weather prompted me to forsake the warm-up suit I had worn all winter, in favor of shorts and the first sweatshirt my searching hand came in contact with in the dimly lit closet. I placed the usual stuff in my pockets: a handkerchief, a pen (in case I have a brainstorm), business cards containing my name, address and telephone number for identification (I don't carry a wallet in the morning) and my keys—I thought.

The walk went fine until I returned home and reached for the keys in my right rear pocket. My hand hit my butt without encountering the expected thickness of my key case. I quickly checked the other pockets of my shorts—not there. I tested the door; it was locked. And Bonny was on a trip so there was nobody in the house.

Well, this was the reason the neighbors had a key to our house. I walked around the block and rang their bell. Fortunately, Karen hadn't left for work yet, but when she looked for the key she couldn't find it. Her daughter, Jackie, who watched the house when we were out of town, had put it somewhere—but where? No problem, I said. I'll go in the window.

I walked back to the house and thanked Mother Nature for keeping the weather warm enough so that I could leave the bathroom window open all night. However, there was a bulky wooden frame covering the window. I went next door to borrow a hammer from

Bob, another neighbor, and with its help I was able to unhook the frame and lift it off the window. I had no trouble removing the screen.

I boosted myself up so that my head was sticking through the small window. My weight was on my forearms, which were on the sill. I could probably scramble through the window and dive headfirst onto the toilet—and break my neck. My torts professor (before I realized I didn't belong in law school) used to say that you have to ask yourself whether the game is worth the candle. It clearly wasn't.

I went next door and borrowed a stepladder from Bob. This gave me enough height so that I was able to insert my legs through the window and squeeze the rest of me through. Feet first, I landed on the toilet and then on the floor, unhurt.

I was relieved, but I still had the problem of finding my keys. Since the deadbolt was bolted on the front door I knew I had carried them outside. I do stretching on the first part of my walk. Maybe the associated movements had bounced the keys out of my pocket. I retraced my path, scanning the sidewalk. No keys.

I returned to the house, wondering whether I had lost my mind. I patted my various pockets, something I do, automatically, when I am mentally checklisting that I have everything. My hand hit a mass over my belt buckle. Sheepishly, I removed the keys from the pocket in the front of my sweatshirt—the sweatshirt I had worn for the first time in many months.

Jackie drove up with the spare key. She had come all the way from school. I thanked her profusely for her trouble and made a mental note to give her something extra the next time she watched the house. I was too embarrassed to tell her what had happened.

Hopefully, most walkers aren't memory-challenged, but even so walking is not without its hazards. Of course, anything we do can be hazardous, including getting out of bed in the morning. Or staying in bed. If we do the latter our muscles may atrophy.

I submit that walking is one of the least risky endeavors in which we can participate. However, it's a good idea to be prepared so I will briefly cover some of the risks of walking. Many of these our mothers drilled into us when we were children, but it never hurts to review.

Rule number one is to wear sunscreen during the hours and the seasons when the UV rating is high. We have all known relatives or friends who had skin cancer so we are aware that the sun can be an enemy as well as a friend. It doesn't hurt to wear a hat, also.

If we walk where motor vehicles travel, the biggest risk is being hit by one. Size doesn't matter. A Geo Metro can kill us just as dead as a Lincoln Terminator—I mean Navigator. So walk on the left, facing traffic. That way we can see what is going to hit us. And hopefully avoid it. In the United Kingdom and other uncivilized countries where people drive on the wrong side of the road, walk on the right. I found this out when I was doing my British End-to-End walk (see chapters 40-43).

Many drivers will give walkers a wide berth, sometimes even crossing to the other side of a narrow road to avoid them. Others doggedly stay in their lane, even if it means giving us a shave when we don't need one. I am always prepared to step off the road. I don't like to walk beside walls or cliffs that offer no escape route. Few drivers play deliberate chicken with walkers, although one driver crossed to the wrong side of the street to buzz my back and honk his horn at me, not far from my home.

Recently, while I was on my morning walk, a commuter trying to save time turned into a driveway of a house on a corner, entering it from one street and exiting it onto the other street, so fast that I never saw the car until it shot past inches in front of me. Another time, a passenger in a car threw ice cubes in my face.

I am not completely passive in dealing with cars. I have been known to slap the fenders of cars that cut in front of me too closely, including a red Rolls Royce once. It didn't hurt the car and, hopefully, woke up the driver. So far, no drivers have made a U-turn and tried to run me down.

Look both ways before you cross a street. I look to the left, then the right, then the left again, in case I missed something. Another reason for looking twice is that one glance just gives us a stroboscopic picture—a photograph. It doesn't tell us how fast a vehicle is moving. With a second look we can see how far a vehicle has moved since our first look, and using our computer-like brains to do some very complex calculations, involving the time between looks and the distance the vehicle has traveled, we can determine its speed and the likelihood that it will hit us before we get across the street.

Again, in Great Britain, Japan and other places where vehicles drive on the left, look to the right first. In London, there are signs at intersections telling us to look to the right. I suspect that more than one tourist has met her demise by looking to the left when she should have been looking to the right. Tom Clancy starts out one of his suspense novels by telling how his hero almost gets killed in London. But an enemy agent isn't the culprit; he looks the wrong way when he crosses the street.

I am not so much worried about non-motor vehicles, such as bicycles. Although bicyclists climb the hills where I live every morning and then go screaming down them, blithely disregarding traffic laws, I figure they are going to be very careful to avoid hitting me because the result would probably be worse for them than for me.

However, several times while I was walking in the dark, a bicyclist without lights narrowly missed me because I had no idea it was there, and vice versa. I wear reflective spots in the dark and on foggy days, but if there is no light to reflect from the spots I might as well be invisible. What really scare me are drivers of cars who don't turn their lights on while driving in fog. Let's say visibility is 100 feet. A car traveling at 30 miles-per-hour goes that far in just over two seconds. Once we spot each other, that doesn't give either of us much time for evasive action. Drivers who think it's safe to drive in fog without lights should picture themselves driving on a busy Interstate while invisible.

In some neighborhoods other people may be a hazard to walkers. It is a good idea to avoid places where gang members are shooting at each other or muggers are out and about. There is safety in numbers; a street where other people are walking is usually safer than an empty one. But if you like to walk at night or early in the morning there may not be many other people around. So use your own judgment. And carry a nine-millimeter. Oops, I shouldn't have said that. I don't want to get into the controversy about gun control.

Where I live the biggest hazard for the walker, next to motor vehicles, is the dog population. I'm talking about dogs on leashes, being walked by their owners. Surprisingly, I haven't had much trouble with dogs not on leashes. Oh yes, I've been followed, barked at, sniffed and jumped up on by dogs not on leashes, but I've never been bitten by one. Sometimes I have avoided them by simply crossing the road. Dogs are territorial and if you stay out of one's territory it probably won't bother you.

One time I returned for a visit to the farm my parents owned in Clarence, New York, near Buffalo. I was walking past another farm where a large dog was chained in the yard. When it saw me it became so excited that it broke its chain and came racing toward me. I stopped walking and affected indifference, which I certainly didn't feel, but by the time the dog reached me it had forgotten why it had gone to all that trouble.

But back to dogs on leashes. Several times, dogs that should have been under the control of their owners have attacked me. One dog bit me on my hand, but I was wearing a glove and it didn't break the skin. In another case a large dog, possibly a German shepherd, lunged for my throat and came within inches of it. Maybe they thought they were protecting their owners.

Becky Corwin-Adams says her husband was attacked by a vicious rottweiler while walking. "He had 21 puncture wounds to his hands and arms. The dog warden and other authorities took the side of the dog owner." But she still walks four to 10 miles a day.

From incidents like these I have learned to keep a safe distance from dogs on leashes, because there is no guarantee that their owners can control them. I will leave a narrow sidewalk and walk into the street to avoid a dog. At one time I would have maintained my course, figuring that it was the responsibility of the owner to restrain her dog, but now I realize that my hide is worth more than my pride.

I make exceptions for dogs I know or small dogs that can't reach higher than my ankle. I figure that if necessary I can always punt them into the next county. Just kidding. I really like dogs. As long as somebody else feeds them, walks them and cleans up their messes.

Off-road walking has a unique set of hazards. Some of these hazards come from plant and animal life. Two plants to avoid are poison ivy and poison oak. I have become well acquainted with poison oak because of several experiences with it (see chapters 6 and 11). Cacti have spines; roses have thorns. Some bushes put out long tendrils that can entangle your legs. I had an experience with them, recounted in chapter 36.

Animal hazards include insects that bite, such as mosquitoes. An insect repellent containing DEET helps. Ticks have become a problem in many parts of the country because of the spread of Lyme disease. Lyme Disease is named after the town of Old Lyme in Connecticut, which is right beside Old Saybrook, where Bonny grew up. Everything in Connecticut is old.

Where ticks abound the recommended action is to wear long pants and socks and spray insect repellent on your legs. Since ticks have a facility for getting onto other parts of your body, as well, after being in a tick-infested area it is advisable to take off your clothes and check yourself all over. Or have a good friend do it.

Larger animals can be a problem for people walking off-road. Look out for snakes. Bonny is particularly afraid of snakes. An encounter she and I had with a rattlesnake is covered in chapter 6. A folk tale I heard from a Sierra Club hike leader is that when hikers are walking in a line the first person will startle a snake, the second will rouse it and the third will get bitten. I don't guarantee this sequence of events.

I saw a dog that had been bitten on the nose by a rattlesnake one time and that wasn't funny. The owner didn't know what to do. Since she was in the mountains there probably wasn't a lot she could do. When Andy was a baby we were camping in Death Valley. Andy was playing in the sand when Bonny saw a small rattlesnake near him. They were coexisting, but there is no guarantee of that, either.

Bonny and I saw a lot of bears in Yellowstone National Park, on our honeymoon, also recounted in chapter 6. I have seen coyotes in the wild, but they are most dangerous when they live in populated areas, and sometimes eat family pets. There are even mountain lions in parts of the country. A friend of ours who has a house near Palm Springs had a stare-down with one who was drinking out of the swimming pool in his backyard—not exactly a wilderness area.

Non-living hazards for hikers include the weather. A number of weather-related incidents appear in this book. One was an encounter four of us had with a thunderstorm, described in chapter 28. That was a screaming good time. Be aware of what the weather conditions may be where you are walking, especially if you are going to be away from civilization, and carry appropriate clothing. Wise words that I should have heeded upon occasion.

As you leave populated areas and the way becomes steeper and slipperier and rockier, and cliffs loom close by, the chance for injury increases. And injuries are more serious when help isn't immediately available. For wilderness hiking it is wise to carry a first aid kit, even if it only has treatment for cuts, blisters and minor foot problems. A small foot problem can put a hiker out of action faster than anything else. I carry tape, moleskin and a small pair of scissors, as well as disinfectant.

Don't hike beyond the limits of your ability and equipment. My father went hiking with me once in the San Gabriel Mountains north of Los Angeles when he was in his 50s. We came to a place where we had to make a short but tricky climb, with quite a bit of exposure. Dad was reluctant to climb the pitch without being belayed with a rope. I didn't have a rope with me. He decided not to do it and we turned back. I think it was a wise decision.

Carry a flashlight and a map of the area. Nowadays, with modern technology, you can carry a cell phone, but be warned that cell phones don't yet work everywhere. I haven't been able to get one to work at the top of Mt. San Jacinto, near Palm Springs, yet.

Which brings us to food and water. Carry plenty of water. The companies that sell bottled water try to make us believe that their water is pure because it comes from mountain springs. Don't believe it. The sickest I ever became from eating or drinking something bad was after I drank water from a spring in the San Jacinto Mountains. Most water—even running water—has to be purified before it can be drunk, by adding iodine or by boiling.

Pack more food and water than you need. You will be glad you have it if you get lost, as I did (see chapter 31).

CHAPTER 8 Fashions on the Beach

About 1970, I heard that European beaches were going topless and predicted that the beaches of California would follow them within three years. As of the date I write this that still hasn't happened for most California beaches. The question is: why not?

You may wonder what this topic has to do with walking. The answer is: plenty. When I walked the coast of California I crossed many beaches. I had an opportunity to observe beach fashions at first hand. Walkers need to think stimulating thoughts to keep the tentacles of boredom at bay. One of the ways I kept my mind occupied was to conduct a scientific and objective examination of beachwear.

First, a few words about male beachwear, because that's all the subject deserves. In the past 30 years male beach fashions have gone from passable to ridiculous. The long, knee-length or longer, bathing suits that boys wear are beyond ugly. I suspect that fashion designers for male swimwear may be imitating basketball uniforms. Over the years the shorts basketball players wear have evolved from trim to tent. Until some sanity is restored to male swimwear (and basketball) fashions, the subject is not worth writing about.

But back to the subject of toplessness, or lack thereof, on California beaches. You must remember that many Californians are descended from New Englanders, or from Midwesterners who are descended from New Englanders. And many if not most New Englanders are descended from the Pilgrims or the Puritans.

The first thing we have to do is to distinguish the Pilgrims from the Puritans. As Bonny, a New Englander with Pilgrim ancestors who came over on the Mayflower, has pointed out, the Pilgrims were not puritans (note the small "p"). The Pilgrims liked to have fun and wear bright colors. They were even known to hoist a bottle upon occasion.

Having said that, I hasten to add that Bonny, herself, is not a raucous person. She would certainly not go topless on a beach. Well, there was the time when she was a teenager that she went skinny-dipping with her girlfriend and the priests came down to the beach, but that is beyond the scope of this book.

The Puritans, unlike the Pilgrims, were grim, humorless people, who were always afraid that somebody, somewhere was having fun. Remember that when Puritan missionaries from New England went to Hawaii, they not only made the natives wear clothes, they also continued to follow their own rigid custom of putting on their long underwear each fall and not taking it off until spring. That may have been an effective way of preventing adultery. And, oh yes, no white shoes after Labor Day.

The Puritans left England and came to America because they were being persecuted for their religious beliefs. Since the first Puritans arrived on American shores in the 1600s, they have spent their time persecuting the rest of us. On the other hand, the English have been celebrating ever since, and I suspect that it's too late to ask them to take the Puritans back.

Like it or not, the prudery of the Puritans has permeated most of the United States like a virus, and has even reached California. That is why, with a few exceptions, there are no topless or nude beaches in California. The hippies tried to change all that in the 1960s, but they have become an endangered species and are now limited to small bands, roving the hills near Eugene, Oregon.

However, in my scientific investigation, I have determined that female beach fashions have changed since the 1970s. Bikinis were invented some time before that decade so the changes have been evolutionary rather than revolutionary. And they have occurred to the bikini bottoms, not the bras, which have remained relatively stable, if not fully supportive.

The major changes to bikini bottoms have been the French-cut sides and the thong, both of which have increased the amount of skin exposed to ultraviolet radiation. Fortunately, the younger generation today is well aware of the hazards of radiation because of the unending vigilance of the federal government, which protects us from everything, since everything eventually causes cancer.

The changes to the bikini bottoms have occurred slowly enough so that the puritans in our midst have apparently been caught sleeping. Whether or not this strategy will work for the tops is debatable. The problem here is nipples. Once you start exposing nipples all hell breaks loose. Apparently, nipples are either too sensual or too pornographic for Americans. In any case we have to be protected from seeing them. If you don't believe me, tell me the last time you saw a nipple on network television.

Nursing babies know about nipples from day one, but when they get to a certain age they must be weaned and kept from seeing a nipple again until they are 17. There have even been court cases to attempt to force mothers to stop nursing their children because somebody said they were too old to nurse.

The guardians of the state are doing their best to protect us from nipples. One time I was walking along a local beach when I saw a burly policeman who had handcuffed himself to a girl about half his size. She was clearly terrified. Her crime? Somehow, she had lost her bikini top. I never found out whether he received a medal of valor for his day's work.

An ordnance passed by the city council of my city, Rancho Palos Verdes, after years of ignoring our nude beach, prohibits people from appearing in public in a manner that exposes, among many other things, "…(for women) any portion of the breast at or below the upper edge of the areola." My American Heritage Dictionary defines areola as "A small ring of color around a center portion, as about the nipple of the breast."

I understand that back in the early part of a previous century ordnances like this applied equally to men and women. However, men stripped off their tops and protested in such numbers on beaches, with their areolas in full view, that these ordnances became unenforceable in regard to them. Perhaps, if ordnances were enacted prohibiting men from wearing anything shorter than knee-length pants on the beach, their contrary natures would arouse them and they would rise up to rid themselves of this fashion nightmare.

Walkers are exposed to all sorts of educational opportunities. While walking the coast of California I became somewhat of an authority on beachwear. I have also developed my own opinions about it and haven't hesitated to voice them. But then I feel that walkers should take an active part in the community.

CHAPTER 9 Giving Directions

"How do I get to Strickler Road?"

I went over to the open window of the car and confidently told the perplexed driver where to go. Motorists have asked me for directions wherever I walked and I have always tried to help them.

This particular incident occurred while I was visiting my parents' farm in the town of Clarence, near Buffalo, New York, where I lived during my high school years. I thought I remembered the local geography. After all, I had walked and driven in this area for five years. Most of the roads run north and south or east and west and the land is relatively flat. How could I go wrong?

Unfortunately, as I continued my walk, I soon realized that I had pointed the motorist in the opposite direction from where he should have gone. I knew he would be upset when he discovered my error and I kept a fearful eye out for his returning car until I finally turned off onto another road. Fortunately, I didn't see him again and so escaped his wrath. Maybe he never figured out I had given him the wrong scoop.

Most of the time I do better. In my local community on the Palos Verdes Peninsula, near Los Angeles, people are always getting lost because of the hills and curves, and I have had vast experience in helping them get unlost. Most cases are fairly simple. Sometimes all I have to say is "Turn left at the next stop sign."

But if the lost souls are trying to find a street address and the directions they were given originally are incomplete I can't help them. One man said that the street he was looking for was "Via something or other." I pointed out that all the streets in that neighborhood were Via something or other. Another was looking for a house number that just flat didn't exist on the street where it was supposed to be.

Another man said he was trying to get to a wedding chapel. Since we weren't in Las Vegas I didn't know about any wedding chapel in the area. It wasn't until after he had gone that I figured out he probably wanted to go to La Venta Inn, a local landmark where a lot of weddings are performed. People who ask me for directions should know that I have a very literal mind.

One couple asked me how to get back to "civilization," meaning the Los Angeles basin below, and when I tried to tell them the most direct route they said they wanted to see the ocean first. I would have had to write a book to explain how to get to the ocean and then to the outside world. I gave them some directions, but as I made them more and more complicated I realized that at some point they would have to stop again and ask somebody else. At least they would no longer be my problem.

A young couple stopped and asked me for directions one day. I couldn't hear the driver, who was on the other side of the car from me, so I poked my head in the passenger window. When I did I received an eyeful of the décolletage of his pretty companion. Most of my experiences at direction giving haven't been that exhilarating.

Recently, a taxi driver stopped and asked me for help while I was on my morning walk. He even had a map, and yet he was several miles and several hundred vertical feet from where he wanted to be. I would think that one qualification for driving a taxi should be the ability to read maps. I hope his fare didn't have a plane to catch.

In Old Saybrook, Connecticut, when I was visiting Ellen, my mother-in-law, a truck driver stopped to ask me for help. I was able to whip out a map of the area and point out his destination to him. He was greatly impressed by my preparedness. Of course, I had been using the map to keep myself from getting lost.

I was even able to shine on my first visit to the Republic of Ireland. On my first morning in the emerald isle I awoke early at a bed and breakfast, not yet accustomed to the time change, and strolled down to the harbor at Wexford, a sleepy village on the east coast whose population was once decimated by Oliver Cromwell. But that was in the days before they had automobiles.

A car stopped beside me just after dawn and a man asked me the way to the railroad station. I had arrived with my family by bus from the ferry terminal the evening before, and I knew that the railroad station and the bus station were at the same place. They weren't more than half a mile from where the driver and I were, but that didn't reduce my pride at being able to give a local resident precise instructions on how to get there.

I had good luck in The Hague, Netherlands, also. I tagged along with Bonny, who was there on a business trip, and when she was conducting her business I had some time alone to explore the local area. I learned how to ride the trams, which are run on the honor system, except occasionally when a "checker" boards and checks to be sure everybody has a ticket.

Twice, good-looking Dutch girls asked me for directions in Dutch (in spite of my white sneakers) about the transportation system. Not wanting to drive them away, I asked if they spoke English. Both of them did and I was able to help them. One wanted to get to the hotel where I was staying so we rode the same tram. My efforts at continuing the conversation beyond direction-giving were not notably successful.

As a walker I try to stay on good terms with motorists so that they won't throw ice cubes in my face, play chicken with me and force me off the road, splash me by driving through puddles from recent rains or attempt to run me down at intersections. Therefore, I have developed some helpful rules for giving directions to errant drivers:

Do not give more than three directions at once. The average person cannot remember more than three directions and will get hopelessly confused while trying to do so. I know this is true because I am the average person and I can't remember more than three of anything at a time, including items to buy at the store, tasks I have to perform or directions.

Be precise. Say, "Turn left at the second stop sign," not, "Turn left near the mountain."

Be terse. This is particularly important when the car is blocking traffic, as is often the case, endangering both the driver's life and your life, since you have to walk into the middle of the street to talk with her. For some reason, drivers who are ordinarily safety-conscious forget about safety when they are lost. Say, "Proceed about two miles and turn right at the light," not, "Well, you go along this road, past the white church, and you'll come to a dairy farm on your left. You'll know it because it has a red barn. Don't turn there. Keep going until you get to..."

Don't flap your arms as if they were chicken wings and point like a weather vane to illustrate your instructions. It only adds to the driver's confusion. In Italy, disregard this suggestion.

If the driver asks you a question, such as, "Do I turn left at Macadamia Street?" say, "Correct," not, "Right." Only use "right" as a direction. If you tell a driver to turn left and he says, "Left, right?" more than once, back away from the car slowly, smile and wish him good luck. And hope he doesn't return to haunt you.

If you aren't able to give directions off the top of your head, ask the driver if she has a map. An amazing number of drivers don't carry maps with them when they venture into areas unknown to them. If she doesn't have a map you may not be able to help her, but at least you can shift the responsibility for being lost back to her.

CHAPTER 10 Walkers Speak

Robert Sweetgall, the dean of American walkers, was valedictorian of his high school class. He was also a junk food junkie with the nickname of Butterball. After he finished college he worked in an office for a number of years and then decided he needed to take action to fight the odds against him because of his family history of heart disease. Robert started his fitness campaign by walking across the USA and then, for an encore, he walked through all 50 states, carrying only a fanny pack. At night he stayed in the homes of kind-hearted people and sometimes he slept in police stations.

Now, having walked across the USA a total of seven times, he teaches other people the health benefits of walking and nobody is more qualified to do so. Robert has written many books on walking. His website is creativewalking.com. He says the good news is that you don't have to be an ultra-marathoner or a race-walker to achieve these benefits; walking just a few miles a day at a comfortable pace will do it.

A foot care tip from Robert: He recommends taking off your shoes and socks and letting your feet breathe every hour or so during a long walk to help prevent blisters. And don't wear cotton socks. Socks made of synthetics or wool are much better for keeping feet dry.

Wendy Bumgardner is the webmaster of walking.about.com, a website that contains all the information you'll ever need to know about walking for fitness, finding the right shoes, preventing and treating injuries, etc. Concerning why she walks, she says, "First, I would definitely weigh over 200 pounds if I hadn't become a walker, based on family traits. It is my main fitness activity. I also use walking for entertainment and relaxation—listening to books on tape while walking, clearing my mind. It is also my main social activity—most of my friends are walking friends I have met at volkssport events (events of the American Volkssport Association (AVA) or International Marching League (IML)). We often walk together, talk, and have a day's outing centered around walking." Wendy walks about four times a week—twice for 30-60 minutes and twice for longer walks of six to18 miles.

I am indebted to Noel Blackham who wrote the book, *One Man and His Dog Go Walkies*, the story of his walk from John O'Groats to Land's End in Great Britain. I followed his route almost exactly. Noel, who lives in Birmingham, England, has also walked around Wales. His daily routine includes four dog-walks, "with occasional rambles of four to 10 miles with dog." He walks for "The challenge. The sense of achievement. Modest self-esteem. The chance to explore, discover nature and feel at one with the universe." He catalogs the benefits of walking as: "Good general health and fitness. Exercise for the whole body without injury to muscles, joints and shock-absorbing systems which can result from the jarring and jolting of running on roads."

Noel told me about an amazing 52-mile, 27-hour walk he did with his dog on June 22nd and 23rd, 1991, in England and Wales. He started at Titterstone Clee and climbed a series of Shropshire summits on his way to Corndon Hill. He walked all night and says, "The feeling of solitude on top of the Long Mynd, in the middle of the night, was a wonderful experience!" At one time, "There was still a pale glow in the sky to our left, and I was unsure whether the sun was setting or rising, for it scarcely dips below the horizon at this time of year."

When the sun came out, "It was encircled by the colours of the spectrum, like a small, full rainbow, or a large, solar corona. When I turned to look again, the sun appeared to be wearing a black sweatband, like those worn by sportsmen across the forehead. It was obviously a thick, or deep, bank of cloud, which was lost in the mist, but which was clearly visible where it crossed the face of the sun. Gradually, it slipped lower and lower, until it disappeared completely, off 'the sun's chin.' Sometimes, the sun would flare up into a dazzling brilliance, when patches of the mist became less dense."

My old army buddy, Bob Harrington, walks more than he used to and admits to having had at least one memorable walking experience: "My most recent memory of a walking experience was walking approximately seven miles during a period of extreme agitation in order to clear my mind and to cope with life. I started at about 9:45 p.m. and finished at around 12:05 a.m. The result was the agitation disappeared, I had a wonderful conversation with myself, I felt free as a bird, and my legs hurt like hell!"

Another army buddy and former roommate of mine, Jim Yates, says he walks three times weekly for up to eight miles, the last part up a steep hill. It allows him time to think and helps him to maintain his weight. For his most memorable experience, he goes back to his youth: "Believe it might have been when I was around 12 or 13. I lived about 120 miles east of St. Louis, out on a farm with no electricity or indoor bathroom. One day I walked with my brother and three or four others of the same age four miles up the railroad tracks to another small town. For some reason, I seem to remember that walk as being one of the most joyous in my entire life—know it was just being with great friends and being at that age in my life. We just talked, threw rocks at things, enjoyed the view of the countryside."

Rose Jensen walks six days a week, three or four miles a day and thinks it is a great way to start the day. She lives on the Palos Verdes Peninsula, where I live, and started going on guided nature walks on the peninsula in the 1980s. She learned a lot about the topography and history of the area. When she traveled with her husband she liked to take an early-morning walk in the villages they were visiting to look at the buildings and observe the people before the crowds came out.

Dick Throne has had a stroke and walks from his house to the corner and back, "to stay alive, keep my heart pumping. And breathe good fresh air." It also gives him a chance to talk to the neighbors and see what's going on in the neighborhood. His most memorable walking experiences with his wife, Eve, were walking on the Great Wall of China in November, when the weather was near freezing, and walking on glaciers in the Canadian Rockies at over 10,000 feet.

Martin Shepherd walks his dogs to help him recover from open-heart surgery. An ex-smoker, he has improved his breathing and stamina, and has strengthened his heart muscle. He is experiencing better general health and physical condition. At the age of five he climbed onto a table and walked up and down the tabletop. He was enjoying his walk until he forgot he was on a table and walked off the edge, necessitating stitches in his scalp. He never walked on a table again.

Lanny Swallow walks three miles with his dog every morning. About walking he says, "It's generally relaxing, unless my dog sees a skunk, and it's good exercise. I also listen to books on cassette while I walk, so I get to educate myself at the same time."

He likes to walk in England. "My favorite day walking was an April day in 1997. It was my first time in England and my wife and I walked in the Cotswolds from Lower Slaughter to Upper Slaughter and finally to Bourton on the Water. It was a beautiful, sunny day and the countryside was gorgeous. We met friendly walkers along the way, had lunch at a pub in a little village and had a great time. We followed an ordinance survey map in a book that I had and we got lost at one point when we weren't sure what a stile was, but it just added to the enjoyment of our walk. The walk lasted about six hours and I still think of it often. By walking we got to see parts of the country that we wouldn't have seen otherwise."

Karen Garland walks three or more miles a day, for exercise, to be outside and to clear her head. She says walkers are very friendly folk. She often prays while she walks and memorizes scripture. Walking gives her a sense of well-being.

My wife's cousin, Marge Hackbarth, has gone bird watching and hiking in more countries than most of us can name. Now retired, she is still traveling and tries to walk two miles each day unless she does some other exercise, such as biking or swimming. She often walks more on weekends. She walks at home for health benefits and in groups for sociability and to enjoy the beauty of the locale. Years ago she sponsored a project to get as many people as possible to walk all the through hiking trails in Connecticut. Those who finished became members of the 400 Club.

One time when Bonny, Andy and I were hiking in the White Mountains of New Hampshire we met Marge at Pinkham Notch (she was there with another group). We had just come down from Mt. Washington, but Andy and I wanted to climb up to Carter Notch and spend the night at the Appalachian Mountain Club hut there. It was drizzling and cool and we were trying to determine whether to wear long pants or shorts. We asked the sage. Marge suggested we wear shorts because "legs dry faster than pants." She was right.

Mary Vandever tries to walk at least a mile every day. She walks because "I have an irrational fear that if I stop moving I'll turn into a marbleized statue, without the beauty or elegance of marble." Walking gives her a sense of freedom and she always feels better after she walks. She fears losing her independence if she can't walk. At one time she was in such pain from osteoporosis that she didn't know whether she could walk the block back to her house. Her doctor prescribed medication and walking, both of which have helped make her bones stronger.

Louise Watkins walks for 45 minutes every day on a treadmill or in her community because, "I can't not do it." It gives her a life force and places her in her universe. Her most memorable walk was a 50-mile trek across Canyon de Chelly with the Navajos.

Darcy Mellinger had her first great walking experience when she trained for and participated in a half-marathon to benefit cancer sufferers. Not only did she enjoy it, she also received support from relatives and friends and raised a lot of money. She came out of it "a healthier, happier woman" and immediately signed up to walk a full marathon in Hawaii, commenting that this was one way for her to finally see Hawaii.

Frank Brown and his whole family walked in an overnight marathon in the Washington D.C. area to shed some light on the national tragedy of suicide. Frank had lost a daughter to suicide. He said that each of the walkers carried a picture or other memento of a loved one. People along their route honked horns and applauded, even at 2 o'clock in the morning.

By the time Alonzo Monk had reached the latter half of his seventies he had competed in 133 marathons. This is made more amazing by the fact that he didn't run in his first one until he was 49. His best time of three hours and six minutes came at age 51. As he grew older he slowed down and looked more like a walker than a runner. But he keeps going six to ten miles a day, "to maintain my physical and mental health." What is the dividing line between walking and running? Does it matter?

Helene Fennessy likes to go on volkswalks (walks sponsored by chapters of the American Volkssport Association). Walking is a way for her to spend time with her granddaughters, away from the TV and other interruptions. Among her walking memories are, "The expression on my granddaughter's face when this city child was offered blackberries off a bush alongside a country road. Stopping to watch a colony of prairie dogs in South Dakota. Coming upon the sight of two pythons sunning themselves in a yard in Florida. And always the ever changing, always delightful, view of our own Corpus Christi Bay."

Kim Grubb began walking as an easy form of exercise to get herself into shape. When a friend found out he had leukemia she signed up to do a marathon in his honor. Now she averages five half and full marathons a year. A walking benefit she has experienced, in addition to health and camaraderie, is knowing that walking for a charity helps save the lives of others. A memorable experience she had was when "the half marathon I did went through Camp Pendleton and I had 30 young army guys screaming my name in encouragement, telling me to pick up my feet, get moving, and that I could win this race, etc."

Celia Miner has always enjoyed walking. "My mother walked a lot when we were young, so sitting in front of the tube was not an early habit. As I got into college I replaced walking with running and eventually became a 'running snob,' looking down on people who moved too slowly and blocked the paths, strolling two or three abreast. Then the knees gave out at age 32 and forced me into running retirement. I went back to walking to keep my weight in check, but I walked as fast as I could, pushing myself with long walks at 12-13 minutes a mile and cramming as many 10K walks as I could into a day. Predictably, my body eventually rebelled, this time with foot problems. I slowed down, let my body heal and rediscovered the 17.5-minute mile."

Celia likes to go on walks sponsored by the International Marching League and has walked in many countries, with "the chance to leave my footprints around the world, seeing places on foot that most people only glimpse quickly as they whiz by in air-conditioned tour buses, with a staticky PA system mangling the tour guide's recitation of facts." On her honeymoon she and her husband participated in international walking festivals in Japan and Korea with 50,000 to 100,000 walkers. As almost the only non-Asians they attracted a lot of attention. Her biggest challenge, also with her husband, was finishing the four-day walk in Nijmegen, Holland, of 50 kilometers per day to earn the Queen's Medal. "The experience ran the gamut of emotions—tears of pain and frustration when the feet screamed for rest to tears of joy when we crossed the finish line on day four."

Margot Nelligan walks three or four miles at a time, three or four times per week. She has walked in the Avon Breast Cancer fundraiser (60 miles over three days) and made walking/hiking trips to other countries. She says active vacations "give me an opportunity to tour an area at a leisurely pace, walking through beautiful countryside and small towns, meeting a lot of local people and getting a flavor for the culture that I couldn't get if I were whizzing through by car, bus or train. The other participants in these tours are generally like-minded, and the camaraderie that develops has been great on all my trips so far. Not to mention the fact that I can truly enjoy the food and wine of the local area without guilt, since I will walk it off the next day!"

Vicki Stemm walks four days a week, in addition to doing strength and flexibility workouts. She walks for health and weight control, and to relax and organize her thoughts. She walked the Avon Breast Cancer fundraiser from Santa Barbara to Los Angeles in memory of a close friend and enjoys walking in beautiful places, such as Yosemite Valley.

Vicki's husband, Eugene, walks 20 to 24 miles per week, and that usually includes one hike. As a physical educator, health educator, coach and athlete, he enjoys the physical and psychological invigoration of walking. It is also part of his rehabilitation program after having undergone quintuple heart-bypass surgery. Nine months before his bypass operation he experienced "an extreme feeling of fatigue and physical discomfort. It was the onset of my artery blockage problems, but I did not recognize it as such or I denied it. If my heart had not been so strong, as my doctors told me later, I might have 'packed it in' at that time."

Stuart Plimpton has a demanding schedule that includes nighttime hikes with the Sierra Club and frequent climbs of Southern California mountains, especially Mt. Wilson and Mt. Baldy (aka Mt. San Antonio). He walks because jogging is too tough, for weight control and something he calls "sweat ecstasy." Some of the things he has seen while walking include, "...American Kestrels catching prey...gray foxes foraging, deer munching and snakes snaking, colorful birds. On moonlit nights, along the shoreline, Black Crowned, night-fishing Herons fishing and black skimmers skimming. I have met interesting new friends and old acquaintances with which to walk and talk to, discovering new observations and opinions. In the higher elevations I have seen such extraordinary vistas that I'm transformed by their beauty..."

Sandy Spaulding and her husband are very active in volkssporting and most of their vacations are programmed around AVA and IML walks they want to do. They have discovered there is no better way to see the United States than on a walk. They also went on the first walk ever held in the DDR (East Germany). "The East Germans were very poor, but very eager to show all a good time. They had hung streamers of cloth from their windows, draping them across the street and all hung out their windows and cheered us on."

Donald Janes walks daily and tries to cover 70 miles a week. One of his memorable experiences was "the first volksmarch conducted in now the former German Democratic Republic (East Germany) that walked along the eastern side of the Iron Curtain with its fortifications, watch towers, barbed wire and mine fields." He talks about his walks on his website: www.der-adler.com.

I was going to use a quote from Terry Vasquez, an old friend and co-worker of Bonny, for this book. In April 2003 Bonny and I flew to Portland and visited Terry, who had moved there from Los Angeles some months before. (We also attended the annual Discovery Walk Festival in Vancouver, Washington, a marvelous walking event. See www.discoverywalk.org.) For three days we walked with Terry beside the Willamette River and along other scenic routes in the Portland area. Unfortunately, two weeks later she succumbed to a hereditary heart problem. We will miss her.

I myself walk because I'm restless. I can't stand being cooped up. When I was in college I would walk around town on winter evenings, peering through the windows of houses and wondering if I could ever be content to live the life of the families I saw there. After college I worked in the computer industry for over a quarter of a century, but fortunately, most of my jobs allowed me to be out of the office a lot, visiting customers. When I had to sit at a desk for an extended period of time I became either antsy or sleepy.

I have to get my quotidian allowance of the outdoors. That's why I don't join a health club. I can't walk on a treadmill when the sun is shining, which it is most of the time in California. Living in a good climate helps, but even when I was stuck at Andy's house in Virginia during the big snowfall of February 2003, he and I went outside and shoveled snow for three days.

I don't want to define myself by my possessions or by my use of technology. Underneath the artificial shells of our clothes, houses and cars, human beings haven't changed much in the last million years. When I walk I feel at one with my ancestors who had to put their hands in cold water and didn't have cell phones and DVDs.

Part II Walking the World

The answer to the question, "Where can we walk?" is "Just about everywhere." From my own experience I tell about some of my favorite walks in some of my favorite places to walk, in many parts of the world. Starting with four great walking cities in the US (Los Angeles, San Francisco, New York and Washington, D.C.) and branching out to the rest of the United States, this is a wonderful country in which to walk. Then cross the border into Canada. Walk with the philosophers and sea captains of ancient Greece or join the fast-steppers in the British Isles (but remember to look to the right when you cross the street). Find out what it was like to walk behind the late but not lamented Berlin Wall and Iron Curtain. Tour the rest of Europe and dip into North Africa at Morocco. Straddle Europe and Asia by walking in Turkey, and take off to the South Pacific—New Zealand and French Polynesia. Then it's on to Japan, China and the rest of Southeast Asia.

Alan Cook

CHAPTER 11 Four Great US Walking Cities

Los Angeles

Walking in Los Angeles is impossible. Well, it's not literally impossible to walk in Los Angeles—although the joke is that nobody does. I mean that Los Angeles is so large and has so many different faces that it is not possible to describe a "typical" Los Angeles walk—because there isn't one.

I have chronicled walking the Los Angeles coastline in chapter 34, "California Coast—Mexican Border through Los Angeles County," and talked about climbing in the San Gabriel Mountains in chapter 27, "Hiking and Rock Climbing in California." Other places to walk in the LA area are described here.

The first walk movie fans may think about is the Hollywood Walk of Fame, and indeed, it does bring back nostalgic memories to see the names of entertainers we have loved on the plaques embedded in the sidewalks. The handprints and footprints in the courtyard of the Chinese Theater are photographed constantly for the same reason. And there is no experience like walking around the lot of a movie studio.

In 1968, while working for a startup software services company (not Microsoft, more's the pity), I managed a project at Warner Brothers to develop computer systems for tracking costs of movies. Incidentally, for those of you who may be fortunate enough to work in the movie business, never accept a percentage of the profits for your work, because no movie ever makes a profit.

John Nownes, the longtime manager of the Warner Brothers computer facility, knew the lot intimately, and we would take walks around it together. On these walks I (and Bonny on a couple of occasions) got to see the permanent sets, such as the western street. We went through storehouses full of antique cars, ornate mirrors and exquisite candelabra, used as props in classic movies. We saw the soundstage where the movie *Blade Runner* was being filmed, with its eerie and lifeless futuristic set, and on other soundstages watched such stars as Ephram Zimbalist, Jr. and Angie Dickinson in action.

One lunchtime, John and I stumbled into a soundstage where a film crew was dubbing in sound for a movie. A man was rubbing his hand on a mattress while a microphone picked up the swish-swish. On a nearby screen a scene from the movie, *I Love You, Alice B. Toklas*, was being projected, involving some rather erotic love-making (for that time) between Peter Sellers and the gorgeous Leigh Taylor-Young. I think John, who was originally from Nebraska and all it stands for, was quite embarrassed by this.

Los Angeles County has flatland, beaches, hills and mountains. The county contains the city of Los Angeles and many other cities, including Rancho Palos Verdes, where I live. Rancho Palos Verdes is one of four cities on the Palos Verdes Peninsula, a hill that rises from sea level to 1,500 feet, 10 miles south of the Los Angeles Airport.

On a topographical map the 700-foot line passes through my backyard. My morning walk is a 4.3-mile loop that goes from my house up to about 1,200 feet. It dips down and then up again before returning home via a series of sharp descents. The walk invigorates me and gets my blood flowing. I walk on streets now, but part of my walk used to be down a canyon trail. A big rain one spring so deepened and widened a ditch that crosses the trail that it became a miniature Grand Canyon. Because I didn't want to take my life in my hands that early in the morning, I changed my route.

As I walk, I can see the Los Angeles basin spread out below me, often with its thousands of lights still twinkling like stars when I start out. I can almost see the several million residents getting out of bed, yawning sleepily, to start another day. I can follow the coastline with my eyes, north to Santa Monica, and then west through Malibu all the way to Point Dume. On a clear day I can see the Hollywood sign and Mt. Baldy, the 10,000 footer that dominates the skyline of the San Gabriel Mountains to the northeast, and if it is clear enough to see a hundred miles I can make out massive Mt. San Gorgonio, farther east, the highest peak in Southern California at 11,500 feet.

There is occasional excitement, even in peaceful Palos Verdes. My cousin, Kimberly, and I were walking through the PV Peninsula Center shopping area one time when we came upon a standoff between Sheriff's deputies and some robbers who were holed up inside a jewelry store. The deputies had serious weapons and were deployed throughout the area. We had to stay behind the police tape and couldn't go into the parking lot that was in the line of fire from the store. The robbers later surrendered.

Another bit of excitement occurred when I was working at the computer division of McDonnell Douglas. A sales rep and I were walking on a San Diego street—not part of Los Angeles, but definitely part of Southern California—when a Volkswagen mini-bus cruised by us—with its rear end on fire. As we watched, the driver pulled into a parking lot and stopped. From everywhere, or so it seemed, half a dozen men materialized, running and carrying fire extinguishers. They put out the fire in a matter of seconds.

I walked the Palos Verdes Marathon twice, in the days when the route went from the shopping area called Peninsula Center, at about 1,000 feet, up to the top of the peninsula, and then steeply down Palos Verdes Drive East to Palos Verdes Drive South, which follows the coast. Marathoner brother Mike would never attempt a run with such an arduous downhill because, as he says, the downhills are a lot harder on the knees than the uphills. However, I didn't have any problems *walking* the downhill portion, which is not as difficult as hiking down a steep mountain trail.

In recent years, the layout of the marathon has been changed. It no longer has any huge downhill or uphill. The route rolls up and down along the south coast of the Palos Verdes Peninsula, with ocean views all the way. Nowadays I walk the half-marathon instead of the marathon because this gets me back to the start/finish line during the same time period as some of the marathon runners. It's more fun to finish with the runners because I can pretend that the spectators cheering them on are cheering for me.

From the marathon route we get a good view of Catalina Island, 26 miles across the sea. I have sailed to Catalina many times. Andy and I stayed at a Boy Scout camp in a remote part of the island when we belonged to the YMCA Indian Guides, and hiked in the nearby hills. Bonny and I have sailed to Avalon, walked around the waterfront village during the day and danced to big bands in the casino at night. At sunset the musicians came out on the balcony and played the song, "Avalon." The haunting strains carried across the harbor to every sailboat moored there.

Catalina has good walks in and around Avalon, where the number of motor vehicles is restricted. Since it is in a bowl, if you go very far in any direction you have to climb a hill. Backpackers can camp among the buffalo and wild goats in other parts of the island. Contrary to what some tourists think, Catalina is not only part of the United States, it is also part of Los Angeles County.

On many evenings I have walked the Sierra Club hike on Signal Hill, near Long Beach, with my half-uncle, Karl. Karl is actually younger than I am because my grandfather remarried late in life, to Maude, a much younger woman, and Karl was the result. Karl contends that I have said I will never call him Uncle Karl. That is probably true.

There's a small mountain in Griffith Park, the massive Los Angeles city park. The peak is called Mt. Hollywood and it is easily climbed from the planetarium/observatory. Some people climb it every day. Back in the days when Los Angeles had bad smog this could be an irritating (to the eyes and throat) experience. But now smoggy days are rare. Residents no longer say they don't trust air they can't see. One time Bonny, Andy and I climbed up to the "Hollywood" sign, also in Griffith Park, and took some close-up photos of it. It may be illegal to approach the sign now so check with your tax advisor.

When I attended UCLA, in West Los Angeles, I walked everywhere because I didn't have a car. I lived for a semester in the men's co-op. We arranged get-togethers with a nearby residence for women. One of these took place in Griffith Park. I was in my element, climbing up steep hillsides and assisting coeds to do the same.

A couple of days later I developed red bumps over much of my body. Most of my body itched, including my genital area. Scratching gave me an intense burning sensation, but I couldn't resist scratching, much as a junky can't resist getting a fix, and as a result I developed open sores. I assumed I had something like three-day measles and spent a day or two in bed (it may have been spring break).

When I couldn't stand it any more I went to the university health service. A woman doctor listened to my symptoms and asked me to drop my pants, not something I wanted to do. After looking at my swollen genitalia she said I had poison oak, which, she explained, travels through the bloodstream. That was my introduction to a hiker's affliction I have caught several times since.

I don't know whether any of the coeds I climbed with caught poison oak. I was attracted to one, a pretty Japanese girl named Joyce, and this would have been a perfect way to follow up with her—to compare blisters if she had any or to gain her sympathy if she didn't. But for some reason I never did this. It's just one of those things that might have been.

I often walked along busy Wilshire Boulevard to next-door Beverly Hills to see foreign films at the Canon Theater on Canon Drive, because the Westwood theaters didn't show foreign movies. In Beverly Hills, a city completely surrounded by the city of Los Angeles, the joke is not that nobody walks but that nobody is allowed to walk. However, I have never been stopped for walking on Wilshire Boulevard, as Ray Bradbury has, prompting his short story, "The Pedestrian," which takes place in a world where nobody walks.

Actually, people do walk in Beverly Hills. They walk in the shopping centers. They walk along the exclusive streets, such as Rodeo Drive, look in the shop windows and marvel at the prices. Of course, no tourist can actually afford to buy anything at these shops. Some of the shops are so exclusive that the doors are always locked and nobody is allowed inside.

When I first moved to California, permanently, I lived for a few months in Echo Park, just north of downtown Los Angeles. I walked around Echo Park Lake, a local gathering place, with pedal boats and no swimming. When the lake was drained one time you wouldn't believe what was found on the bottom. There are hills in the area that rival those in San Francisco for steepness and if you can navigate the sharp ups and downs you can walk from Glendale Boulevard east to Chavez Ravine, where the Los Angeles Dodgers play.

In spite of rumors to the contrary, Los Angeles does have a downtown area. It used to be that the highest building in the city was the city hall, but then height restrictions were lifted and now there are a number of futuristic metal and glass skyscrapers that look too clean to be real. The theory is that we have learned how to make earthquake-resistant buildings. I hope that's true.

The beautiful downtown library building, rebuilt after a fire gutted the original building, contains an extensive collection of literature for all ages and interests on a number of levels, reachable by a series of escalators in an open atrium. At the other end of the age spectrum is the Bradbury Building, built in 1893, with an interior that is an architectural marvel.

At street level the sights that bombard the eye of the walker are much more grubby and real. And you will never encounter most of them in the suburbs. During the day, at least, the hubbub of commercial activity and a continuous flow of pedestrians mark this as a true city. There is the garment district where I used to buy discounted suits, a diamond district and other "districts."

Many of the streets are center-city seedy, with pawnshops, small cafes and other places where you can buy just about anything at a discount. This is the part of town that makes you appreciate how lucky you are that you don't have to live here, and in fact most of the people who work here live elsewhere.

But there are also the people who don't officially live anywhere. When I worked for Chrysalis, a nonprofit organization that helps homeless people get back into the workforce, some of us took a walking tour of the area centering on 5th Street, which at the time was a campground strewn with tents and blankets. It was a city within a city, where cigarettes were a medium of exchange, but dollars were also greedily accepted.

These people walk because they don't have any other method of transportation, unless they can raise bus fare. And if they have the money for bus fare they may spend it on drugs or liquor. We toured the missions that gave them food and a place to sleep, sometimes at the price of following the rules laid down by the staff, which may include doing volunteer work and studying the scriptures. But many of these people are homeless because they don't like society's rules.

We saw one agency that will accept people in any state of sobriety, no questions asked, and let them sleep on a cot for eight hours. At the end of that time they can still linger in the courtyard in front of the building.

That is a dark side of Los Angeles. Every large city has a dark side. However, LA is so diverse that many residents never see the dark side. Perhaps it's a good idea for us to visit the dark side once in a while because it makes us appreciate the light side.

San Francisco

For my money, the greatest walking city in the world is San Francisco, although I wouldn't want to live there (but that's another story). Chapter 35, "California Coast—Ventura County through San Francisco," describes my walk along San Francisco's ocean coastline and across the Golden Gate Bridge, but that isn't the part of San Francisco I like most.

What I like—love—about San Francisco are its hills. I am a hill person. Why I'm a hill person I'm not sure since I was born in the flatlands of western New York. My father liked hills; maybe that's the reason. As my brothers and I grew older he took us to progressively higher hills and mountains (see chapter 3).

The city and county of San Francisco have the same boundaries. The area within is as compact as a snowball, whereas Los Angeles is as spread out as the tentacles of a jellyfish. The hills of San Francisco are contained within a few square blocks inside the city. It is possible to climb all the major hills in San Francisco in one day, if you have enough stamina, whereas one day is barely enough to let you get started seeing Los Angeles by foot (or any other way).

Walking the urban hills of San Francisco is different from walking in rural hills or mountains. Mountains offer trees, rocks, dirt and occasional wild animals. San Francisco offers concrete, asphalt, cable cars, motorcars and buildings. The wild animals are the people.

San Francisco (calling it Frisco will brand you as an outsider) has the noise and pollution of a city, but it also has spectacular views of the bay, with its famous bridges. That is, if you can see the bay. For San Francisco also has fog. The joke is that San Francisco has one season—winter. Well, maybe early spring. Because it doesn't snow there and it doesn't get really cold. But with the fog and rain and wind it can be miserable. On the other hand, I have been in San Francisco on the most beautiful sunny day the earth has ever seen.

Driving in San Francisco can be hazardous to your health. Picture Steve McQueen, in the movie, *Bullitt,* racing his Mustang up and down the hills during the chase scene, spending more time in the air more than on the road. Flying over the tops of hills and not being able to see if there was anything below him. Imagine that you're driving his Mustang and see if your stomach stays in place.

Parking in San Francisco is a bad joke. What parking places there are on the hills are so precarious that cars parked perpendicular to the street look as if they could be tipped over with one finger. Therefore, the only reasonable transportation alternative, besides the cable cars, is walking.

Walking in San Francisco is just hazardous to your wind. But I still enjoy it. I enjoy walking up the section of Lombard Street, self-proclaimed as "the world's crookedest street." Passing the houses along the street that cling to the cliff, built by people hoping that the San Andreas Fault and the many smaller faults will stay relatively quiet for another century.

I enjoy visiting the Cable Car Museum, to see the cables that pull the cars and learn how the brakes work. It isn't how the cable cars go that worries me; it's how they stop.

I love to walk through Chinatown, humming "Grant Avenue," from *Flower Drum Song.* The sights and smells of these few blocks may not be gathered together anywhere else in the world, not even old China.

The restaurants have delicious names like The Golden Dragon, or is it the Golden Lotus? The Grand Palace or perhaps Imperial Palace or Imperial Emperor. The food stores sell spices, herbs, meat, chicken and fish, and odors emanate from them that can be overwhelming to the delicate western nose.

Shop windows contain fantastic sculptures carved in jade and other semi-precious stones. And enough ivory is on display to supply most of the elephants remaining in the world with tusks. Luggage stores offer steep discounts on a variety of bags—where do they get them?—and the ubiquitous souvenir shops peddle poorly made miniature cable cars and tons of T-shirts.

Continue on to the corner of Broadway and Columbus and the Condor Club, remembering when Carol Doda first danced topless on the piano there in the sixties. And when you could go to the nearby clubs like the Hungry i and the Purple Onion and listen to the Limeliters for three dollars. This really dates me, doesn't it?

Climb Telegraph Hill and when you get to the top of that climb Coit Tower, with its 360-degree view. Towers are like hills to me—they are there to climb. Finally, coast down the hills to Fisherman's Wharf, past the row houses that always seem to have inviting secrets hidden behind their similar exteriors. Visit the National Maritime Museum, eat seafood at DiMaggio's—is it still there? Where have you gone, Joe DiMaggio?

The best view I ever had of San Francisco came just after sunrise, from an airplane. Bonny and I were flying from Tokyo to Los Angeles. The flight was memorable for another reason: The whole flight took only 8.5 hours. At times our ground speed approached 700 miles-per-hour. We were riding on a hurricane. We reached the California coast at San Francisco on a clear morning. The hills, the buildings, the bridges, the bay were all in sharp three-dimensional focus, like an IMAX movie. Who wouldn't want to walk in a fascinating panorama like that?

My San Francisco may be a figment of my imagination and my memory, but then, there are as many different San Franciscos as there are people who have lived in or visited the city. All of them are worth walking through. And walkers have left their hearts in all of them.

New York City

Although I grew up just 400 miles away, in western New York, I didn't get to New York City until my high school's senior class trip in 1955. We blanketed the city by subway, bus and on foot, seeing all the usual sights. We were dazzled by the neon lights of Times Square and my friend, Mickey, and I saw several plays and musicals, including an original-cast production of Cole Porter's *Can-Can*. Whatever happened to the French female lead, Lilo? Wow! But a young Gwen Verdon almost stole the show.

I have walked and sightseen in New York several times since my first trip (see chapter 5), but one of the more memorable visits was with Bonny in April 1995. Bonny was invited to go to New York to receive the prestigious President's Award from Xerox Corporation. Xerox put us up at the Waldorf Astoria Hotel and gave us the run of the city. We chose to walk, however: to the New York Public Library guarded by stone lions; through Central Park; to the Gershwin Theater, where we saw a superb performance of *Showboat*.

It was pouring when we exited the theater and we decided to hail a taxi. Lo and behold, even though the yellow taxi is the predominant species of vehicle in that part of Manhattan, we couldn't entice one to stop for us. We ended up walk/running back to the hotel in the rain. Our good clothes were sopping and shapeless, but our bodies were none the worse for wear. We laughed, stripped, showered and jumped into bed to warm up.

Like other great cities of the world, New York has a magnetic quality about it that attracts people. I'm not sure what this quality is—a blend of energy and hope, perhaps—but a trip there is always exciting for me.

Washington, D.C.

The United States was founded with a unique vision of individual freedom. If we, as US citizens, are to retain this freedom, we must have an understanding of what it means. A walk around Washington, D.C. will help us gain this understanding.

Son Andy and his family live in Virginia and he works in Washington, so my grandsons have already been there, but those who are not so fortunate should make an effort to go. Older grandson Matthew started taking an interest in the presidents at age five and one half. He could name them all and knew much about them. Andy joked that he was one of the foremost authorities on the presidents. Although I am proud of Matthew, my fear is that Andy may be right—at least when it comes to this country's teenagers. If we don't protect our freedom we will lose it.

A sightseeing walk around Washington includes many impressive buildings: the White House, the Capitol, the Supreme Court building, the Washington Monument, the Lincoln and Jefferson Memorials, the Smithsonian Institution. My hope is that the people who take this walk and tour these historical landmarks will be stimulated to learn or remember our country's history and will come to understand what individual freedom means to them and their families. If they do they should be willing to fight to protect the vision of our founding fathers.

CHAPTER 12 United States and Canada

Since 1964, when Bonny and I were married, our family vacations have never been devoted exclusively to walking, but walking has always been a byproduct of the way we travel. Our son, Andy, joined us in 1968 and participated in our vacations for the next 20 years. Bonny and Andy are history buffs so our trips have been educational as well as fun.

When Bonny was young her parents owned a laundry in Clinton, Connecticut. During the summers, all members of the family, including Bonny and her two brothers, worked long, steamy hours in that sweatshop and dreamed of being just about anywhere else. Bonny would say to her mother, Ellen, "Stick with me, kid, and we'll go far." Ellen started to travel with us after Andy was born and continued to be part of our entourage into the 1990s, seeing a substantial part of the world along the way. During those trips Ellen always walked her five miles each day, the distance we figured we averaged just from sightseeing alone.

We spent the 1960s and 1970s touring the United States. By 1978, Bonny and I had been in every state. It took Andy a little longer. He finally picked up his last two states, Indiana and Kansas, in the summer of 1991 when he drove to Los Angeles from Washington, D.C., where he had been working as a government intern.

Starting in 1980, we have been touring the rest of the world. And there's such a lot of world to see. And I might add, there are such a lot of great places to walk. A few of them are noted in this and other chapters.

*　　　*　　　*

In 1967, Bonny and I toured Arizona, New Mexico and a bit of Colorado, with an emphasis on cliff dwellings, which by their nature provide interesting walks just to get to them. But the walking highlight of the trip was our hike into the Grand Canyon down to the Colorado River.

My brother, Steve, and I had made this hike in 1962, when we walked down the Bright Angel Trail to Phantom Ranch, on the canyon floor, ate lunch and then walked back up the steeper Kaibab Trail. The following year Steve hiked the canyon from the south rim to the north rim with his college buddies. Somewhere along the way he caught a horrible cold. When they arrived in Los Angeles he collapsed on the floor of my apartment and stayed there recuperating for several days while his friends went on without them. He finally flew to San Francisco and rejoined them.

Bonny and I also walked down the Bright Angel Trail. The trail is about four feet wide and we shared it with the mule trains carrying tourists down to the river. I'm not sure the tourists had the best of the bargain because the backs of the mules are uncomfortable and the beasts tend to walk along the edge of the cliff, overlooking numbing drops.

We ate lunch beside the dark green Colorado River, with its fierce current. The temperature was about 80 degrees F on this October day, but in mid-summer it reaches 110 degrees or more. Canyon hiking is the opposite of mountain hiking because you go downhill first and uphill last. This was emphasized during our vertical ascent of more than a mile when Bonny got blisters on her heels. She called the final part of the climb "dreadful."

As we were coming back up the trail, we met several female schoolteachers going down. They had no water and no concerns and were clearly ill equipped for the rigors of the canyon. We advised them not to go any farther without water, but they shrugged us off and kept going.

We stayed that night at a motel in Cameron, Arizona, with a shower stall just big enough to hold one of us if we didn't try to turn around. But at least the water was wet and cleansing.

A few days later we toured Chaco Canyon National Monument in New Mexico. To quote our log, "We hiked up a steep Indian trail through rock crevices to get to the mesa overlook above Pueblo Bonito. From here we were able to clearly see the D shape of the pueblo. From the overlook we hiked along another Indian path across the mesa to another group of ruins. It was along this path that we found numerous pieces of ancient broken pottery, a piece of human vertebrae and a pile of winnowed grain that had turned to stone. The wheat still formed a perfect cone shape, like someone had just finished working on it."

*   *   *

In 1970, Bonny, Andy, Ellen and I toured Utah, camping along the way. We went to a number of parks, including Monument Valley, which is owned and run by the Navajos. They have their own rangers and police force. The more famous of the monoliths, such as the mittens, have been featured in many movies and advertisements. John Wayne knew them well. Arches National Monument also offers some of nature's most spectacular artistic works, with stone arches up to 300 feet across.

Our tent proved to be almost waterproof and that was fortunate because we encountered near-record rainfalls. One morning Andy, already a "reader" at the age of two, sat up in the tent and started looking at his books. Figuring that it was still dark because of the rain I got out of my sleeping bag. It took us a while to figure out that it was only 3:30 a.m., at which point we all went back to sleep.

In the evenings, beside the tent, Bonny, Ellen and I played Acey Deucy for pennies. Although I considered myself to be a smart gambler, I never won much money from them and occasionally Ellen, who played intuitively, took us for a ride. This is a relative term, however, because the largest pot I can ever remember anyone winning was $1.16.

Two other national parks we saw were Zion and Bryce, both known for their impressive scenery, consisting of amazing rock formations, among other things. At Zion Andy and I took a walk, with him in the backpack, along the Virgin River, where teenagers clad in bikini bottoms and panties rode tire inner tubes with the current, free from the restrictions of civilization.

*   *   *

In 1973 and 1974, we went to western Canada and Alaska. We drove our white Volkswagen camper with the "bubbletop," and "Cook's Nook" painted on the side. Andy and Ellen slept on the top bunk and complained about each other's snoring; Bonny and I slept on the bottom.

One of our more unusual walks occurred in Vancouver, British Columbia, when we walked over the Capilano Suspension Bridge. It is 450 feet long and spans the Capilano River, 230 feet below. The bridge swayed with a wave motion and creaked as we walked across it. We trod lightly and didn't look down. The natives originally had a rope bridge across the canyon. That must have been fun for somebody with acrophobia to cross.

We walked through Butchart Gardens on Victoria Island, an artist's palette of color and design. Juneau, the capital of Alaska, is a good walking city, with hills and bridges. It is isolated, since no roads lead to Juneau from the outside world, or vice versa, making it a strange location for a state capital. There was a movement at that time to relocate the capital to Anchorage or some other place more accessible, but it didn't succeed. We arrived in Haines via the Alaskan State Ferry and walked to a show featuring local actors. Andy, then age six, said to the astonished female ticket seller, "Haven't I seen you before? Don't you sing and dance? Aren't you on TV?"

We went through the gorgeous Canadian parks of Jasper and Banff. In Jasper Village we saw a bear amble through town and chase a resident into his house. In Jasper National Park the four of us (including five-year-old Andy) hiked with a ranger up a three-mile trail to an alpine meadow. We could see Angel Glacier across the valley. Part of the trail went through a transverse moraine deposited by the glacier. We also took a snowmobile (a large vehicle with tracks instead of wheels) tour of the Columbia Ice Fields, on top of hundreds of feet of ice, feeling that this was not a good place to walk. At a campground we saw a ranger show about wolves at night, but it was too late for us to go "wolf-howling" afterward.

In Calgary, Alberta, we toured the Dinosaur Gardens at Calgary Zoo. Forty-six life-size replicas of dinosaurs and prehistoric animals lived in the garden. Live animals that we saw on these trips included bears, deer, moose, elk, mountain sheep, coyotes and beavers.

*   *   *

In 1976, we took our camper all the way from Los Angeles to Illinois and back, via a circular route. On this trip, Andy and Ellen usually slept inside while Bonny and I slept outside in the tent. That is, except when it rained or we had a bear scare.

We discovered cave walking on this trip. We toured Jewel Cave in Custer, South Dakota, with its colorful stalactites and stalagmites. The tour started with an elevator ride down the equivalent of a 23-story building. One part of the cave is "dead," meaning that it is not changing anymore. Another section is "alive." It is growing, aided by dripping water. At one point the guide turned out the lights and we were in absolute darkness and silence. No cars and no TVs. The temperature is 47 degrees all year round. Cave walking on established paths should not be confused with spelunking, which is exploring uncharted caves, using helmet lamps and ropes. Spelunking can be dangerous, and is frightening for the claustrophobic. I never did any, although I had a friend who tried to talk me into it.

Other places in South Dakota, reachable by a combination of car and foot power, include Crazy Horse Monument, a huge rock sculpture of the Indian chief; Mt. Rushmore, with its presidential heads; Deadwood, where Wild Bill Hickok was killed during a poker game; and Lead, with the largest gold mine in the US. Eastern North Dakota and parts of Minnesota have some of the flattest land in the world. It was scraped flat by many glaciers. The elevation change is less than two feet per mile. That is flatter than the floors of your house. Much flatter than some of the old houses we have visited in our travels. You could see forever if it wasn't for the curvature of the earth.

Later, Andy spent a year of college in the flat country as an exchange student, at Moorhead State University in Moorhead, Minnesota, just across the state line from Fargo North Dakota. The biggest problem he faced wasn't the flatness—it was the winter cold, but he proved he could take it. Better him than me. I grew up near Buffalo, New York, which is cold enough, but I escaped from there as soon as I could.

There are some hills in Minnesota. Between Fergus Falls and Alexandria we hiked to a hilltop called Inspiration Point—and it was. We could see seven lakes in three different counties. Minnesota is the land of lakes. At Alexandria we saw a local museum, famous for Viking artifacts, which the Viking explorers left in 1362 A.D., 130 years before Columbus came. The Vikings also left a carved stone telling about how 10 of their number died nearby.

I recommend a visit to the Mayo Clinic medical museum in Rochester, Minnesota. We saw many interesting human anatomical displays, including bones and a skull that we could pick up and look inside. If you want to take care of something properly you need to know how it works. And that goes for our bodies, which should be first on our list of things to take care of.

In the northeast corner of Iowa we visited the ancient Effigy Indian Mounds. The mounds were built between 2,000 and 1,700 years ago by at least two different Indian cultures. Some are shaped like animals and some are round or oblong. We hiked a short trail up a hill to see them and also to see a spectacular view of the Mississippi River.

We spent some time in Abe Lincoln country. My mother's maiden name is Lincoln. We are not directly descended from Abe—all his direct descendants are dead—but we are probably cousins. Abe lived in New Salem Village in Illinois, near Petersburg, with a population of about 100, from 1831-1837. He arrived here when he was 22 and first on his own. He was postmaster for a time and went

77

into business with a friend. It later failed. He learned how to be a surveyor and spent time reading books by the light of the wood chips burning at the blacksmith shop. He lived at Rutledge Tavern for a while and supposedly was in love with Ann Rutledge, who died in 1835, at the age of 22, of pneumonia.

We stopped at the prehistoric site called Cahokia Mounds, in East St. Louis, Illinois, on the Mississippi. People first inhabited this site in 700 A.D., and it grew to a population of 30 or 40,000 about 1000 A.D. It was an urban development and a center of trade for much of mid-North America. The mounds were constructed from dirt carried by the basketful. It is estimated that the inhabitants moved more than 50 million cubic feet of earth to build them. They also built four large circles using wooden posts, which are similar to the circles at Stonehenge, in England. These are lined up with phases of the sun and were probably used as calendars.

Bonny's claustrophobia showed itself during the rides up and down the 630-foot St. Louis arch. We rode in one of eight cars, or cages, if you prefer. Bonny didn't. The cars have to keep leveling themselves during the trip up the curving arch. A claustrophobic has an overwhelming urge to escape confinement, but there was nowhere to escape to during the rides. Bonny didn't like being panic-stricken in front of her mother.

We walked around Mountain View, Arkansas, where at a dozen or more shops local residents demonstrated how they have worked their crafts since coming to the area. We saw how lye soap was made, plus woodcarving, dried apple dolls, quilting, weaving, spinning, blacksmithing, caning, canning, candle making, broom making and pottery.

That evening we were treated to a show, put on by the residents, aged 10 to 85, who entertained us with fiddling, pickin' and grinnin'. They played guitars, banjos, bass fiddles, violins (called fiddles) and dulcimers. One boy of about 12 fiddled and jigged at the same time. A 13-year-old girl named Brooke Breeding sang, "Michael Rowed the Boat Ashore" and other songs beautifully and with feeling. She accompanied herself on the dulcimer.

Bonny and Andy indulged their love of history—especially military history on Andy's part—as we toured Pea Ridge National

Military Park, where one of the decisive Civil War battles was fought in March 1862, by 26,000 troops. Cannons are still sitting in the fields and there is a National Park Museum to give details of the battle.

Muskogee, Oklahoma is the tribal headquarters for the "Five Civilized Nations." The five civilized nations are the Cherokee, Seminole, Choctaw, Chickasaw and Creek. The museum at Muskogee had a fine display of artwork created by Native Americans. There were paintings and artifacts showing individuals walking the Trail of Tears, the term used to describe the resettlement of the tribes from Georgia, North Carolina and Tennessee to Oklahoma in 1838-39. Over 4,000 men, women and children died along the trail. Not all walks are happy ones.

The National Cowboy Museum at Oklahoma City contains many paintings and sculptures by artists such as Remington and Russell. The Helium Monument at Amarillo, Texas, contains time capsules filled with artifacts and helium. Aren't they afraid the capsules will float away, like birthday balloons?

Just after we pulled our VW into a campsite in Las Vegas, New Mexico, a wild thunderstorm, with hailstones as big as golf balls, peppered us for half an hour. The hailstones sounded like giant drums on the roof of the camper, and lightning flashed all around us. Horses in a nearby field ran about, aimlessly, trying to escape the onslaught. The cloudburst accompanying the storm sent rivers running through the campground. In order to keep our spirits up while the storm raged, we drank beer and ate cheese.

On our walk around Santa Fe, New Mexico, we also saw a famous wooden stairway in the chapel of St. Loretto, built in answer to prayers. The chapel stairway was handmade with wooden pegs and has no central support. It spirals two complete circles. Architects from all over the world study it because it is so sturdy and so unusual. The carpenter who built it is unknown since he disappeared after he finished his work.

Acoma Pueblo, in New Mexico, is called the Sky High City because it sits on a mesa, 365 feet above the surrounding valley. It is the oldest continuously inhabited place in the US, having been founded in 1600. The Painted Desert and Petrified Forest, in Arizona, were formed 180-200 million years ago, a few years before.

At Whiteriver, Arizona, on the Fort Apache Reservation, we visited Raymond, a boy we had been helping through the Save the Children Federation. This was the second time we had visited him. On the first trip, some children took us to a powwow, where Raymond's family was partying, in exchange for a ride in our camper. Tantalizing odors issued forth from large cooking pots, stirred by women. We took some of the kids to an Indian rodeo. Raymond and his sister, Patty, spent the night with us and slept in our tent. Andy showed them his book of Indians. They didn't know that tribes other than the Apache existed.

On this trip we picked Raymond up after school and took a walk with him, during which he killed a snake. Two cars full of local residents with rifles stopped at our campsite near the White River. The men told us that a black bear had been spotted there that morning. After dinner it was dark so we all retreated into the camper and slept inside, including Raymond. Men prowled the campground off and on all night, with flashlights, guns and dogs, but the bear wisely didn't show itself again. The men had killed a bear in the area a short time before.

*   *   *

Our 1977 trip was to the southern United States. We continued our cave exploring by taking a two-mile self-guided tour through the historic section of Mammoth Caves, in Kentucky. Prehistoric natives used the cave over 4,000 years ago. Some unusual animals live there, such as fish, crickets and crayfish that have no color, as they don't need camouflage, and who are blind or even have no eyes at all.

We walked through the French Quarter of New Orleans while the mosquitoes converged on Andy and me, the more edible members of the family, and covered our legs with bites. We walked into the Florida Everglades, among the alligators, fish, birds and bugs. In addition to alligator babies, larger versions of the reptiles lounged nearby, regarding us with unblinking eyes. Talk about creepy.

In Florida, we gathered shells on the beach and watched the pelicans. Our first night there we set up camp on the island of Navarre Beach, near Pensacola. Andy tried surf fishing for a while before dinner. At first the sky was clear, but then it became blacker and blacker. Bonny, who had been in hurricanes in Connecticut, warned us that something bad was coming.

We jumped into the tent about 7:30 p.m., when the rain and wind hit. The wind partially collapsed the tent, and fearing that we would be blown away we took down the tent and put everything into the car, getting soaked in the process. The rain stopped half an hour later and we set the tent up again on the lee side of the concrete-block restrooms. We found out later that a fragment of Hurricane Anita had passed through.

We met two of my brothers, Mike and Phil, and their families at a campground in North Carolina. At night the adults drank wine and laughed a lot, disturbing other campers. One day, seven members of the group, including nine-year-old Andy, climbed Mt. Mitchell, the highest point in the US east of the Mississippi River (6,684 feet). The climb is 3,700 feet in 5.5 miles. Other members of the family drove up the road.

*   *   *

The four of us toured Hawaii in 1978, the 50th state for Bonny and me. Soon after we arrived, much of our camping equipment was stolen out of our rental car as we slept in a tent in a campground on Oahu. We were set up, perhaps by the person who made the reservation for us. Although our Coleman stove was taken, and the orange jackets covered with patches from the places we had visited were irreplaceable, we tried not to let the thefts daunt us.

On the big island of Hawaii we walked near the live volcano, Kilauea. It erupts more or less continuously, and solidified lava covered the road in some places. On the island of Kauai, Andy and I were able to walk two miles into the roadless northeast Na Pali coastal area, to a place called Hanakapi'ai, where clothes are an afterthought.

We had our big hike on Maui. We camped near Haleakala Crater, intending to drive to the top before dawn and witness the sunrise. At dawn it was raining and we were inclined to go on sleeping, but we finally struggled out of our sleeping bags and got to the top just after the sun came up.

Andy and I walked into the crater on a trail, amid the rare silversword plants and the beautiful but stark multi-colored rocks that rose up around us. I figured that as we went lower and lower into the crater we were roughly paralleling the descent of the road from the top of the mountain. What we discovered was that we had to climb about 1,300 vertical feet on rather steep switchbacks to return to the road. Fortunately, Andy was up to the task.

*   *   *

In 1980, we toured the eastern provinces of Canada. For those who have read *Anne of Green Gables*, by L. M. Montgomery, or watched the miniseries, a tour of the "Anne" house on Prince Edward Island is a must. In Halifax, Nova Scotia, we watched a bagpipe band, called Wilde Thyme Pipes and Drums. Some of the bagpipers and drummers were girls and very stylish.

In the combined province of Newfoundland and Labrador, both of which are accented on the last syllable by the locals, who are few and far between, we went to Corner Brook (accent on Brook) and ate a meal at a picnic table built for giants. Fortunately, we didn't meet any of these height-challenged beings.

At the Bay of Fundy, between New Brunswick and Nova Scotia, we had our most unusual walk. We found we could venture far into the ocean, along the bottom left waterless at low tide. Don't be caught away from shore when the tide is rising, however, because the difference between high tide and low tide here is among the greatest of any place in the world, reaching 14 meters in some spots.

In the city of Quebec, in the province of Quebec, we took a tour of the Citadel, with the aid of a vivacious female guide, who was more French than English. The guides and guards were students, working their last day before returning to school (it was September 1). Our guide participated in taping the mouth of one of the guards, who was not supposed to speak or move. They were just having a little fun, she explained, after having to be serious all summer. The alternative to walking in the old city near the Citadel was to ride in an open buggy pulled by a broken-down horse. Considering the cost, the auto traffic and the condition of the horses, it wasn't a very appetizing alternative and we passed.

CHAPTER 13 Greek Mainland

APHRODITE, PAN AND EROS

(Based on a statue in the Athens Archaeological Museum)

Here's Aphrodite, goddess of love,
attempting to fight off the goat-god, Pan,
while Eros, her son, hovers above
her shoulder, ever a child, never a man.

The marble likenesses, still fresh,
for two millennia have stood,
almost alive, almost flesh;
they look as if they'd like to move—and could.

The goddess defends herself with a shoe—
a shoe! a puny weapon indeed.
Is this just for show, a false hullabaloo,
before she succumbs to Pan—his lust and her need?

And what of Pan, goat-legged and horned;
why must he make one conquest more?
Does he fear he'll be belittled and scorned
because of his looks, and so he must score and score?

You can't trust Eros, that little imp;
he has no pity for even his mother.
He's full of tricks, a matchmaker and pimp,
and he'll play one person off against another.

Is it naked lust or love in bloom
that's pictured in this Greek tableau?
It's time to let the action resume,
so cue the actors and let's get on with the show.

THE OLYMPIANS

They are the gods and goddesses of today,
Descended from the Olympians of Greece.
From every land on Earth they come to play;
Though there be wars and strife they come in peace.

They meet to test their skills in many a sport;
Their bodies, tuned pianos, are perfection.
With poise and graceful rhythm they cavort;
To all the struggling world they give direction.

Through years of training, physical and mental,
They work with love and hope and discipline.
Though strong as lions, with children they are gentle;
Their smiles when they compete are genuine.

They jump and vault and shoot and swim and throw;
They somersault and run and skate and ski.
They give their all to win and yet they know
It is the game that counts, not victory.

Our souls cry out for heroes, let us follow;
From chains of hate the imprisoned seek release.
Each deity, Athena or Apollo,
Will lead us to a world of love and peace.

Bonny was greatly influenced by one of her teachers, Miss Goodwin, who lived in an apartment above a store on Main Street in Old Saybrook, Connecticut and never married because "nobody ever thought to ask me." She rode her bicycle to school and loved everything to do with ancient Greece, although she never actually visited Greece. But she instilled this love in Bonny, who did so well on a test in college about Greek gods and goddesses that the professor accused her of cheating. Bonny proposed that for our first trip outside the northern hemisphere we tour Greece.

We did so in 1981 and liked it so much that we have returned four times since then. On our first trip to Greece, Bonny, Andy, Ellen, and I flew to Athens on a now defunct airline called World Airways. Several of our bags didn't arrive in Athens with us and we didn't see them again until weeks after we returned home. That taught us a lesson about international trips—travel light. In fact, except that Bonny and I had to buy some underwear, we did better with our reduced baggage.

We exchanged money at the airport at 58.5 drachmas to the dollar. Then, quoting from our 1981 log: "We took the yellow bus from the Eastside Airport (where we had landed) to Syntagma Square. We walked around to the south side of the Acropolis and got a room at the Phillipos Hotel on Mitseon Street. In Syntagma Square I saw two boys with T-shirts reading, 'Palos Verdes PE.' We took the penthouse suite on the 6th floor for 2,000 drachmas (less for stay of three days or more). Magnificent view of the Acropolis from the balcony outside our room."

At sunrise the next morning I went out on the balcony and photographed the Acropolis, bathed in the light of the dawn. I got some of the best pictures I have ever taken of the Acropolis in five trips to Greece.

We ate dinner at Socrates' Prison, a restaurant on Mitseon Street that disappeared during the day. At night, tables and chairs magically appeared on the sidewalk. Their food was delicious and we returned to eat there again and again on other trips to Greece.

Another restaurant we liked was just down the street from the peculiarly named Hotel Austria, where we have stayed on recent trips to Athens. In 2000, we toured Greece with my brother, Phil, and his wife, Judy. At the restaurant, Dina, a blond who spoke English better than we did, waited on us. Greek salad contains green peppers, tomatoes, olives, onions, feta cheese and olive oil. Dina's Greek salads were the best we have ever eaten, and on the rest of that trip we compared all other Greek salads to Dina's. The second night we ate there Dina at first wouldn't allow Bonny and me to order the chicken with orange a second time, but she relented after we told her how delicious it was and begged her to let us order it.

The other problem we had with World Airways in 1981 was that the DC-8 that was supposed to take us back to Los Angeles never arrived in Athens. It got held up in Shannon, Ireland, with engine problems. We waited all day at the Athens Airport with the other passengers until two chartered Britania Airlines planes arrived to ferry us to London's Gatwick Airport. From there we were bused down to Brighton, on the south coast of England, and Bonny and I stayed in the Marie Antoinette Suite of the aging but still swanky Metropole Hotel for a few hours of much-needed sleep. Andy and Ellen had their own suite.

The Metropole might have been a fun place to stay under other circumstances, but we didn't have time to properly enjoy its amenities, including showerheads so high on the wall that taking a shower felt more like standing in the rain. We also didn't have time to appreciate Brighton's ambiance as a resort community, with its ornate piers dating back to the 19th century. It took us 48 hours to get home, but it was an adventure.

Athens is one of the world's best walking cities because of its antiquities. And our whole family loves antiquities. The biggest problems in Athens are the same as those of most of the world's mega-cities: the motor vehicles, the noise and the pollution. The most important antiquity is the Acropolis, on a hill that is visible from much of the rest of the city. Bonny achieved one of her childhood dreams when she had her picture taken, sitting on the steps of the Parthenon.

There are other interesting hills, including Likavitos, which has a funicular (tram) going to the top for those who don't relish the stiff climb. One of the bonuses of reaching the top of Likavitos is a great view of the Acropolis, but the view of the Acropolis is even better from the top of Filopapou Hill (also called Academy Hill because Plato had his academy there), which can be reached only on foot.

Earthbound walkers who also like to shop will appreciate the Plaka, with its myriad of shops, *tavernas* and places of entertainment, built along narrow, winding streets, at the foot of the Acropolis. Walking is the only way to see it as very little motor traffic is allowed. We have seen female tourists dance with the local men and get repeatedly flipped, end-over-end. Here, you can buy anything Greek your heart desires, from the famous pottery made on the island of Skyros to statuettes of some of the more randy creatures from Greek mythology.

One of my favorite statuettes is a copy of a statue in the National Archaeological Museum. It depicts Aphrodite, Pan and Eros. Aphrodite is ineffectively trying to ward off the attentions of the goat-god, Pan, with a shoe, while Eros, who is her son in addition to being the god of love, hovers above her shoulder. (See the poem at the beginning of the chapter.)

The port of Piraeus is an easy metro ride from downtown Athens. It has ships, of course, and its own archaeological museum, featuring magnificent bronze statues of Apollo, Athena and Artemus, found in a storehouse in 1959. Would you believe they had been there since 86 A.D., when they were hidden to prevent them from being stolen by enemies of Greece?

Andy collected beer cans in 1981 and he looked for them wherever we walked. Sometimes we even shipped them home. The collection sat in our garage for years, but recently he gave permission for much of it to be recycled. Surprise—the five-cent California redemption fee for cans doesn't apply to cans not made here so we sold them by weight.

We have rarely had problems with hotels in Greece, but one time in Athens we were leaving at 4:30 a.m. in a taxi to catch a flight to an island, when the desk clerk told me we owed some hundreds more drachmas (we had paid the bill the night before) because the night clerk had given us too much change. This was not true and I argued my case, but I felt like Leonidas, the Spartan who defended the pass against the Persians at Thermopylae, while my traveling companions made their escape through the hotel doorway to the taxi. Then I quickly followed them.

*   *   *

Another one of our favorite places on the Greek mainland is Delphi, built on the side of Mount Parnassus. Because of this, much of the walking in the village, itself, is on stairways, and the main site of the ruins is just as hilly. The oracle of Delphi made incomprehensible predictions here, probably after becoming high while breathing the fumes from funny smoke that wafted through the cracks in the rocks.

The ruins include the Temple of Apollo, the treasuries of the various city-states, the large odeon (theater) and the stadium, which is above everything else on the hillside. The stadium has special seats with backs, at the center of the field, perhaps for nobles or judges. It is long—well over a football field in length—and scores of children were running in it the last time we were there, pretending they were competing. A few adults joined in the fun. Each tier of the stadium's stone seats has a level part for rear-ends, behind which is a depression for the feet of the people seated on the tier above.

In 2000, we toured Delphi with Phil and Judy. We were eating at a *taverna*, sitting near participants in an auto race that utilizes the mountain roads in the area. Judy asked them what we should do if we were driving and one of the racecars came up behind us. A driver said, in accented English, "Drive fast." Phil and Judy climbed partway up Mount Parnassus the morning we left Delphi, but didn't have time to make it to the top.

*   *   *

Olympia, site of the original Olympic Games, has interesting ruins, including the stadium. On our first Greek trip, in 1981, Andy stood on the ancient stone starting lines, used for the foot races, and pictured himself as an Olympian.

We traveled by bus to get there and had to change at Nafpakto. While waiting for the bus, I washed my hands at a faucet beside the street. My wedding ring slid off my finger and into the gutter. Bonny and I searched for it, frantically and unsuccessfully. We accumulated a number of sympathetic helpers, including a newsstand operator who produced an iron bar, with which he proceeded to pry up the grate from the sewer.

An Italian girl got down on her hands and knees and fished the ring out of the muck in the sewer. She put it on my finger, in return for a hug. There was general rejoicing and some joking that we were now married. The girl was asked whether she was married to her traveling companion, a male Italian, but she answered that with an emphatic no. All this through translators and sign language, since she spoke no English.

*   *   *

In 1996, Bonny and I drove from Athens north to Thessaloniki on E-75, the National Highway. We stopped along the way at the statue of the real Leonidas, who held off the Persians at the pass of Thermopylae, with a small body of men, until the Spartan army escaped. We ate a lunch at Dion, under Mt. Olympus, which was in the clouds. None of the gods was in evidence.

We went to the museum in Dion and walked around the archaeological site, featuring the villa of Dionysos, with well-preserved mosaics. A statue of Aphrodite, in good condition, had been recently found in the mud at the site. The original was in the museum and a copy was on the site. Plays by Euripides were performed at the Greek theater in Dion. Both Philip and his son, Alexander the Great, spent time here.

We found a hotel room in Panorama, a wealthy suburb of Thessaloniki. The downside of this was that kamikaze mosquitoes came in through the open windows at night (it was the first of September and too warm to close them) and attacked us in waves, piercing the sheets to suck our blood. In the morning Bonny's face looked as if she had measles.

We drove into the heart of Thessaloniki without a detailed map. We got completely lost, but with the help of several local residents (some were more helpful than others) we finally got ourselves straightened out.

We went to the archaeological museum, which has important artifacts from Philip's tomb, discovered recently in nearby Vergina. Included is his skeleton, with damaged skull, where he was hit near the eye with an arrow, and shin guards. One of his legs was shorter than the other. He was assassinated at a wedding by one of his bodyguards. A lot of gold was found in his tomb. The statue of Alexander on a horse is right beside the water, and the White Tower, built in the 16th century, is nearby. We climbed its circular staircase and had a good view of the harbor area.

We drove east through the Chalkidiki Peninsula, the bottom one of the three fingers that jut out toward the east from Thessaloniki. It was filled with green mountains and pretty valleys. We saw sheep, goats, hogs and cows, and much of the land was farmed. We went as far as Ouranopoli, the resort village near Agios Oros, the self-governing area at the end of the peninsula, with many monasteries and no women.

Ferries leave from Ouranopoli and tour the coast of Agios Oros, which is as close as women can get to it. Men can apply for a four-day stay, if they have the proper religious attitude. They stay in monasteries or the lone hotel and hike between them during the day. Access and egress are by boat only. I was not tempted to apply and Bonny wouldn't have let me, anyway.

CHAPTER 14 Greece—Poems about Crete

The following two poems tell different versions of the same myth. This is the myth of the Labyrinth at Knossos Palace in ancient Crete. My poem, "Bull Leaper," is based on the story of Theseus, as told in the book, *The King Must Die*, by Mary Renault, and on a wall painting at Knossos Palace, depicting bull leaping. Although the Minotaur, which was supposed to have roamed the Labyrinth, is not mentioned in the poem, the story is probably closer to the truth of what really happened in the Labyrinth than "The Minotaur," a more traditional telling of how Theseus slew the Minotaur.

BULL LEAPER

Stripped to the waist, with body oiled
and painted tips of budding breasts
alluring, yet I am unspoiled
by touch of man for none molests
the sacred female dancers of the bull.

Goddess-on-Earth our team salutes
as we prepare to do our dances;
we're oblivious to the shouts and hoots
of patrons betting on our chances,
for when our team performs the Bull Court is full.

Limber and strong, we are seven boys
and seven girls brought as tribute to Crete
from other lands; we left the joys
of childhood behind and now compete
in the Bull Court with our bull, mean-tempered and fierce.

Knossos reverberates with cries
from the Labyrinth as our bull appears;
we gauge his mood for who missteps dies,
then approach and dance with him. Our fears
abate as we perform, though his horns could pierce

bodies not grown oh so easily.
Our dance is applauded by the crowd,
and now the focus is on me.
Though I'm the star I must not be proud;
I owe my life to the members of my team.

Eyeing each other, my bull and I,
we do the dangerous dance with grace.
I grab his horns and launch and fly
and somersault to outer space,
then land upon his back, my elation supreme.

Dismounting, I do another flip;
I'm caught by one who stands below.
He steadies me if I should slip,
protects me from the horns, from throe
of death. Euphoric, I bow—and still survive.

Presents will come from adoring fans,
the highborn ladies of the court.
They collect their bets while making plans,
seduction their goal; to them it's sport,
but we who dance thank the gods that we're alive.

THE MINOTAUR

A fearsome monster lived in ancient Crete,
The Minotaur, who dearly loved to eat
Young girls and boys; they were a tasty treat.
This monster had the body of a man,
But head of bull, so picture if you can
A most ferocious beast, from which all ran.
King Minos made the monster spend its days
Inside the Labyrinth, a tortuous maze,
Well hidden from the sun's bright warming rays.
Its father was a gorgeous bull, snow white,
Which rose beneath the sea into the light,
Poseidon's gift to Minos for a rite.
The bull was given for a sacrifice,
But Minos couldn't kill a brute so nice,
So kept it for his own, against advice.
Poseidon, angered, wished to foster strife
For Minos, thus caused Pasiphae, his wife,
To love the bull and bring a child to life.
And that is how the Minotaur was born,
Part man, part bull, with long and curling horn;
The kind of child that makes a mother mourn.
King Minos asked a tribute for the beast
Of seven youths and seven maids, at least.
It fell to Athens to supply this feast.
Once in nine years this offering was paid.
Aegeus, king of Athens, was afraid
Of mighty Minos so he always made
These bloodstained gifts, and sent them one by one.
How could this mischief ever be undone?
It's time that we met Theseus, his son.
The third such gift of kids was coming due
When, lo, young Theseus, who often slew
A monster in good cause, both tried and true,
Announced that he would go with them to Crete.

94

"Once there I will engage and then defeat
The Minotaur, nor will I once retreat."
So he, with youths and maids, to Crete set sail,
To slay the Minotaur and not to fail.
There, Ariadne met this handsome male.
Now Theseus had Aphrodite's aid;
She helped him gain the love of this fair maid.
That was his secret in this escapade.
The daughter of King Minos fell in love
With Theseus, and prayed to gods above
That he would find that she was worthy of
His love, also. She pondered this for days,
Then went to Daedalus, who built the maze,
And learned its secret in return for praise.
Next, Ariadne gave a ball of string
To Theseus, directing him to bring
It to the maze, but not to tell the king.
He went into the maze with length of thread.
It helped him find the beast, asleep; he shed
Its blood with piercing sword until 'twas dead.
And now that he had won without a doubt
He traced the thread as it snaked all about
Until at long long last it led him out.
Sweet Ariadne asked if she could flee
With Theseus and kids across the sea.
She hoped for love, but this was not to be.
For on the isle of Naxos, while asleep,
She was deserted, left alone to weep,
With just her fleeting memories to keep.
But then the wine god, Dionysus, spied
Her there and raised her up to be his bride.
Immortal, she lived happy, by his side.
And Daedalus? Confined to his own maze
With Icarus, his son, he was to raise
Them up with wings he made; to where the blaze
Of sun was hot they flew, but sad to say,
The wings of Icarus would melt away.

He died, but Daedalus survived the day.
And Theseus returned upon his ship
To Athens, joyed by his successful trip,
But quite forgot to, per agreement, strip
His sail of black, replacing it with white,
A signal to his father that his fight
Had ended well and he'd come out all right.
Aegeus thus, when he the black sail spied,
Despaired of Theseus and thought he'd died,
And threw himself into the raging tide.
Then Theseus, of Athens became king.
He always was where things were happening,
And had adventures of which poets sing.
And so we end this myth of yesteryear
That tells of love and lust and hate and fear,
Of gods and men and beasts, recorded here.

CHAPTER 15 Greece—Echo and Narcissus

Bonny and I saw the story of Echo and Narcissus depicted in a mosaic floor of a palatial home, uncovered near Paphos, on the island of Cyprus.

ECHO and NARCISSUS

What causes an echo, an echo, an echo,
When you shout in a canyon or cave?
Come listen, come listen, I'll tell you a tale,
A tale for the meek and the brave.
There once lived a Nymph, a beautiful Nymph,
Arcadia was her home.
Like all beautiful Nymphs she enhanced her beauty
With flower and ribbon and comb.
Her name was Echo, was Echo, was Echo,
A good Arcadian name.
And she had just one fault, but a grievous fault,
Which led to her downfall and shame.
She liked to talk, to talk and to chatter
On subjects sublime and absurd.
Whenever she talked, she chattered and argued,
And she had to have the last word.

One day with Hera, Queen Goddess Hera,
Echo talked and chattered away.
Now Hera had wished to surprise her husband,
King Zeus, with the Nymphs at play.
Because of the chatter, Queen Hera was thwarted,
And you don't thwart a goddess who's queen.
So Hera said, "Echo, I'm taking your voice;
Starting now you're not heard but just seen.
I'll make one concession," (an ironic concession),
"Since you always must have the last word,
You'll still have the last word, but only the last,
And you have to repeat what you've heard."
So here was poor Echo, poor Echo, poor Echo,
Would she be resigned to her fate?
She still had her beauty, but lacking in words,
How could she win a mate?
One day in the forest when she was out walking
She saw a beautiful man.
And Echo thought, I will win his love
Or I'm not an Arcadian.
His name was Narcissus, and he was searching
For a friend, for a friend who was lost.
And he called, "Where are you? Where are you? Where are you?"
As the paths of the forest he crossed.
Now Echo wished to tell him she loved him,
But all that she could do
Was whenever he called, "Where are you? Where are you?"
She repeated the last word, "You?"
This puzzled Narcissus; from where came this voice
As gentle as a breeze?
This voice that repeated, repeated his words;
He searched among the trees.
Though Echo was hiding, was hiding, her heart
Was burning with red-hot fire.
Her urge to stay hidden was overcome
By her intense desire.
From behind a tree she ran and wrapped

Narcissus in her arms.
She hoped, she hoped that he would love
Her for her many charms.
Alas, Narcissus knew nothing of love;
In him there burned no flame.
Aloof and proud, he lived life as
A mechanical, passionless game.
Narcissus was frightened and ran away
From Echo's sweet affection,
And Echo, poor Echo, poor Echo was crushed
Because of his rejection.
Ashamed and alone, despondent, despairing,
She hid in the back of a cave.
She wasted and wasted and wasted to nothing;
That cave became her grave.
And what of Narcissus, the heartless Narcissus,
What fate had he in store?
Well, Aphrodite, goddess of love,
Found someone for him to adore.
It's not what you think; the goddess blamed
Narcissus for Echo's demise.
And so she determined a clever plan,
For goddesses are wondrous wise.
One day she caused him to come to a spring,
And when he knelt to drink
He saw a beautiful face in the water.
Whose? Well, whose do you think?
He saw Narcissus, Narcissus, Narcissus,
He saw his own reflection,
But he thought it was a water spirit
Upon a close inspection.
He tried to embrace it, embrace it, but when
He touched it it disappeared.
He stayed by the pool admiring his image
Because he greatly feared
He'd lose it, he'd lose it, this beautiful face,
If he should go away.

And so he sat and pined and sat
For many and many a day.
Like Echo he wasted, not eating or drinking
Until he had left just one breath.
And with it he said goodbye to the image,
And then collapsed in death.
The faithful Echo heard the goodbye,
And she answered, she answered, "Goodbye."
And Echo, sweet Echo, will answer your words;
Her voice will never die.
Where Narcissus, Narcissus had been by the pool
A lovely white flower grew.
And we call that flower Narcissus today,
Enjoyed by me and you.

CHAPTER 16 Greek Islands

ATLANTIS

They call you Santorini—
a crescent floating on the azure sea.
They come by ship and ride
your patient beasts of burden awkwardly
up steps of promise to engulf
themselves in swarms of souvenirs.
They dine at cliff-side restaurants
while you hold back your brimming tears.
They sunbathe on your beaches and
imbibe sweet Santorini wines,
extracted from the dew-flecked grapes,
handpicked from slope-strewn twining vines.
They love your rugged beauty, but
care not about your storied past,
nor that you've seen a golden age,
so bright, so light, it could not last.
For once you were Atlantis—
your songs were sung in grand mythology.
Your slopes climaxed in lofty peak,
your captains sailed the azure sea.
They talked with kings and carried home

treasures from both far and near.
Your artists painted scenes of life
that were too soon to disappear.
Your women, confident and proud,
kept breasts uncovered, heads held high.
Your scientists, before their time,
knew secrets of the earth and sky.
When rumbles shook your verdant slopes
these people boarded ships and fled.
So when the great explosion came
no one remained; there were no dead.
But monster waves were messengers,
announcing doom to east and west;
announcing end of golden age,
when life was lived with boundless zest.
Where once your mountain raised its head
there ebbs and flows the azure sea,
and all your radiant people are
long since consigned to history.
They call you Santorini—
they gambol on your sun-drenched shore and cliff,
while you, engrossed in glories of
the past, repeat the one word: "If…"

ERATO

Erato is my muse—
the muse of lyric poetry,
of metaphor and simile,
of images galore.
This is poetry that brings
a tear or smile, but always sings.
The words that paint the sunset skies;
they tell of joy and wicked lies.
Here are poems of lovers, by the score.
The poet writes of love that's won

and love that's lost,
and love that's tossed upon the shore
and is buried by a breaker with a roar.
Of love unrequited, love benighted,
lovers this and lovers that,
lovers, lovers, love, love, love…
until it becomes a crashing bore,
and Erato cries, "No more! No more!"
Erato is my muse—
the muse of erotic poetry,
the poetry of lust and sex
and how our passions soar.
And so erotic poems I'll make
if this will keep my muse awake,
for she is jealous and complex
and always keeps a score.
I'll write of the lusts of man and mate
in verses that will titillate,
for I have learned I must not abuse
the patronage of my vain muse.

What we like best about Greece are the Greek islands. Bonny and I have visited eight islands, but there are many more. Olympic Airways flies to the major islands. In all our travels in Greece we have taken a ferry between islands only twice (from Kos to Rhodes and Mykonos to Delos and return) because we didn't want to spend all our time on boats. Some of the ferry trips are overnight.

In 1981, we flew to the island of Kos from Athens on Olympic Airways. On our way to Kos we read about a Los Angeles earthquake in the international edition of the Herald Tribune, between 5.1 and 5.8 on the Richter scale, with an epicenter close to where we live. For the rest of the trip we worried about whether we had a house left, but didn't actually do anything about it because we were enjoying our trip too much. We arrived home to find that our house had suffered no damage.

On Kos we (Bonny, Andy, Ellen and I) followed a man on a bicycle home and rented two rooms on the third floor of his narrow but new three-story house. The next day we rented bicycles and rode four kilometers to the Asklipion, where Hypocrates taught natural medicine. My bike had a partially flat tire and shook at speeds over five miles-per-hour, which was fine because I also shake at speeds over five miles-per-hour. We took a walking tour of the Castle of the Knights of St. John, built in 1250 A.D. It is large and impressive, right on the water's edge, complete with moat.

Andy and I walked from the city of Kos along the beach to the west, until stopped by somebody who looked enough like a soldier to gain our respect. It wasn't clear whether he stopped us for military reasons or because there was a nudist colony beyond that point. Although nudity is officially illegal in Greece, girls on the public beaches are not bothered as long as they are at least wearing bikini bottoms, and there are also designated nude beaches.

*   *   *

We took the ferry from Kos to Rhodes, a short trip that goes within spitting distance of the coast of Turkey. On Rhodes we went to a show featuring Greek folk dances, held at an open theater within the old city. To get there from our rented room at a pension we followed signs through the dark, narrow, winding streets. It was eerie. Afterward, knowing we would never be able to retrace our steps, we walked to one of the main streets and made our way back to our room from there. The dancing was well done, but it was very windy, and we got cold in our shorts and T-shirts (this was in early September). The next afternoon a strong wind cleared the west-facing beaches of people.

The Colossus of Rhodes, which was one of the Seven Wonders of the Ancient World, was a huge statue of Apollo, with his legs straddling the harbor. It was destroyed long ago by an earthquake and has been replaced by statues of deer on each side of the harbor.

*   *   *

During our 1988 trip to Greece, Bonny, Andy and I flew to Mykonos, one of the most touristy of the Greek islands. Our hotel room overlooked the harbor and the whitewashed buildings of the village. The narrow, twisting streets of the village were supposedly designed on purpose to give raiding pirates a hard time; they certainly gave us a hard time. Andy was the only one of us who mastered their navigation and we depended upon him to guide us. Since Petros, the official Mykonos pelican, moved around, spotting him didn't help. One of the main attractions of Mykonos, other than almost continuous partying, is that the beaches are designated for different sexual preferences and dress preferences.

*   *   *

Another attraction is its proximity to the sacred island of Delos, which is but a short boat ride away. French archaeologists are the only people who live on Delos. They have been excavating the extensive ruins for over 100 years. We enjoyed tramping through the ruins and climbing Mt. Cynthus, the highest and most sacred point on the island at 112 meters.

We saw the "large, drooling lizards" (to quote the guidebook) that inhabit the ruins and discourage people from camping, which they're not supposed to do, anyway. The lizards must be there to preserve the sacredness of the island. We also saw a small owl sitting in the ruins. It was undoubtedly Athena, keeping an eye on us.

*   *   *

From Mykonos we flew to Samos, which is but a short ferry ride from Turkey. Pythagoras (of the theorem) and Aesop (of the fables) hailed from Samos. A man named Eupalinos built a 380-yard tunnel through a hill before 500 B.C. to provide drinking water for the village of Samos. It is another of the Seven Wonders of the Ancient World.

Walking through the tunnel is permitted now, but the entrance is barely wide enough for one person to enter and the roof over most of the tunnel is so low that walkers have to stoop. Bonny, Andy and I entered the tunnel. Bonny, who has claustrophobia, immediately saw her mistake and tried to get out, but other people had come in behind her. She literally climbed over everybody between her and the entrance in her panic. Then she waited for us outside.

*   *   *

One of our favorite Greek islands is the largest, Crete. Bonny and I have been to Crete three times. We always visit Knossos, the ancient Minoan palace and home of the Labyrinth. Bull leaping, an ancient sport, is depicted in well-preserved frescoes. A walk through the ruins of Knossos takes us back 4,000 years. Knossos is easily reachable by bus from the city of Heraklion, which has a major airport, meaning that real jets fly there, not the puddle-jumpers that fly to the smaller islands.

There are ruins of other palaces on Crete that are well worth seeing. These are accessible by rental car. Some of the main roads on Crete are narrow, two-lane affairs, and in 1992 there were still stretches that were unpaved, but it is much easier to drive on Crete than in the vicinity of Athens. Going through the villages is fun. At one village we had to wait for the local owners of parked cars to be summoned from the shops and *tavernas* so that they could move them out of the way of a truck and bus coming through in the opposite direction from the one in which we were traveling.

In 2000, we went to Crete with Phil and Judy, my brother and sister-in-law, and drove to Plakias, a beautiful beach on the south coast of the island. They had to cancel a planned walk to another beach when a fair-weather hurricane came up—a 70-mile-per-hour wind on a sunny day. Instead, we toured the Preveli Monastery, on a hill above the sea, whose monks helped a number of Australian and New Zealand soldiers escape from the Germans via submarine in 1941.

At the nearby village of Spili we walked up one of the narrow streets (a footpath made of concrete and flagstones) until we were above the village. We saw lavish displays of bougainvillea, olive orchards and rugged peaks, and ate lunch at the famous Lion Fountain. Back at Plakias, we tried to walk over the hill to Damnoni Cove, but the wind was so violent that we came back instead of continuing to the next beach. At times, all we could do was to stand with our backs to the wind and brace ourselves. On the beach the blowing grains of sand felt like needles penetrating our skin.

To escape the wind we drove to the port city of Chania, ravaged during World War II, on the north coast of Crete. Although it does have a restored Venetian harbor, the best thing about Chania was Anastasia, the daughter of the owner of the hotel we stayed at.

South of Chania, we walked from Meskla to near Therisso. It was an enchanting country walk, almost all uphill. Fortunately, we reached the village of Zourva before we became too hungry and had lunch at the only *taverna* there. Thus fortified, Phil, Judy and I trudged onward on an unpaved road (it was paved, if narrow, up to here) to the highest point, while Bonny returned to the car. We saw goats, sheep, flowers and lovely views of mountains and olive groves.

*   *   *

Our favorite Greek island is Santorini, also called Thera, a crescent that used to be a round volcano before it blew up in approximately 1628 B.C. Fortunately, the 200,000+ sea-faring inhabitants had plenty of warning and escaped in their boats. Some people think that Santorini was the fabled Atlantis (see the book, *Unearthing Atlantis*, by Charles Pellegrino).

Santorini is still a volcano and steam can be seen rising out of the caldera, which is now underwater. It is a fragile paradise, held together by prayers and concrete. A destructive earthquake, in 1956, scared away half the population of 12,000 and destroyed most of the buildings. The inhabitants have been rebuilding their white structures ever since and paving the top of the island with concrete.

Twice we have stayed in a hotel in Firastefani, near the monastery. The monks can make sleep difficult as they chant and rock and roll during the night. In addition, the bells of a nearby church would awaken us in the morning.

The archaeological dig at Akrotiri is steadily uncovering the houses of the ancient Minoan civilization, which had running water, indoor plumbing, natural air conditioning, frescoes on the walls (preserved in the local museum), plus other signs of affluence and advanced thinking, such as a working storage battery (don't ask me what they used it for). Bonny and I have followed the progress of the dig during our four visits to Santorini, from 1988 to 2000.

We have also made the hike from Fira, the center of population, to Oia, at the north end of the island, all four times we have been there. Andy did it with us in 1988, Phil and Judy in 2000. The rugged hike of several hours follows the rim of the caldera and features breathtaking views of the cliffs and the water below. Black stone walls crisscross the hills for erosion control. Were they built by the Romans?

The path at various times is made of rock, concrete, flagstones in concrete, lava and volcanic ash. Parts of the path, composed of small pieces of lava (black) and volcanic ash (white), are loose. On the steep downhill, where the trail momentarily comes down to the road, this presents a footing problem. Other stones are red.

At the end of the hike we always have lunch and beer in Oia, at a *taverna* overlooking the water. On one visit to Oia, Bonny and I purchased a painting of the nine Greek muses, holding hands and clad in frothy white dresses. I asked the artist which one was Erato, the muse of lyric poetry, because they all looked pretty much alike. Upon finding out that I was a writer she pointed to the muse in the middle.

The hike from Kamari Beach to Mesa Vouno, site of ancient Thira, is a stiff climb of four kilometers to a cliff top near the highest point on the island, on a road that is mostly paved rock. Bonny and I found it to be a challenge in the hot sun. However, the ruins are extensive, some from 600-800 B.C. and some from 100 A.D., featuring carved relief animals in rock, and names carved by the boys who danced naked for the gods (and the local men).

Another interesting hike is from Fira down the 587 or so steps to the harbor, dodging donkeys and donkey dung. Passengers on cruise ships have three alternatives for getting up the cliff to Fira: walk, ride a donkey or ride the cable car. Since we always fly to Santorini, we don't have to fool with the steps at all, but we did so to find out what was at the bottom. Bonny and Judy rode the cable car down and up. Phil and I walked down and up and were wringing wet with sweat by the time we reached the top. Another year, I walked down the steps by myself to examine the largest yacht I have ever seen.

There are many beaches on Santorini. Some of them are sandy, but others are hard on the feet. Some are known by the color of their surfaces. There is a Red Beach, a White Beach and a Black Beach. Walking on the beaches in shoes is easier on the legs and the eyes (because of the girls) than some of the other walks on the island.

Our favorite restaurant on Santorini is called the Flame of the Volcano. It is situated on the edge of the cliff at Fira, overlooking the caldera. We can sit there and watch the sun set into the water. For a little while all of our problems go with it.

*   *   *

The island of Cyprus was not completely Greek when we toured it in 1992. Turkey occupied part of it. We went only to the Greek portion. There was also a strong British influence. The unit of currency was the Cyprus Pound and people drove on the left.

One of Bonny's three great wishes had been to sit in a ruin under a full moon, and on Cyprus she was granted that wish. At Kourion we saw a performance of *Romeo and Juliet* at the Roman amphitheater, while sitting on the granite seats. And, by exquisite timing, there was a full moon. The crowd of about 3,500 mostly English-speaking people was enthusiastic, but not so much so that the spectators forgot to eat the food and drink the wine they brought with them. The cooler of the man in front of us took up as much room as a person. We didn't find out whether he had purchased a ticket for it. The amateur cast spoke English and did a good job. There wasn't a cloud in the sky to mar the performance of the moon.

We saw the spot where Aphrodite was born. She walked out of the water near some rocks that are still standing. Aphrodite's Temple is nearby. Near the city of Paphos we saw ancient mosaics that were on the floors of mansions near the harbor. Many are based on tales from Greek mythology, such as the story of Echo and Narcissus.

At Omodos, where lace is made, we were shopping in the central market area when an old man accosted us and motioned for us to follow him. He didn't speak much English, but he looked harmless enough so we acquiesced. He took us downhill on a residential street. He picked lemon leaves for us to smell. Then we came to a donkey inside a building and we fed the leaves to it. Next he picked some mint leaves and we sniffed them. Just when we were wondering where he was taking us he turned a corner and motioned us into a courtyard. This was his house. He pointed out where he made wine.

His wife appeared, dressed in the traditional black of older Greek women. They led us into the main room of the house and uncovered—lunch. Lunch consisted of bread, cheese, tomato, cucumbers, raisins, almonds, kumquats, Turkish Delight candy, kebab (pieces of nondescript meat, no skewer), cold chips and homemade wine. We ate while the man kept saying, "Very good," which was most of his vocabulary. The woman produced a lace doily, which she informed us cost three pounds. They showed us pictures of other "guests" who had been there.

Since this was obviously costing us money, we ate heartily. We left with the doily, two bottles of wine, and lighter by eight Cyprus pounds. Unfortunately, we were out of film at the moment and it was too far to go to the car and return. I faked taking a picture of the couple with Bonny before we left.

In Nicosia, the capital, we walked to the barrier between Greek and Turkish Cyprus. Although not exactly the Berlin Wall, a physical barrier was in place and armed United Nations soldiers guarded the major streets. Photos were prohibited. I decided not to fake a photograph here.

One of the most interesting artifacts in the Pierides Foundation Museum in Larnaca was a safety pin made in 1200 B.C. Presumably, the patent of the inventor had expired by the time the modern patent for the safety pin was granted.

CHAPTER 17 British Isles

People walk a lot in the British Isles. Walking paths crisscross the landscape. Some go for hundreds of miles. Although many of the paths cross private property, the owners don't usually bother the walkers, as long as they stick close to the paths, don't harass the farm animals and don't commit acts of vandalism. Walkers are also responsible for following safe practices, such as staying away from mad bulls.

Walking has a long history in Great Britain. The poet, William Wordsworth, was a walker; he wrote about walking in poems such as, "Stepping Westward." His sister, Dorothy, walked a lot and also wrote about it. She did some of her walking with Samuel Taylor Coleridge. John Keats was a walker, as was Robert Louis Stevenson who, although born in Scotland, walked in many places. He told about a walk he did in France in *Travels with a Donkey in the Cevennes*. A vintage British musical, *Me and My Girl*, features an exuberant number at the end of the first act called "The Lambeth Walk," that always stops the show.

However, I suspect that many residents of the British Isles don't walk as much as they used to, especially in some of the more remote areas. I have taken an informal survey in places such as northern Scotland and have determined that the average weight of the inhabitants indicates a definite lack of exercise. Could this be because it is easier for them to jump in the car than walk several miles to town?

On the other hand, residents of the larger cities, such as London, appear to be extraordinarily fit. They are thin and wiry and walk very fast, especially when they are near entrances to the Underground. We have found ourselves in danger of being trampled by a horde of commuters rushing to catch a train.

This leads me to the startling conclusion that people who use public transportation are in better shape than people whose primary means of transport is the automobile. On our first trip to the British Isles, in 1983 (other than the few hours we spent there while trying to get home from Greece in 1981), Bonny, Andy, Ellen and I got to test this theory because we depended exclusively on public transportation for our travels, including trains, buses, ferries and the London Underground. It wasn't until several years later that I got up enough nerve to drive on the left side of the road, and not until 1999 that Bonny did the same.

It irritated Bonny that her mother, Ellen, trusted 15-year-old Andy to guide her around London on the Underground, but not Bonny, when Ellen and Bonny went off on their own without us. There must be a moral here that feminists can latch on to.

We got to know the dos and don'ts of public transportation quite well. At one rural railroad station we were waiting to change trains when I saw a sign suggesting that passengers stand back from the edge of the platform nearest the tracks. I idly wondered why until a train whooshed through the station at 80 miles-per-hour. Oh.

Bonny dressed us in identical blue warm-up suits for the 1983 trip and had us carry daypacks, which contained most of our sparse luggage. Ellen, the former owner of a laundry, rolled her clothes so neatly and compactly that she never had any problem finding room to pack them.

We walked a lot during the trip. We flew into London's Heathrow Airport, right over Windsor Castle (I had just time to grab my camera and get a shot of it from the air), but the next day we traveled to the Republic of Ireland by train and ferry. We spent our first night in Ireland at Wexford. Early the next morning I took a walk by the harbor and was pleased to be able to give directions to a man trying to get to the railroad station (see chapter 9).

From Wexford we ventured on to Waterford, where we toured the glass factory that had been reopened in the 1950s after having been closed for 100 years. The apprentices practice very basic glass-blowing operations over and over for seven years. I would go out of my mind.

In Cork, we watched in amazement from the top deck of a double-decker bus as the driver maneuvered us through the narrow streets of the city, around impassible corners, to Blarney Castle. Andy was the only one to kiss the Blarney Stone, lying on his back, head and shoulders extending over the edge of the rock floor, while attendants held his legs. It wasn't the unsanitary condition of the stone that fazed the rest of us—it was just plain fear of heights.

From Cork we took the train to Dublin's fair city ("where the girls are so pretty"). We were fascinated by the Book of Kells at the Trinity College Library, a beautifully illuminated manuscript of the Latin Gospels, believed to have been written in the eighth century.

We took the ferry to Wales and train-hopped along the north coast. Andy and I walked all the way around the city wall of Conway. We were transported hundreds of years back in time, but not as far back as we had been when walking among Greek ruins. There aren't many places where an almost-complete city wall still stands. Chester, England, which is south of Liverpool, is one of them. Canterbury has a piece of its wall remaining, from which you can get a good look at its magnificent cathedral.

After exiting Wales, we traveled north into Scotland. We stopped in Glasgow, but the tourist service said there were no rooms available, so we immediately jumped back on the train and continued to Balloch, at the south end of "the bonny, bonny banks of Loch Lomond." Bonny and I have returned to Balloch several times since 1983 because that is where I finished my British End-to-End walk (see chapters 40-43).

Loch Lomond figures in my family history because the Buchanan clan, from which I am descended, owned a castle on the eastern shore. I can feel the shades of my highland ancestors when I am near the loch. We took a boat trip on it and saw the rocky mass of Ben

Lomond, towering above. Rocky masses always challenge me. When the boat stopped near the mountain, Andy and I got off and hiked partway up, passing many sheep on the trail. Time did not permit us to go all the way to the top.

On our way north we stopped at Stirling and toured the castle there. It sits on a cliff and from below it looks impressive and impenetrable. We ventured north as far as Inverness and took a boat ride on Loch Ness, but did not see the elusive monster then or on our return in 1999, when I walked along most of the north shore of the loch (chapter 40).

As we made our way south we spent several days in Edinburgh, touring its castle and being appalled by the extremely ugly memorial tower to Sir Walter Scott, one of my favorite authors. Later, we toured Sir Walter's impressive home, near the border between England and Scotland, which he named Abbotsford, and on which he spent a lot of money he didn't have. He died prematurely, cranking out pages just to make a buck (or a pound), surely a caution to other writers.

The annual Edinburgh arts festival was in progress while we were there. Although we didn't actually see any of the official shows, the participants did a lot of acting outdoors in the parks, adding life and cheer to the city.

We did see the splendid Tattoo show at the castle, with its music, marching and color. The four of us walked back to our small hotel after the evening performance and couldn't make the key to the room work. The desk clerk called the woman manager, who showed up in an ugly mood and accused us of breaking the lock. She finally called a workman, who had to take off some of the molding around the door in order to get us into the room, well after midnight.

*   *   *

We have enjoyed walking in many other parts of the British Isles. Here are some of our favorite spots, going out from London: Windsor, with its spectacular castle, and nearby Eton, with its famous school; Oxford University, with its many colleges, including New College, where my brother, Mike studied in the 1960s, founded in 1379, only

600 years ago (in an earlier generation my Uncle George attended Magdalen College at Oxford); Stonehenge, where ancient astronomers built a circle of stones that still puzzles and delights people; Salisbury, with one of the largest cathedrals; and Bath, with its Roman baths.

Canterbury, the site of another huge cathedral, is near Dover. Touring the south coast of England, from east to west, one finds: Dover, with its white cliffs ("There'll be bluebirds over the white cliffs of Dover"); Hastings, where William the Conqueror (an ancestor common to Bonny and me) defeated Harold, king of the Saxons, in 1066; and Brighton, (where we unexpectedly found ourselves after our first trip to Greece, in 1981), with its ornate piers, one of which has since been partially destroyed by fire.

Immediately west of Brighton, in the area of Worthing and Littlehampton, Bonny uncovered a covey of cousins while doing her genealogical research. They had been separated from the American branch of the family for 120 years. We have now visited these cousins twice. We have also visited others from the same roots in Sheffield, near Manchester. All have shown us marvelous hospitality.

Continuing along the south coast of England to the west is Portsmouth, which has Admiral Nelson's 104-gun flagship, Victory, on display. Nelson died on Victory at Trafalgar in 1805, while defeating combined French and Spanish forces.

On our 1994 trip, with my mother, not far from the coast we stumbled into New Forest, by mistake. It was serendipity that we found the Walter Tyrrell Pub here, dedicated to Bonny's ancestor who is supposed to have shot King William II with an arrow while hunting in 1100. According to historical sources, it was no big loss. Nearby, the Rufus stone commemorates the spot (Rufus is from the Latin and refers to William's red hair). Walter was exiled to France, but later returned to England and had the bottom half of the three lions on his coat of arms excised.

*   *   *

We finally went to Northern Ireland in 2002, largely because of a couple we met in Lancaster, England, a few days after September 11,

2001. Kieran and Diane were sitting beside us at dinner, having just dropped their daughter off at a graduate school in Birmingham. Kieran is a policeman (constable), whose usual territory is south of Belfast, but when things start heating up there he is called in, along with everybody else. They assured us that we would be safe in Northern Ireland.

We flew to Belfast from Glasgow and spent our first night at Ballycastle, a farm bed and breakfast in Newtownards, County Down (made famous by the song from the movie, *Around the World in 80 Days*, which mentions County Down in the same breath as gay Paree, old New York and London town). Margaret and Ronnie Deering, the owners, were having a party that evening, to celebrate the 50th anniversary of Queen Elizabeth's rein, and invited us. They had food, music featuring Nat King Cole, sack races and an old-fashioned dance in the barn, cleared of the tractors Ronnie collects, some dating back to 1920. What fun.

Then we hooked up with Kieran and Diane. They took us to Newgrange, near the Boyne River in the Republic of Ireland, a 5,000-year-old mound of rocks, with a burial chamber inside. At the winter solstice the rising sun shines through a hole above the entrance and illuminates the chamber.

On the ride back to Banbridge, where Kieran and Diane live, many people lined the side of the road, dressed in green (some in costumes), celebrating the 1-1 tie of the Irish football (soccer in the US) team, in the match against Germany, during the World Cup competition. I have never seen such jubilation for a tie, unless it was the celebration in England for a nil-nil (0-0) tie a few days later that put the English team into the next round of the World Cup. No wonder the colonists revolted (or maybe they were revolted).

Kieran and Diane drove us into Belfast and told us where we could and could not go. The police stations look like forts; they have been attacked with mortars in the past. We had good meals with them at Harry's Bar, in Banbridge. On our last night in Northern Ireland we stayed at a small hotel in east Belfast. Riots took place on the same street several miles to the west of us.

Much of our walking in Northern Ireland took place in cemeteries, where Bonny was looking for additional ancestors. The writing on many of the older gravestones is worn and difficult to read. Some of the cemeteries are not well cared for and some of the stones have fallen over. We drove west to Omagh and toured the Ulster American Folk Park, which has examples of houses, shops, schools and churches in both Irish and American history. We walked through the Ulster History Park on a Saturday morning and had the whole place to ourselves.

We watched for fairy trees. Fairies have a special affinity for blackthorn trees in Northern Ireland. The trees shouldn't be cut down because the fairies get upset. We saw blackthorn trees standing alone in farmers' fields. Kieran and Diane reported coming upon one in the middle of the road, without warning. You can't mess with the fairies.

*   *   *

London is one of the world's great walking cities, as long as you remember to look to the right for cars (signs at major intersections advise you to do this) and have your Underground day-pass with you so that you can jump on a train now and then. Like Los Angeles, London is just too vast for a walker to cover it all.

Some of my favorite places to tour in London include the Tower of London and the double-decked Tower Bridge next to it; other sights and bridges along the River Thames (keeping in mind that the original London Bridge is now at Lake Havasu, Arizona); Buckingham Palace; the many museums; Kensington Gardens; Hyde Park; Leicester Square, where discount tickets are sometimes available for shows (we have seen many excellent productions); and Covent Garden, with its street performers. We like to stay at the Balmoral House Hotel, on Sussex Gardens Road, one block from Paddington Station, which is family owned, reasonably priced, cozy, and features good breakfasts.

On our first trip to London, in 1983, Bonny, Andy, Ellen and I had just sat down for dinner in a restaurant when a man sat down at the table next to us. He ordered a piece of pie a la mode. He then took his knife and fork and attacked the pie, growling like an animal all the while. First he cut it up into pieces; then he shoveled the pieces into one big pile; then he mashed the whole mess down. At this point he took a huge bite, missing his mouth with half of it, and left a gob of ice cream on his cheek. The ice cream remained on his cheek while he shoveled the rest into his mouth. Finally, he wiped his cheek with his tie.

We also ate dinner at the Borshtch 'n Tears, which featured placemats with wry comments. Samples: "The salt and pepper will be found towards the centre of the table. Your bill will be found despite your efforts to hide it." And, "Sex is better exercise than walking. A miss is as good as a mile!" Hey, I never denied that.

During our 1983 trip we averaged close to five miles a day walking, much of it with packs on our backs. Ellen carried her ten-pound pack without complaining and often had more energy than other members of the troop. At the end of the trip she said, "What I need is some good exercise. I'll be glad to get home so that I can mow the lawn."

In 1994, I had a stopover in London for a few hours on my way to Nice, France, to meet Bonny. I didn't feel like hanging around the airport so I checked my luggage and took the Underground to Covent Garden. I was spaced out enough by jetlag so that a young, female street performer was able to induce me to attempt to spin a hula-hoop, something I never learned how to do when the fad was at its peak. She also got another guy and me to do other things much too silly to mention here. Then I walked across the Tower Bridge, took the Underground back to Heathrow Airport and flew on to Nice.

CHAPTER 18 Walking Behind Curtains and Walls

BERLIN WALL (1961-1989)

Over and under and through the Wall they came,
parched with a thirst they couldn't quench.
Tunneling, flying, leaping, crawling, hidden
in car seats and carts, determined to wrench
themselves free from tyranny's stench.

Oppressed, tortured, imprisoned, shot—
still the thirsty would not could not be denied.
The spring of freedom beckoned, so close, so far;
yards, feet, nay inches away they died—
and friends and loved ones cried.

Some made it! a baby hidden in a bag in a cart;
desperate men who leapt on a moving train;
a hollow car seat, tunnels, boats,
a makeshift glider, balloon and plane;
putting an end to the thirst and pain.

And then one day, one wonderful day,
they hammered and shattered and tore down the Wall!
Thirsting, singing, shouting, laughing, hugging,

chunk by chunk they watched it fall—
and the terrible thirst was quenched for all.

In 1985, our traveling quartette (Bonny, Andy, Ellen and I) flew into Budapest, Hungary, "the pearl of the Danube," carrying minimum luggage, a practice learned from our previous trips. That sounds romantic, but Budapest was still behind the Iron Curtain at that time and we didn't have hotel reservations.

Our travel agent could have gotten us reservations at the Intercontinental Hotel at a rate that would have forced us to sell our firstborn (and only born) son, Andy, but we passed and said we would wing it. Fortunately, Bonny had studied the guidebooks and knew exactly what to do. She herded us onto a bus, where Ellen and Andy promptly fell asleep. The bus took us to the Centrum, or center of town, and from there we walked to the IBUSZ tourist office.

The clerk, who looked like Nastassia Kinski, as did many of the women there, found us adjoining rooms, with shared bathroom facilities, at the Panorama Hotel, at one-quarter the Intercontinental price. The price included breakfast and a beautiful view of the city, neither of which the Intercontinental price included. The hotel was on the Buda side of the Danube River (the other side is called the Pest side).

Walking in Budapest centers on the Danube and the hills beside it. Many buildings were still damaged from World War II fighting. From our hotel window we could see Gellert Hill, named for St. Gerard, who converted Hungary to Christianity, and the Liberation Monument at the top, also called Hungary's Statue of Liberty, honoring the heroic Russian liberators who freed the city from German occupation. An ironic note is that in the 1956 uprising, more than 2,200 people died and 200,000 fled to the West, including Gabe, a man I worked with at McDonnell Douglas.

Many young folks were sunbathing on the concrete steps lining the Danube, some in their underwear. We took a boat ride on the Danube that went under some of the eight bridges. From the boat we saw the impressive Parliament Building and Santa Margarite Island, where the Romans built spas. Hungarian men invited Ellen and Bonny to dance on the deck to folk music. They decided that this was too strenuous for them and declined, but it was the only time we heard the people really laugh and sound happy.

People seemed to spend a lot of time waiting in line (including us when we purchased train tickets). They waited quietly, with anxious expressions on their faces, probably because they were wondering if they were in the correct line. The clerks who serviced the lines spent a lot of time writing in four copies, the last one illegible, stamping documents with official-looking stamps and looking slightly puzzled. The red tape wound slowly.

We took the train to Prague, in what was then Czechoslovakia, also an Iron Curtain country. During the first hour or so of the ride we were beset upon by no fewer than eight sets of uniformed functionaries, checking tickets, customs for Hungary and customs for Czechoslovakia. One uniformed woman was intent on moving us to a second-class compartment (we had first-class tickets and reserved seats), but another person finally stopped her.

We didn't have hotel reservations in Prague, either. It was raining when we arrived so we left Ellen and Andy standing in a doorway near the railroad station, promising we would return soon (they must have had a lot of faith in us), and walked to the tourist office. The name of the first street we saw was Georgi Washingtonian.

The clerks at the tourist office tried to put us in an expensive hotel. Saying no thank you, we walked to a nearby hotel and found it full, but one of the clerks there called her friend at a third hotel that had rooms available. We walked there and the friend offered us half off if we paid in dollars, instead of the local coronas. Realizing that this was probably illegal, I only paid for half the room in dollars, so I only committed half a crime. The black-market rate for dollars was as much as three times the official rate. When we paid for our last dinner in Prague I ran out of coronas and offered a dollar to pay the rest. I received much more change than I anticipated.

The central square of Prague features an astronomical horology clock, built about 1400, with its parade of apostles on the hour. A skeleton rang the bell to show that time is fleeting. The maker of the clock was blinded so that he couldn't make another. While we were looking at the clock a man stuck a camera in Bonny's face and took a picture of her, then disappeared into the crowd. The facades of the buildings in the square are unique, featuring impressive artistic creativity. The Charles Bridge over the Vltava River is a footbridge lined with statues. It was built by Charles II in the 1200s and in 1985 still had gaslights lit by the old lamp lighter.

We visited an old synagogue in the Jewish area, dating back to the 12th century, with a small graveyard where 12,000 Jews are buried under a jumble of headstones, much like rock piles on a mountainside. There was an exhibit of drawings made by Jewish Czech children in a concentration camp during the early 1940s. They featured childish figures of people reaching for each other, hugging, dancing and holding hands. There were rainbows, birds and flowers. The children were all liquidated by the Nazis.

While we waited for the train at the Prague railroad station the guards repeatedly harassed and intimidated students who were sleeping in sleeping bags while they also waited. Apparently, sleeping wasn't allowed in railroad stations. We took the train from Prague into Austria and endured hassling by the cousins of those guards, as they inspected our packs and the water closet in our first-class compartment. It was a relief to get to Vienna, on the other side of the Iron Curtain.

*   *   *

When we toured Berlin and East Germany in 1993, the Berlin Wall was gone, except for a section left as a reminder, and there were still reminders of World War II. The Kaiser Wilhelm Memorial Church was badly damaged during the war and left that way as a warning. Another cathedral, Berliner Dom, had just opened for the first time since a bomb crashed through its dome in 1944.

The ornate Brandenburg Gate is worth seeing and is located on the East Berlin side of the late-but-not-lamented Berlin Wall. At Checkpoint Charlie, perhaps the best known of the checkpoints where people passed through the wall, a section of the Wall remained, with a warning memorial consisting of a guard tower and some signs.

The nearby museum contained stories of many of the people who escaped from East Germany and some who didn't make it. They went over the wall and under the wall, by water, by air, through checkpoints concealed in little cars and shopping bags, and just about every way imaginable. I watched a poignant movie showing the demolition of the wall and the events leading up to it. I guess people who have lost their freedom are the ones who most appreciate it.

Berlin has many delightful museums, including art museums, the Pergamon Museum, with relics from Turkey, and the Bode Museum, with Egyptian relics and paintings. One museum contains the actual bust of Nefertiti, who was obviously a babe. There is a reconstruction of the Ishtar Gate, from ancient Babylon, built by Nebuchadnezzar II (reigned 604-562 B.C.), made from beautiful blue stones and covered with lions that are also part snake and part bird. There is a wall from the palace at Assur, 9th century B.C., and Cuneiform tablets. The Charlottenburg Palace contains a huge golden ballroom and other gorgeous rooms and furnishings.

We picked up a car in Berlin and drove to a number of cities in the former East Germany. Many East Germans appeared to be driving new cars, in spite of a dismal employment situation. It may have been because the West German government exchanged West German marks for East German marks at par.

Potsdam features Sans Souci, the Prussian palace, complete with ornate rooms and furnishings. Voltaire lived there for a while. We drove to Halle, where my father's mother was born, on a bumpy autobahn with a speed limit of 100 kilometers-per-hour, instead of no speed limit, which is usual on autobahns. Few people observed the speed limit, just as in Los Angeles.

Our first impression of Halle was a gray, dismal, rundown city, with buildings in disrepair. We got caught in a traffic jam heading toward the *zentrum* (city center) and broke away from it when we could. We decided not to attempt to look up the residence of my second cousin, who still lived there.

My father took a number of trips to Germany, before and after marrying my mother. He wrote in his diaries about visiting relatives, including a mysterious female German cousin. My father was strait-laced and, as one friend noted, completely without guile, but my mother, the one time I heard her talk about Dad and his cousin, said only, "He always came back to me."

In Leipzig and Dresden, which were pretty much leveled during World War II, there was a lot of new construction in progress, but we were told that it hid deep economic problems. We stayed in Dresden on the 10th floor of a hotel that had been redecorated and walked to the central plaza. In a buffet-style eatery we pointed to some dishes, attempting to find out about them, and before we knew it we had plates of these dishes in front of us. The chicken, stuffed cabbage and potatoes covered with paprika were quite tasty.

Bamberg, in West Germany, was the prettiest city we went to on the 1993 trip, with a river, multitudes of flowers, and well-cared-for old houses. The old town hall is on a bridge in the center of the river. A caution for all U.S. travelers in Europe: In Frankfurt, Bonny plugged her curling iron into the 220-volt socket and burned her hair. Then the plastic in the iron started to melt. She didn't do that again (at least not with that iron).

*   *   *

In 1988, when Bonny, Andy and I toured Turkey, we tried to get to Bulgaria three different ways. Bulgaria was still behind the Iron Curtain at that time and I'm not sure what our fascination was, but we failed on all counts. First, we rented a car in Izmir, Turkey and asked whether we could drive it into Bulgaria. The answer was an emphatic no. Next, we checked airline schedules from Istanbul, but there were no flights to Sofia, Bulgaria.

We thought our third try was going to be successful. We booked a bus tour to Sofia at our hotel in Istanbul, or so we thought. When we arrived at the travel agency we were informed we were going to Varna, a resort on the Black Sea, instead of Sofia. If we had wanted to go to a resort, it wouldn't have been in a Communist country. We asked for our passports back. A man showed our passports to us (we had given them to the hotel clerk the night before) but he refused to return them and said they were being taken to the Bulgarian Consulate to get a group visa (we already had individual Bulgarian visas we had obtained in the US). He immediately left the building with our passports and many others.

We waited, determined not to leave without our passports. Very little English was spoken. I was put on the phone a couple of times with a person who spoke slightly more English. Somebody told us to wait half an hour because there might be a bus to Sofia that day. Thirty minutes and more went by. People constantly came into the office and argued with the agents, usually in loud voices, which seemed to be the primary method of communication in Turkey. Some of the people may have been unhappy because the departure of the buses was delayed until the passports and visas arrived back on the scene. The place was a madhouse.

Finally, the tourists were allowed to board the buses. Our passports were returned to us and we were informed that there was no bus to Sofia that day. By this time we had decided we didn't want to go to Sofia at all and asked for our money back. We were told to get it at the hotel. We eventually did, all except for about $10.

*   *   *

By 1996, Bulgaria was no longer Communist, but some of the effects lingered on. Bonny and I made advance reservations to fly to Sofia from Athens. Upon our arrival at the Sofia Airport, we each had to pay a $20 entrance fee in US dollars. Bulgaria was suffering from hyperinflation and every opportunity was taken to obtain hard currency.

Our Balkantourist guide, Dani, and her driver, Basil, were waiting for us in the airport lobby. They drove us to the Park Moskva Hotel, where our three-night stay was prepaid. Our room on the 11th floor of the hotel had an old TV set and received CNN part of the time. The food at the hotel restaurants was good, and inexpensive. There weren't many guests at the hotel.

Dani and Basil met us at 9 a.m. the next morning. They gave us a quick driving tour of downtown Sofia (accent on the first syllable) and then Dani continued guiding us on foot. We toured St. Alexander Nevski Memorial Church and learned a lot more about it than we cared to know. We saw various other churches and public buildings and an excavated Roman road. Dani, who had been a guide for 20

125

years, talked nonstop and gave us a thumbnail history of Bulgaria. Turkey controlled it for over 500 years, until 1878.

The streets of downtown Sofia are paved with yellow bricks— literally. It is depressing to think that this might be the origin of the Yellow Brick Road in *The Wizard of Oz*, and I suspect L. Frank Baum never went to Bulgaria. We saw bricklayers patching holes in the streets with yellow bricks. I don't think there was any gold in them.

After the overthrow of Communism in Bulgaria in November 1989, the Communists were reborn as Socialists and still managed to control the government, possibly because the substantial number of pensioners feared losing their government pensions. Hyperinflation destroyed the value of their pensions, anyway. Many of the older women dyed their hair red, but nobody smiled much. It was a grim society.

On our own we toured the National History Museum, a huge building with many employees, dedicated to making sure that we didn't damage or steal anything, but almost no visitors. Lights were turned on as we entered rooms and turned off as we left. We also toured the national art gallery, but the pictures there were the most depressing collection we've seen anywhere. Even the nude statues looked unhappy.

The tram went through a forest to get from our hotel to downtown Sofia—actually a park, of which Sofia has many. We did a lot of walking in the park and took some pictures. We also studied the flea markets, part of the extensive underground economy, purchasing embroidered cloth and hand-painted and lacquered boxes. Bonny bought two sets of nested dolls, one inside another, five deep—called *matroshka* (little mother). We paid partly in dollars. We had problems with head shaking because a nod means no and a shake means yes. We decided the best policy was not to move our heads at all but to pretend they were in neck braces.

Bonny's carrying bag was slit, probably with a knife while we were shopping in an underground area near the Sheraton Hotel (much too high-priced for us). A man who pressed us to change money was the likely suspect. I told him to go away, but he was hard to get rid of. Nothing was taken and we were glad we carried our valuables in pouches underneath our shirts. We also didn't change any money on the streets because it was a scam—most of the bills given out were worthless.

We ate lunch at the same Italian restaurant three days in a row. During that time the price of the spaghetti dish we liked increased from 299 leva to 343 leva. A glass of sparkling water rose from 15 to 18 leva. Our hotel, which had been buying dollars at 184 leva when we arrived, offered 205 when we left, but we could have gotten 228 leva downtown, without resorting to the black market. Dani and Basil drove us to the airport when we left. We tipped Dani in dollars and gave Basil the remainder of our leva. I hope he spent it fast.

For more on Communist countries and formerly Communist countries, see chapters 23 and 26.

CHAPTER 19 Europe

In 1985, Bonny, Andy, Ellen and I traveled to Vienna, Austria, by train, from Prague, Czechoslovakia. It was a relief to get back to the free world. Walks in Vienna feature palaces, museums and the opera house, where Bonny once had visions of dancing at the annual ball. Seeing the limited space available for dancing, envisioning the crowds of people filling it and picturing having to stand up all night because we couldn't afford a box seat ended that vision.

We ate in a restaurant whose menus were written in German. Andy had taken three years of high school German, but he still ended up with a plate of raw hamburger. It was quite good, however.

In Austria we picked up a rental car, which made our travels more flexible. The car was great for driving from one city to another, but we quickly found that when we entered a moderate-size city that was new to us, if we parked the car and walked around we could usually figure out how to navigate the streets and get to wherever we wanted to go within half an hour. This was far superior to attempting to decode the tangle of narrow and winding streets while driving in heavy traffic.

In Salzburg we walked along the Salzach River and toured the castle, which is a short funicular ride up from the Residenz Plaza. The plaza features a giant chessboard, whose pieces are rolled around by the players. How can they attain the perspective of the whole board when they are in the center of it? There are lots of places to walk in Austria, but walking is not allowed on the bike paths. A woman bicyclist yelled at me when all I did was step onto the path to take a picture.

Mad King Ludwig almost bankrupted Bavaria by building exquisite palaces and castles. They are fun to visit, but I wouldn't want to have to pay for them. At Linderhof, we escaped into his fantasy world as we toured the castle, grotto and kiosk. The grotto, inside a cave, features a lake with a seashell-shaped rowboat, covered in gold leaf, and three sets of lighting to change the mood.

Neuschwanstein Castle looks like a real castle because it is the model for the castles at Disneyland and Disney World. The walk to the castle from the parking lot is a kilometer, steeply uphill, but it is worth seeing from close range or from across the lake, with its impractical design and slender towers. Of course, for Americans it is cheaper to see what it looks like in the US, compliments of Walt Disney. King Ludwig, incidentally, died under mysterious circumstances. I suspect that not many of his subjects mourned him.

Our tour went over the Brenner Pass into Italy in our rental car and finally reached Venice, after a horrifying introduction to Italian drivers. A driver wishing to pass us would stay about six inches from our bumper. When an opportunity presented itself for him to pass, as often as not a third car would simultaneously pass him. Then a motorbike would come along and swerve far over to the left-hand side of the road to pass all three of us. Italian drivers drive as though they belong to a religious sect that guarantees a dozen lives, of which this is the least important.

We stayed in Venice Mestre, on the mainland, at the Venezia Hotel. I mention this because the desk clerk there was the best at her job of any we have ever seen, anywhere. This shorthaired young woman spoke excellent English, acted as if she had been expecting us and in her charming way extolled the advantages of staying at the hotel. She noted our *Frommer's* guidebook and asked if we were from California, explaining that Californians had the brightest smiles.

A walking tour of Venice means walking alongside the canals and across the bridges, such as the impressive Rialto Bridge. Although Venice is smelly, crumbling and slowly sinking into the sea, some of its former glory shines through. Most of the tourists and pigeons are found at the Piazza San Marco, where the cathedral is located. Only Ellen could tour the cathedral, since she was the only one properly attired (shorts not allowed), but we all toured the Palace of the Doges.

We crossed the Bridge of Sighs (the sighs of those about to be executed), featured in the movie, *A Little Romance*, where a very young Diane Lane and her French boyfriend run away to Venice with the idea of kissing under the bridge in a gondola at sunset, abetted by a thief, played by Laurence Olivier. Olivier has the best line in the movie: "What are legends, anyway, but stories about ordinary people doing extraordinary things?"

We rode the *vaporetto* (water bus) the length of the Grand Canal, eschewing the gondolas because they are expensive and compete with the motorized traffic, which takes a lot of the romance out of being poled along in an ugly boat.

Our 1985 trip continued on through a corner of France to Geneva, Switzerland. We took a nice walk along the Rhone River to Lake Geneva, where a 300-foot-high water jet spews forth, an engineering feat of which the locals are justly proud. Geneva is the world headquarters for lots of impressive-sounding organizations, including the defunct League of Nations. Currently, the European HQ of the United Nations is located here.

Zermatt, Switzerland, is one of those picture-book places, located in the Alps, that don't really exist, except in books like *Heidi*. Just kidding—Zermatt really does exist and the houses really are alpine chalets and they don't allow cars, except for electric cars. Zermatt is at an altitude of 1,620 meters, surrounded by peaks, most notably, the Matterhorn, which we could see from the doorway of our hotel.

Andy and I took a tram and a cable car to Schwarzee, which means "black lake," in honor of a black lake, at 2,582 meters, and from there we made our assault on the shoulder of the Matterhorn. We hiked up to the Matterhornhutte, at 3,260 meters, which is the jumping-off place for climbs to the summit. It is a hotel and restaurant. When we saw the helicopter flying up the mountain, with something hanging below it, we figured it was on a rescue mission. However, the hanging cargo turned out to be cans of soda. The magnificent view from the hut includes peaks that are higher than the Matterhorn (which is 4,478 meters).

Of the dozens of people who hiked to the hut, we were the only ones wearing sneakers, as everybody else wore boots with certified lug soles. Our minimalist packing didn't allow for boots. Even so, Andy was easily the fastest person on the mountain, as his cross-country training stood him in good stead. The books advise the use of a guide to climb to the top of the Matterhorn from the hut and the Zermatt cemetery is full of people who didn't take that advice. We hiked all the way back down to Zermatt. There were a great many people on the lower trails, which are dotted with restaurants and even small hotels.

On a trip to Switzerland with my mother, my father attempted the hike to the hut by himself. However, he did it at a time of year when there was glare ice on the trail. After falling down and fearing that his next fall would be over the edge, he wisely retreated to the safety of Zermatt.

On the 1985 trip, we wended our way to Amsterdam, a city with many canals, much graffiti and zillions of bicycles. It is easy to get around, with a combination of walking and trolleys. We drove into the city at rush hour, which was a mistake, parked in the red-light district, where Andy got an eyeful of the girls showing off their wares, and walked to the railroad station. Here, two women accosted us. However, they were not hookers; they had rooms to rent. We ended up on the third floor of a house with steep and narrow stairs. The houses have permanent outside pulley systems for lifting furniture to the upper floors.

Anne Frank's hiding place was open to the public, including the bookcase used to conceal the annex from prying eyes. There were pictures of Anne and her family and actual samples from her diary. The pictures of movie actors and actresses she collected were still on the walls and there were even pencil marks, indicating heights of the children at various ages. It was a very moving experience. The Van Gogh Museum has a terrific collection of that artist's paintings. Other museums feature artists such as Rembrandt.

*   *   *

In 1993, Bonny and I found ourselves in Europe again. We started out in Belgium. In Brussels, we walked past the ornate guildhalls from another century and saw the famous statue of the boy peeing. Although he is reputed to have over 400 costumes, he was naked. Perhaps, he couldn't make up his mind what to wear. At the Grand Place we listened to a number of oompah bands, in uniform. The musicians paraded around the square at dinnertime and stopped for drinks at restaurants. Wineries and breweries sponsored them.

In Antwerp, we saw the largest cathedral in Belgium/Netherlands, which is very large. But then, there are many large cathedrals in Europe. If you wonder what people did during the Middle Ages, the answer is, they built cathedrals. When they weren't building castles. We also toured the palatial home of Peter Paul Rubens (1577-1640), which contains much artwork. There is a special exhibit of sketches by him and others to demonstrate aspects of human anatomy, so they could properly paint people.

In The Hague, Netherlands, you can take the tram practically everywhere, and walk to where the tram doesn't go. While Bonny was doing some work for Xerox, I sought out the world's largest sand castle, on the beach at Scheveningen. I walked the short distance to the beach from the hotel in lovely weather (it was early June), and then walked along the beach to the castle, which had a sign in front, proclaiming it to be in the Guinness Book of Records. It was 15 meters high, large around the base, with professional sculpture that appeared to be based on ancient Mayan art.

The Hague also features an aquarium with a walk-through tunnel, surrounded by water, but it wasn't as good as the one we saw in Auckland, New Zealand. The Netherlands runs on bicycle power. As in Austria, I got warned to stay off the bike paths. The girl riders often wore skirts that buttoned in front, but they weren't always buttoned. Beachwear was also very informal.

*　　*　　*

In 1995, Bonny flew to Rome on Xerox business and I tagged along. We arrived at Rome's Fiumicino Airport in the late afternoon and took the train to Rome Termini station. From there we walked several blocks to a hotel. I went into the hotel while Bonny waited outside with the luggage (we didn't have reservations). A boy reached his hand around the corner of the building and grabbed one of the bags. Bonny yelled and chased him; he dropped it. She reported the incident to the hotel management, but they only shook their heads. Apparently, the boy lived in the area.

Bonny had several free days so we saw St. Peter's piazza and cathedral and then toured the huge Vatican Museum, along with hordes of others. Every school child in Italy seemed to be there (it was Friday, March 31, possibly spring vacation). St. Peter's contains the "Pieta," a statue Michelangelo finished when he was just 25. The vibrant colors of the newly restored paintings by Michelangelo in the Sistine Chapel showed what a wonderful artist he was.

We went to the Trevi Fountain, which was the inspiration for the song, "Three Coins in the Fountain." And the Spanish Steps, which seemed to be a gathering place for all the tourists in Rome. In the nearby Metro station we were swarmed by a group of young children. Previously warned that they were pickpockets, we distanced ourselves from them.

The Capitoline Hill is near the Colosseum. The piazza there was designed by Michelangelo and is surrounded by old government buildings, now museums. They contain many sculptures of heads of famous Romans and copies of Greek statues, as well as paintings by the masters (Titian, Rubens, Tintoretto). Santa Maria ara Coeli, the church next door, has a statue of baby Jesus, whose lips change color. Many ruins remain in the Forum, including a number of pillars and arches. The Colosseum, itself, is the grandest spectacle of all, with the floor excavated to reveal the rooms below, where the animals were kept. It bears a strong resemblance to the Coliseum in Los Angeles (or vice versa).

We walked along the Tiber River and the Circus Maximus, where chariot races were held. We toured Castel Sant Angelo, on the Tiber, just east of the Vatican. There are good views from the top of the castle. At Gesu Church, depicted in bold relief is the assertion that while Catholics are lifted up to heaven Protestants and other heretics are beaten down to hell.

On a crowded Metro, a man managed to unzip my fanny pack, even though it was in front of me; he also unzipped Bonny's purse. Fortunately, he wasn't able to get anything out. Once again, we were thankful for the pouches we carried under our shirts, containing our valuables.

We changed to the Hotel Parco dei Principi, in the park Villa Borghese, right next to the zoo, for the Xerox business part of the trip. From here we walked to the Pantheon, designed by the emperor Hadrian (A.D. 118-125). Then we saw the extensive art collection at the Palazzo Doria Pamphili.

One day we went by Metro and bus to Anzio, the site of an Allied landing during World War II, in which Bonny's Uncle Dick participated. In fact, he participated in many catastrophic events during the war. Most of the members of his company didn't come back. The beach still had crumbling brick fortifications from the war. The city is a resort area now, complete with a marina.

On two days that Bonny had business meetings I went sightseeing with Carol and Adele, a wife and fiancée of Xerox employees. We toured the catacombs at San Callisto, where 500,000 early Christians were buried on five levels. We took a tour that went down two levels. Then we walked along part of the Via Appia (Appian Way)—a bad part, unfortunately, since it was narrow, with lots of traffic, and not from chariots, either. On another day the three of us went to the Baths of Caracalla and toured them.

Bonny and I took the train to Florence with two other couples, including the Benners, Carol (one of my sightseeing partners) and her husband, Dave. Rich and Bonnie Kirchner also went with us. As we waited to get into the Uffizi Museum, we saw a local costume parade, representing historical figures of the area. We also saw a man going from car to car along a street, testing to see whether any were unlocked.

The Uffizi contains Botticelli's painting, "Venus on the Half Shell," and the premier collection of Italian Renaissance art. We went to the National Gallery to see Michelangelo's "David," nicely lit, and his slaves—five statues he was working on when he died (he had not had time to free them from the stone). At the Duomo, the great cathedral, I climbed the bell tower. The Bapistry of St. John is the oldest building in Florence. The Ponte Vecchio (bridge over the Arno River) has shops along its length.

CHAPTER 20 France

THE CLIFFS OF PALOS VERDES

The cliffs of Palos Verdes
Fall steeply to the sea,
So like the cliffs of Pointe du Hoc
In far-off Normandy.

The Palos Verdes palette
Blends hues of brown and green,
And the gray of Palos Verdes stone
For a rich, pastoral scene.

With bouquets of yellow mustard
Dancing in the spring;
A cornucopia of color
That only peace can bring.

These cliffs were never red
Like bloody Pointe du Hoc,
Where robot soldiers killed their brothers,
In a ghoulish, cosmic joke.

On the cliffs of Palos Verdes
No crosses mark the spot;
No graveyards full of fallen heroes
Exist in Camelot.

The cliffs of Palos Verdes
Fall steeply to the sea,
Creating a sublime facade
Of peace and harmony.

On our 1985 European trip, Bonny, Andy, Ellen and I drove through the seven-mile-long Mt. Blanc Tunnel from Italy to Chamonix, France. Hikers in Chamonix have to be willing to contend with the snow on Mt. Blanc, the highest mountain in Europe (4,807 meters), and the surrounding peaks. We chose, instead, to ride the "world's highest cable car," which ascends in two stages to 3,842 meters, the last part almost straight up. Talk about breathtaking. From the top we could see hikers camping on the snowfields adjacent to us.

On the same trip we also spent a night in Metz. Metz was one of the most important cities of Roman Gaul. Two of the crusades stopped here and it was a major cultural center during the Renaissance. In the 12th century it was one of the richest and most populous cities in Europe. Metz was annexed by the Germans as a result of the Franco-Prussian War (1870) and was not returned to France until 1918. It was heavily damaged during World War II. We went inside the huge Metz cathedral and admired the intricately carved figures on the outside. There is a plaque on the outside wall in memory of Marshall Foch, of World War I fame, who was instrumental in returning Metz to France.

*   *   *

After Andy left home to start college at the University of Oregon in 1986, Bonny and I took another trip to France so that we wouldn't be alone in our empty house. In order to get around we rented a Mercedes—by mistake. We had requested a car with automatic transmission because of Bonny's tendonitis, and probably got the only one in France. Although it wasn't a large model, it proved difficult to drive through the narrow streets of some of the villages. It also came with a security system; we had to enter a four-digit code to start the car.

Security systems, like much of modern technology, can complicate our lives. We picked up the car at Charles De Gaulle Airport and headed north to Senlis in early evening. Our first problem occurred when we parked the car in a dark area to look for a hotel. When we tried to start it again we couldn't read the digits on the security keypad.

We had a worse incident later, in Lyon. We had to leave the car in a parking garage. The attendant wanted us to leave him the keys because our car was blocking another car. We knew that the employees of the garage would never be able to start our car again to move it out of the way once we left. Our two or three words of French were completely inadequate to explain the problem and only served to irritate the parking attendant, who walked away in disgust. Finally, Bonny prevailed upon a man who spoke French and a few words of English to help defuse the situation.

Senlis had cobblestone streets, which aren't made for walking. I doubt that horses like them, either. It also has a huge cathedral (like every other French city). This one had long plastic sheets hanging from the high ceiling because it was being renovated. Since we were the only ones in the cathedral, the atmosphere felt like something out of the Addams family.

Chantilly, home of the famous Longchamps racecourse, was more fun. We walked around the huge stone stable and the palatial estate, formerly owned by one of the dukes of the ruling family. It is filled with magnificent paintings of well-known artists, such as Raphael, Fouquet and Ingres, and there are swans in the moat.

Rouen is a port city on the River Seine. We toured the museum Beaux Arts, which has paintings by great artists, including some by Monet. The painting Bonny liked most, however, was by a woman from Hartford, Connecticut, Mary Mac Monnies. I took a picture of it. We saw the horology clock, built in 1390, on a square now barred to traffic. Joan of Arc was burned at the stake in Rouen. I won't mention that we toured the 13th century cathedral. I am not going to mention cathedrals again for the rest of this chapter, except in an emergency.

Bayeux has the Bayeux tapestry (actually an embroidery), 70 meters long, created about 1077 and depicting in 58 scenes the triumph of our common ancestor, William the Conqueror, at the Battle of Hastings in 1066. In her genealogy research, Bonny has found that she and I have many common ancestors, which makes us cousins. However, we suspect that most people whose ancestors hail from Britain and/or France are cousins.

Bayeux has a museum that tells the story of the Normandy landing, from June 6, 1944 through August, with movies, newspapers and a large number of relics. It is a very well done memorial to the people who fought there to preserve our freedom. The allies liberated Bayeux on June 7.

If you like poignancy with your walks, tour some of the Normandy beaches, where the D-Day landings took place. On Gold Beach, many pieces of the man-made harbor named Port Winston, built for the landing, still remain. To get from here to Omaha Beach, head west through country filled with farm buildings and stone walls hundreds of years old. What did the people who lived here do during the landings? Where did they go?

Visit the American cemetery near Omaha Beach and look down the too-neat rows of thousands of white crosses and Stars of David. Remember that each of these stones represents a young man whose life was snuffed out in his prime. Contrast this peaceful scene with the horror of the pictures you have seen of the battle, itself.

Walk on the top of Pointe du Hoc, the cliff scaled on D-Day morning by a force of 225 Americans to knock out the German guns emplaced there. Although the guns had already been moved when the attack took place, only 90 men remained when the unit was relieved two days later. Pointe du Hoc looks enough like the cliffs of Palos Verdes, where we live, that I wrote a poem about it.

After we had our fill of war we drove south through cornfields, apple trees and cattle and stopped for the night at Laval. We ate dinner in a quaint restaurant by the River Mayenne, just below the 12th century chateau that belonged to the Counts of Laval. The next morning we walked along the river and then drove east along the Loire River.

As we drove the back roads and were forced to take some detours, we got lost and unlost all afternoon. Driving through the ancient villages is like negotiating mazes. There are often signs, but not always where you can see them. The streets get very narrow, at times allowing only one-way traffic and sometimes that is a tight squeeze. Allowing cars on these picturesque cobblestone streets is a shame, anyway.

This was chateau country. In Azay le-Rideau we toured the local chateau, which has water provided by the Indre River. It was built about 1518, more for comfort than security. Next we toured the chateau at Chenonceaux, east of Tours, home of Catherine de Medici and Diane Poitiers, wife and mistress of Henry II respectively. They both lived here but at different times (Diane first—Catherine kicked her out when Henry was killed). The chateau straddles the Cher River and is largely restored. There are many cave dwellers living near the manor and near Chenonceaux. Often the caves have a facade with windows, and sometimes several rooms are contained in front of the opening in the rock.

In Amboise, we toured Le Clos Luce, the manor where Leonardo da Vinci lived the last four years of his life. It featured exhibits of many of his drawings, along with models of the machines depicted (courtesy of IBM). He was left-handed and wrote mirror image. One of his ideas was the concept of the manual transmission in an automobile. I'm sure the French (and maybe the Italians) feel that if God had meant cars to have automatic transmissions he/she would have had da Vinci invent it.

In Sarlat, which is off the beaten track, we took a stroll in the 17th century, through narrow, crooked lanes, bounded by the original buildings. This area is known for its pre-historic cave drawings and *fois gras* (goose liver). The 14th century bridge in Cahors makes a pretty picture, reflected in the Lot River. The old section of Cordes is at the top of a fairly steep hill. We parked at the bottom and walked up. The atmosphere was spoiled, as it is in most of these old villages, by the cars snorting up and down the narrow cobblestone streets. At the square on top, the villagers were preparing for some sort of Rabelaisian celebration.

Albi is where Henri de Toulouse-Lautrec was born. A museum here has a great many of his paintings, posters and sketches. He is most famous for depicting life in Paris during the late 1800s, especially in Montmartre, where the cancan dancers reigned supreme. Many of the buildings in Albi are brick, including the cathedral (sorry—that slipped out).

Arles is a Roman city on the Rhone River. We saw its colosseum, still in use today, and then went to a museum featuring drawings by Picasso, which he executed in 1971 and then presented to the museum.

Aix-en-Provence is near Marseille, in a much more populated section of France than where we had just been. We went walking on the main street, Cours Mirabeau, which has large Plane trees on both sides and ancient fountains in the middle, making it much more attractive than most main streets. Everybody else was out walking, too. The next morning we walked to the area near the city hall (Hotel de Ville), where the early-morning market was set up to sell flowers, fish, fruit and vegetables. Very early morning. It was just closing when we got there at nine. We did manage to buy a box of strawberries, however.

In Lyon, scene of the incident at the parking garage, we walked around for a couple of hours, checking out both its rivers, the Rhone and the Saone, which run parallel to each other. We also looked at some art galleries. Lyon is the third largest city in France after you-know-who and Marseilles.

The next morning, while we were waiting for the Fine Arts Museum to open ("the most important museum in France, after the Louvre in Paris, for late 19th century and 20th century art," quoth our guidebook), we wandered into the building housing the Lyon Stock Exchange (Bourse). It was started in the 1500s and was the first one in France. Unfortunately, it wasn't open for trading yet. We even came back after we finished seeing the Fine Arts Museum at noon and it still wasn't open. That's better than the proverbial Bankers' hours.

Dijon also has a Fine Arts Museum, housed in the palace of the Grand Dukes of Burgundy. It contains an enormous art collection.

While in Dijon we ate dinner in a cellar of unknown origin, but dating from about the 13th century, with four large pillars supporting a stone ceiling. Talk about atmosphere. The food was good, too.

When we arrived at Fontainbleau we found a room on Rue du Parc. The hotel is literally right beside the park. We walked through the park and palace grounds until the inside of the palace opened for the afternoon at 2 p.m. Bonny posed on the stairs where Napoleon said goodbye to his troops. The tour of the inside took us over two hours and that didn't include Napoleon's private chambers, which were being remodeled. In some of the rooms every square inch of space is decorated with a variety of art. It took our collective breath away. Typically, after a tour like this I can't remember the details of what I have seen, but the aura stays with me for a while. And I think that, somehow, some of it gets permanently impregnated in my brain, making me a more cultured person.

Niece Heather was studying in Paris for a semester, so we took a hotel next to her dormitory on Rue Bernardins, in the Latin Quarter on the West Bank. Two days later we had to move (the hotel was closing for remodeling) so we went to the Hotel California. Later, we found out that my parents had stayed at the Hotel California in 1964.

With Heather, we toured Notre Dame Cathedral. By toured I mean we walked all the way to the top of the towers that Quasimodo, the Hunchback of Notre Dame, used to frequent (pant-pant). There are great gargoyles at the top. The view was magnificent, in spite of the fact that the air was very murky. For example, we could just barely see the Eiffel Tower. After walking back down the endless spiral staircase we went to the Georges Pompidou Centre and toured the Museum of Modern Art, featuring works by Picasso, Matisse, Miró, Rouault and many others. Spontaneous street-shows of various types kept erupting in the courtyard and these attracted good-sized crowds.

After eating dinner with several of Heather's friends, the three of us took a one-hour cruise along the Seine, west as far as the Eiffel Tower and east past the small island, Isle de Cite. The boat had strong searchlights to light up the points of interest on the banks of the river and there was a commentary in three languages.

The next morning the three of us set out on foot on a murky and cool day. We went to the Louvre, where we spent several hours enjoying some of the enormous art collection. We saw the "Mona Lisa," "Coronation of Napoleon," by David, "Venus de Milo," and the statue of the "Winged Victory of Samothrace," as well as other works too numerous to mention.

After eating lunch at a sidewalk cafe we walked through the Tuileries gardens and then toured the Musee de L'Orangerie, which has paintings by Renoir, Picasso, Cezanne and many others. The highlight is the series of murals by Monet called "Les Nympheas," done in celebration of peace after World War I. Then we walked the whole length of the Champs Elysees to the Arc de Triomphe and saw the eternal flame burning for the Unknown Soldier under the Arc.

After dinner we took the Metro to Monmartre. We climbed several flights of stairs to the Basilica of Sacre Coeur (Bonny rode the funicular) and after a brief tour of that we set off to find the starving artists, who congregate in the square. Nowadays they draw your portrait while you wait. They were particularly anxious to draw Heather's portrait. Some of them were good painters and their wares were on display, both outside and inside the local shops. Montmartre is the highest spot in Paris and we could see city lights as well as the Eiffel Tower. It was midnight when we returned to our respective abodes.

Several days later, after Heather left for a holiday trip to Switzerland, Bonny and I returned to Monmartre and had dinner at Chez Eugene, on the square. Before dinner we saw a painting we liked, of the square, with a number of fanciful nude dancing girls in it. We couldn't bring ourselves to pay the asking price. I justified not buying it by arguing that it would be too large to carry.

During dinner we changed our minds. After dinner we looked for the artist, but she (I believe she was a woman) had left. We settled for a slightly smaller, slightly less expensive painting of the square, showing Chez Eugene, with people dressed in 19th century fashions, but without the nude dancing girls. The painter wouldn't discount it much because, as he pointed out, he had to eat. Trying to make us feel guilty, eh?

On the day we went up the Eiffel Tower I climbed the stairs to the first two stages while Bonny and Heather took the elevator. We all took the elevator to the third stage (walking wasn't allowed) and enjoyed the magnificent view in the rain. Because of the rain we all took the elevator down.

The Jardin du Luxembourg is a garden originally built in the early 1600s for Marie de Medici, widow of Henry IV, who lived in the adjoining mansion, Petit-Luxembourg. Children were sailing boats in the large pond when we visited it. Another interesting place is the Invalides, where Napoleon is buried. It has a museum, with mementos from both World War I and World War II. In addition, there are numerous well-preserved suits of armor for knights and horses. Hotel de Cluny, a medieval residence of the abbots of Cluny, contains ruins of a Roman bath and some remarkable tapestries (e.g. "Lady and the Unicorn").

Those were the days before we were rich enough to allow ourselves to be robbed by the Paris taxi drivers so we rode the train to Charles De Gaulle Airport when we left. We walked our bags to the RER station (suburban trains), about half a kilometer from the hotel. The first train was so jammed we couldn't get on it, and it was just as well because we found out it was the wrong train.

When the correct train came we pushed our way on. I had trouble getting my suitcases inside the train, but finally made it just before the doors closed. At the next stop I stood my ground while people exited around me, fearing that if I once stepped off the train I'd never get on again. By this time Bonny had made it to a seat. I moved to the opposite doorway, thinking I was safe there, but at the next station the doors opened on that side and I had to fight to stay on the train again. Finally, I made it to the aisle and eventually a seat.

*   *   *

In 1994, I flew into Nice, France, all by myself, since Bonny was on business in Amsterdam. Having to exist without her for a day, I bought baguettes and fruit and made my own breakfast and lunch. The ATM machines dispensed cash at the best possible exchange rates. Traveler's checks had become passé. I walked along the stony beach, humming Jacques Brel tunes. The beach is several miles long, part public, part private, all stony. Locals wore long pants or skirts while walking on the promenade next to it. Tourists and joggers wore shorts.

As for the beach, itself:

> The topless young ladies of Nice
> Are honored in war and in peace.
> No one can measure
> This national treasure,
> Which brings tourists to Nice without cease.

I climbed the hill on the beach, to where the original fortified city was, dating from at least the sixth century, A.D. Nice comes from Nike, the Greek word for shoe. Sorry, I mean the Greek word for victory.

Bonny arrived, and after she worked in Nice for a day, we ate dinner at a small restaurant in the "old village," l'Auberge des Arts. The owner, Yves Boltasso, showed us a letter he had received from *Bon Appetit* magazine, in Los Angeles, requesting his recipe for "Chilled Strawberry Soup with Ginger." I wrote a draft of a letter for him to send to the magazine, including the recipe. His hope was that the recipe would be featured in the magazine. The next night we returned to the restaurant and I proofread the letter, which *Monsieur* Boltasso had gotten typed.

After we left Nice, we drove to Monte Carlo via the hilly shore route. We walked into the casino foyer and lost one franc in a slot machine. It costs a lot more to actually get into the main casino, so we passed.

Back in France, we drove north toward Paris, touring cathedrals as we went. I give up trying not to mention cathedrals. In Avignon we toured the cathedral, Notre Dame de Doms. In Orleans we toured the Orleans cathedral. In Chartres we toured one of the three largest cathedrals, which sits on a hill. Third largest in the universe? I don't know. We had heard size claims like that before. The cathedral is colorfully decorated, with banners and pennants of local nobility.

At Triel-sur-Seine we toured the Saint Martin cathedral. All the cathedrals have similar designs, with flying buttresses, columned interiors and stained glass windows. Bonny's ancestor, founder of the Terrell clan, probably got his name from Tirel, a version of Triel. The village is located on the River Seine, west of and below Paris.

In Paris, we met my mother, who flew there from Toronto. She was still living on the family farm near Buffalo at that time. We walked her all over Paris. Later, she claimed that all the walking and stair climbing (in Paris and London subways) fixed a hip problem that had bothered her for some time. We took the famous walk again, from the Place de Concorde to the Arc de Triomphe, along the Champs Elysee. The Arc had been given a face-lift, recently. The lines were too long at the Eiffel Tower to take the elevator because it was a French holiday.

As Bonny, Mother and I made our walking tour of Paris, red carpets were being laid on sidewalks for the 50th anniversary celebration of D-Day (June 6, 1994), creating a tone of excitement and nostalgia. Our museum day-passes let us get into places like the Musee D'Orsay, in the rain. This former railroad station has an outstanding collection of impressionist paintings and many other items.

The Conciergerie is where people (including Marie Antoinette and Robspierre) were held prisoner prior to being guillotined. Sainte Chapelle is a small church with fabulous stained-glass windows. Notre Dame was undergoing an external facelift. I climbed the stairs to the top and stood among the gargoyles for the second time. We toured the nearby ruins, where over 80 different layers of civilization have been found, and saw the memorial to 200,000 Jews sent to concentration camps from France.

The morning we went to the Louvre, its opening was delayed because of a strike. Fortunately, strikes in France, although frequent, can be very short. An hour later we returned and were admitted. This was the second time we had seen Leonardo da Vinci's "Mona Lisa" and I concluded that it is overrated. It is small and not a great work of art. Da Vinci did far better paintings and his inventive drawings of future technology make him one of history's most creative thinkers.

Rubens did a spectacular job on 24 huge paintings depicting the life of Marie de Medici, egotistically commissioned by her.

The Basilique Saint Denis is named after the saint who was beheaded in the sixth century at Montmartre. He carried his head to Saint Denis, where he was buried. Many kings are buried here, including Bonny's and my joint ancestors, Charles Martel and Pepin le Bref (he must have been short).

We flew from Paris to London and this time we did get robbed by a Paris taxi driver. He took all our French francs and wanted more. I finally gave him some dollars and swore at him, even though I don't usually swear in front of my mother.

CHAPTER 21 Spain and Morocco

INCIDENT IN ALGECIRAS

Algeciras, Spain—
exotic name for an exotic place;
near Gibraltar, where the British reign,
across the strait from Tangier,
Morocco, green hills and space.
We wait for Hertz to open
after siesta. A couple,
not young, not old, approaches—
on a hunch? Are we kind-hearted
Americans, waiting to be plucked?
Austrians, from Salzburg, they are,
home of salt and *The Sound of Music*.
We greet them with smiles; Salzburg's neat.
Have they lucked out with us? They've traveled far,
come on the ferry (we did too),
but their pack and money were stolen.
Slept on a park bench, with nothing to eat.
Newly married, she is pregnant.
Is she? How can they get back
to dear old Salzburg? 6,000 pesetas
is the key, a train to Madrid,

then the embassy. The Hertz man comes;
we duck inside, get lost amid
the paperwork. We get a car.
The bride and groom still here?
We hoped they'd disappear.
Only a jerk would leave them now.
Around the corner I get change—
8,000 pesetas, enough for food.
Are we naive? Profuse thanks,
a trickling tear. They will arrange
to pay us back. But months go by;
the mail is silent. We wonder why.

In 1990, Bonny and I went to Spain and Morocco. We flew into Madrid and rented a car. El Escorial, our first stop, is a comfortable drive from Madrid. Built by King Philip II from 1563-85, it is a combination palace, church, burying place and library, the largest such structure in Spain. The most impressive display was a huge military mural on a very long wall. The library has books dating back to the 5th century. It also has a model of the universe, showing the earth and Spain at the center.

In Segovia, we toured the Alcazar (military castle), built in the 15th century. It is famous because Isabella and Ferdinand had their first date there. Then they lived in the castle while they drove the Moors out of Spain. They must have done a good job. We walked up the 140 winding steps to the highest rampart and looked over the green countryside below the cliff on which the castle is situated, but there wasn't a Moor in sight. Segovia also has a great cathedral and a 2000-year-old Roman aqueduct, which is still being used.

The city of Toledo is located in the hills, and walking in the old part includes a lot of up and down. El Greco's painting of the death of the Count of Orgaz is on display at the church of San Tomé. It is supposed to be his best, but Bonny, our resident artist, didn't care for it. Isn't El Greco the painter who had astigmatism and painted his people with elongated figures?

Walking in the narrow streets is as difficult as driving and a lot more dangerous, because of the cars, which don't have much room to pass, and the motorbikes, some of which are driven by hotrodders. Medieval streets are often just 10 feet wide or narrower.

Spaniards eat dinner very late. Bonny and I are early eaters. We would be standing at the door of a restaurant, waiting impatiently, when it opened at 8 p.m. As likely as not, we would be the only diners between eight and nine, while members of the staff stood around, wishing more tourists would show up.

May 1st is a national holiday in Spain. On the morning of May 1st we walked to a viewpoint, near our hotel in Toledo, and saw crowds of people on a hill across the Tagus River, celebrating. We could hear what sounded like a cannon being fired.

Our route took us through La Mancha, which is Don Quixote country, where we saw a number of tiltable windmills and some castles. A popular song from my youth, back in another century, talked about dreaming for the day the singer could look for those castles in Spain.

In Córdoba, we walked from our hotel to the huge mosque, built in the 8th century, and the largest outside of Mecca, but somewhat spoiled by the cathedral built right in the center of it. We also climbed both towers of the Alcazar and saw its beautiful garden. The Alcazar overlooks the Guadalquivir River. It was here that Columbus received Isabella's commission for the voyage west.

We stayed in a hotel in Córdoba on the night of the May 1st holiday. Sometime after 10 p.m., we heard music coming from near the hotel. Bonny sent me to investigate. Following the sound of the music, I rounded the corner of one of the narrow streets, characteristic of old Spanish cities, and came upon a small plaza, filled with wall-to-wall people, mostly young. Flamenco music blared from a speaker that sat in a fork of the lone tree.

In the center of the plaza, in a line extending out from the speaker, dozens of teenage girls and a few boys were dancing the flamenco, by the glare of several spotlights. The girls were dressed mostly in jeans or miniskirts; a few wore longer skirts, but none of them was wearing anything resembling the traditional full-skirted flamenco costume.

However, in spite of the spontaneity of the dancers, they were in almost perfect synch with each other. It was apparent that they had been dancing the flamenco from birth. The music would start; they would be talking to their friends, seemingly ignoring it. Then, at a certain point in the song everyone would start dancing, simultaneously, usually in couples, but sometimes alone.

They would go through a series of movements to the pulsing beat, stamping their feet, clapping their hands, circling alone, then circling their partners with an arm arched above their heads. Looking across the plaza, I could see all the arms raised together. The Rockettes couldn't have done better. At the end of a number of bars of music they would all stop, laugh self-consciously and resume their conversations. I retrieved Bonny from the hotel and we watched them, fascinated, for over an hour.

In Sevilla, we parked our Citroen rental car just off the main street and walked into the center of town, as was our custom in a new city. We went to the Plaza de la Encarnacion and took a room at a hotel, recommended by our *Frommer's* guidebook. As we returned to the car we drew a careful line on the map, showing a path through the narrow, one-way streets. If we could have marked our route with a string, we would have. Once we navigated this route with the car and parked it in a lot across the street from the hotel, we didn't move it again until we left Sevilla.

During our walking tour of Sevilla, we went to the Tower of Gold, on the Guadalquivir River. From here, a chain was placed across the river by the Moors to stop attackers. The Contract House is full of archives of voyages to the Americas, West Indies and other Spanish holdings, including drawings and layouts of buildings in the new world. To some extent, these are a forerunner of National Geographic. Columbus returned to Sevilla after his first voyage.

The Alcazar is richly ornamented and the cathedral is the third largest in the world (but you've heard this before, haven't you?). Columbus is said to be buried there. We climbed the tower by a series of 38 ramps and had superb views of Sevilla in all directions. We saw two genuine shell games in progress, complete with three walnut shells, a pea and men waving money—probably shills. The scene looked funny to us, but we weren't the ones losing our money.

One of the more amazing cities we saw was Ronda, which is divided in half by a 500-foot deep canyon. A Roman bridge crosses the canyon, and, as much as I respect Roman engineering, I was glad it had been rebuilt a number of times over the years, so that it can accommodate cars. Buildings cling to the sides of the cliffs.

* * *

We took the ferry from Algeciras, Spain, to Tangier, Morocco, for our first look at Africa. As we walked from the ferry terminal to the Hertz office in Tangier, a man walked along with us and told us he had been to New York. We suspected he was trying to sell us something and told him we didn't need anything. He eventually left us. The child entrepreneurs are very enterprising. They size you up and then speak to you in one of half a dozen languages.

We drove our Renault 4, a sardine can on wheels with the gearshift on the dashboard, to Rabat, the capital of Morocco, and then on to Fez. We were shocked at what appeared to be a disregard for human life. One example: Several people, including an older woman covered from head to toe in traditional Muslim garb, were trapped between lanes while attempting to cross the highway, while cars zoomed by them on both sides at 60 miles-per-hour, all going in the same direction.

Our guide through the medina (old city) of Fez, Hamid, wore a fez, djellaba (long cloak) and slippers. He was slender, and shorter than Bonny. We met him the day before, when we stopped to buy gasoline at a station outside of Fez. He introduced himself to us, showed us his official guide license and medallion and led us to our hotel in his car. He refused a tip, but we contracted for his services at that time.

After Hamid left us at the hotel, a young man, who had obviously seen us arrive, said that he was the brother of the guide and that the guide would not show up tomorrow morning. Fortunately, we ignored him.

Our walk through the medina of Fez was a walk back in time. The oldest section dates from 800 A.D. Hamid led us through a rabbit warren of alleys, in which we would have become hopelessly lost by ourselves. We could have wandered for days and never found our way out.

Hamid continually pointed out picture-taking opportunities to me. Muslims often object to having their pictures taken, fearing that their spirits will be stolen, but with Hamid, who knew everybody, with us, it appeared to be okay. We saw the inside of a mosque from the entrance (nonbelievers cannot enter), a sacred burial chamber, also from the entrance, schools with beautiful mosaic walls, and viewpoints where we looked over the whole city. We stopped at two *caravanseri*, where camel caravans used to rest on their market routes. We passed the oldest university in the world, Qaraouyine, now a museum, dating from the 800s, several centuries older than Oxford.

Hamid guided us to shops selling tablecloths, silver jewelry, copper products, clothes and rugs. Shopkeepers gave us high-powered sales pitches in each of them, and mint tea in one. Bonny bought a belt with gold thread, after bargaining assisted by Hamid (even though he received a commission on sales). We emerged from the other places unscathed. The whole tour lasted more than four hours. Since we hadn't bought much we gave Hamid a 100 percent tip.

The yard where leather tanners tan and dry the hides was the most odiferous place we went to. The stench nauseated us and the sight didn't do much for our stomachs, either. Pigeon dung was mixed in with the colors in the various dyeing vats, in order to set the color in the hide.

Some sights we saw in the souk (marketplace): burros carrying loads several times as large as themselves; medieval business stalls as small as six feet by 10 feet, filled with sitting workers; and workers engaged in shoemaking and repair, woodwork, making saddles for burros, embroidery, sewing, rug making, and leather/hide work. Stalls had minimum light and no comforts.

Various parts of animals were for sale: brains, tripe, lungs, hooves, horns and the standard cuts of meat we can relate to. Also for sale were snails, fish, nuts, fruits, spices, clothing material, lace, pottery, brass work, silver work, jewelry, copper cooking pots, belts, candies, holy candles, kaftans, djellabas, chalk for whitewash paint, clothes, and water in a goat skin.

Fountains periodically appeared in the walls, where both people and animals went for water. We saw people leading their burros, covered with containers, to the water supply. Shopkeepers used balance scales to weigh just about everything; they placed stones representing weights on one of the weighing pans. Live chickens were being weighed at one shop.

There were a number of Koran schools for boys and girls, aged three to six, who were taught separately. The children recited their lessons in unison and giggled a lot. Many of them walked and ran, barefoot, through the narrow, covered, dirty alleys.

Five hundred thousand people lived in the old town out of a total Fez population of 2,000,000. The streets or alleys were much too narrow for cars. The donkey or burro was the local truck and the critters were forced to carry huge loads of just about everything imaginable, including lumber for construction.

There was one Moroccan walk we didn't take. We drove south to the Middle Atlas Mountains and decided to walk to some cascades, mentioned in the guidebook. As we drove down a hill on a narrow road that was in bad shape and kept getting worse, children and adults began walking and running along the road, heading for the cascades. They were Berbers and we assumed they wanted to act as our guides to the cascades. However, as their numbers grew, we became more and more nervous, since there were only two of us. When we reached the parking area, we didn't get out of the car. We turned around and headed back up the hill. At least we had driven through some beautiful scenery.

Once we did stop to attempt to take a picture of some Berber children. They began grabbing at Bonny's glasses so we brushed them off and got back in the car. We took the picture of a lone Berber girl, in exchange for a dirham (the unit of Moroccan currency).

We stopped at the ruins of Lixus for lunch, one day, and climbed the hill first built on by the Phoenicians in 1,100 B.C. Later, the Carthaginians and Romans both added their improvements. It offers a superb view of a river estuary at the ocean.

*   *   *

We took the ferry back to Algeciras, Spain, and were waiting for the Hertz office to open, after the afternoon siesta, when we experienced what we now refer to as the Algeciras Incident. We gave 8,000 pesetas to an Austrian couple, but never saw them again (the pesetas or the couple). All is explained in my poem, "Incident in Algeciras," at the beginning of the chapter.

The main tourist attraction in Granada, Spain, is the Alhambra, the citadel and palace on a hill overlooking the city. Built by Moorish kings in the 12th and 13th centuries, the Alhambra is the finest example of Moorish architecture in Spain. We spent three hours walking through it, as there is a lot to see. A thunderstorm came up while we were there, giving the lie to the idea that the rain in Spain stays mainly...

Isabella and Ferdinand are buried in a tomb in a Granada cathedral. We saw some of Isabella's personal art collection. Most of the paintings depict a bleeding Jesus being crucified. It was here that Columbus reported back to Isabella, after he returned from his first trip.

Madrid has wide streets and they go for long distances. We found that out when we were carrying our luggage and looking for a hotel. Previously, we had taken a bus from the airport to the Plaza de Colón (plaza of Columbus). However, we found a nice hotel on the seventh floor of a building on Gran Via, the Hotel Andorra.

The day after we arrived in Madrid, we toured and toured the Prado (it is huge). We loved the paintings by Valezquez; he was a true master of the use of light. Goya painted unflattering portraits of his royal patrons; he also painted funny cartoons, used for tapestries, and, in his later years, dark paintings, in blacks and grays. Unfortunately, his "Naked Maja" was on loan to a London museum. In the annex to the Prado we saw Picasso's famous painting of "Guernica." I guess you either like Picasso or you don't. On the walk back to the hotel for our siesta we had a beer at McDonald's.

We toured a factory where tapestries were still made by hand the same way they had been for 200 years. The weavers were still weaving the Goya cartoons that we saw the originals of at the Prado.

The Plaza de España features statues of Don Quixote and Sancho Panza. Pedestrians jaywalk in Spain, whether or not cars are coming.

If cars are slow to start up when a light turns green, people will walk right in front of them. As walking tourists, Bonny and I were tempted to fall into the same dangerous habits.

We toured the royal palace in a group, with an English-speaking guide. We saw the throne room, the banquet hall and other rooms, 15 of the 2,800 rooms, altogether. Nobody lives here, but it is used for official ceremonies. We saw the museum of armor, also on the grounds, and wondered whether the suits had air conditioning.

We walked to the royal gardens and saw the museum, containing royal carriages used by various monarchs. One carriage and one car were riddled with bullet holes, souvenirs of a successful and unsuccessful assassination attempt. There are no crown jewels and the king and queen do not wear crowns, although the queen wears a diamond tiara on state occasions.

CHAPTER 22 Turkey

In 1988, after Bonny, Andy and I visited Greece, we rode the ferry from the Greek island of Samos the short distance to Kusadasi, Turkey. From there we rode a *dolmush* (minibus) to Selcuk. While waiting for the bus, Bonny read to us about the low crime rate in Turkey, but the guidebook said to watch out for pickpockets in crowded places. We were in a crowd because there were day-trippers going to visit the ruins of Ephesus. Just about then, somebody tried to pick Andy's back pocket. Fortunately, it was empty. His valuables were in a pouch, underneath his shirt.

The guidebooks also warned us about the conservative dress code in Turkey, because of the predominance of the Muslim religion. The first beach we passed in the *dolmush* was topless. Oh, well, you can't believe everything you read.

We walked to Ephesus from Selcuk, the nearest village. The ruins show what a truly magnificent city Ephesus was, the richest in the world during the glory days of the Roman Empire. As an example, the theater seated 24,000 people. The public toilets had running water for both sewage disposal and hand washing (kept separate, of course).

We were treated to an elegant meal at a restaurant in the middle of a street in Selcuk, for a nominal price, with service and presentation equal to the finest that New York has to offer. The dessert was pistachio nuts flambé. After the meal the waiter poured lemon water on our hands. The only downside was the bite of pepper that Bonny ate. It set her mouth on fire and she tasted it for hours afterward.

We took the train to Izmir for less than 50 cents per person. On the train several young people carried on a conversation with us, using sign language and a few words of English and German. Bonny exchanged earrings with a girl. The lavatories were just holes in the floor, with elephant feet beside them. The Turkish children refused to use them.

As we drove north from Izmir to Istanbul in a rental car, we toured two historic sites. Pergamon has an Acropolis and two large amphitheaters, one of which seated 50,000 people. The library used to have 200,000 books, second only to Alexandria, but Marc Antony took them as a present for Cleopatra after the Alexandria library burned. Parchment was invented here. Galen, the physician from Pergamon, had his views accepted for 1,600 years.

The ancient city of Troy actually had many lives, in different time periods. It has been much excavated since Schlieman discovered it. We saw a full-size replica of the Trojan Horse. The ruins themselves were not terribly exciting and the sea is no longer close by, having retreated over the centuries.

The city of Istanbul, where we stayed for a week, has many fascinating sights for walkers. When we were there, street vendors peddled a variety of products, including sweat socks by La Coste, Puma and Adidas. It seemed as if every child we passed had a handful of them to wave in our faces. Other items peddled on the street included shirts, belts, long underwear, shoeshines, weight and blood pressure measurements, letter-typing services, a drink of water or a puff on a water pipe.

We took a ferry up the Bosporus. It zigzagged from Asia to Europe and back again. This was the first time any of us had been in Asia. We got off at Sariyer. After lunch at a fast-food restaurant we took a *dolmush* over a hill to Kilyos Beach on the Black Sea. We walked down to the water and performed the traveler's ritual of sticking our hands in it.

The Grand Bazaar in Istanbul is very grand and mostly indoors. There are 4,000 shops on a maze of alleys, selling carpets, jewelry, leather goods, copper goods, artwork and many other products. The crowds of people on the sidewalks sometimes made navigation difficult.

We bargained more or less skillfully for the items we purchased. One clerk said he had to go ask his boss at another shop before he could okay a price. I went with him because I thought he might be employing a negotiating tactic used by car salesmen called "higher authority," but sure enough, he asked his boss and the deal was quickly concluded.

The Agia Sofia is now a museum, but through the ages it was either a Christian church or a mosque, depending on who was in charge. Most of the gold and valuable artworks it contained were taken from it at one time or another. The crusaders did their share of damage. It is an architectural wonder, however, with a huge, unsupported dome.

Topkapi Palace is a wonder, because of its size, with many buildings set on a large piece of real estate. We saw an arms museum and an awesome display of jewels, with egg-sized sapphires and an 86-carat diamond. The jewel-encrusted Topkapi dagger was made famous outside of Turkey by the movie, *Topkapi*. We did not see the newly refurbished harem, but we were assured that there are no longer any women there. We did see the building where the white eunuchs lived.

We went underground to see the cistern, dating from the 500s, with 400+ columns. Classical music that was being played in the dimly lit cavern helped to create a spiritual atmosphere.

We had to take off our shoes to enter the Blue Mosque. It is the greatest architectural wonder of all, with its magnificent dome and four internal columns, each 15 feet in diameter. People wearing shorts had to wrap their legs in cloths, but there did not appear to be a requirement for women to have their heads covered. Since it is still a mosque, people were praying inside.

We stayed in three different hotels, each one cheaper than the last, as we shopped around. We ate lamb shish kabob at a little restaurant in Istanbul that was around the corner from our final hotel, several times. The chef cooked all their food in a large oven heated with logs. The food was moved in and out of the oven with long-handled paddles. The employees got to know us and shook our hands when we walked in. They had a television set that played reruns of US TV shows dubbed in Turkish.

One morning Andy came back from a walk in Istanbul, all smiles, and proudly announced that he had found a place where he could get a shave for the equivalent of 25 cents. He took me to the shop the next morning and, sure enough, the price was right and the shave was good. The barbers even splashed on after-shave lotion, combed our hair and put on hairspray.

Turkey's large cities, such as Istanbul and Izmir, were very noisy, with lots of horn honking and pollution from motor vehicles. Traffic in Istanbul was chaotic and the drivers didn't follow any recognizable traffic laws. This made for a scary time for pedestrians, as the cars played "chicken" with them, but pedestrians jaywalked a lot, to add to the fun.

CHAPTER 23 Baltic Countries

The cruise ship, Royal Princess, was named after Princess Diana, who also christened it. In August 1997 Bonny and I took a cruise to the Baltic Sea on the Royal Princess, owned by Princess Cruises. After we disembarked from the ship at Dover, England, at the end of the cruise, we spent a couple of days in London. On the morning of Sunday, August 31, we awoke at about 6:15 a.m. and retrieved a copy of the London Times from outside the door of our hotel room. The headline said that Princess Diana had been in a car crash in Paris in a tunnel by the Seine and had been badly injured. We turned on the telly and learned that she had died.

The cruise began, uneventfully. We boarded the Royal Princess at Dover on Saturday, August 16. Our cabin was on the second deck from the bottom, called the Plaza Deck. There were ten decks, altogether. We mustered for a life jacket drill before we left port, which occurred promptly at 5 p.m.

We signed up to eat dinner at the first seating because we are early to bed and early to rise people. Our tablemates for dinner were Sue and Rob, from Dayton, Ohio. This was their 12th cruise. It was our first cruise. A third couple assigned to our table missed the boat and boarded at Oslo. However, they only ate two meals in the dining room, which were the meals Bonny missed because of a malady, so she never met them. We met other couples who spent most of their lives cruising. One lady was on her 97th cruise. Maybe she was on the lam from the police.

Each evening, after dinner, we attended a show of professional quality. Sometimes we danced to a big band sound, impersonated by a small band. One night we danced to the "Anniversary Waltz," along with one other couple, because our anniversary occurred during the cruise. During one show, while I was sitting in the front row, I was pulled up on stage by one of the female dancers in the middle of a number. I faked it and skipped around with her, but I could have used 15 seconds of rehearsal.

Typical of the exciting daytime activities was a class in napkin folding, but one afternoon I took part in the talent show, reading 13 limericks I had written about members of the entertainment staff. I even got some laughs. It seemed that everywhere we went photographers lay in wait to snap our picture. A day later the prints would be posted and we would have the opportunity to buy glossy 8 x 10s of ourselves enjoying life on the Love Boat.

I went through the orientation on the treadmill in the workout room, so that I could learn the secret code, which was necessary if I wanted to tread on my own. However, I much preferred walking laps of the promenade track (four laps = 1.1 miles) on the Dolphin Deck, so that I could acquire Cruisercise bucks, which I exchanged in the ship's store for free caps and T-shirts. I walked a lot of laps during the cruise.

*　　*　　*

We were very happy to see land the morning the ship glided through the fjord that leads to Oslo, Norway. Bonny was feeling under the weather so I explored Akershus Castle, which was right beside the ship, on my own. I saw two homeless men, which I thought weren't allowed in Norway. In the afternoon we took a tour to several museums. Bonny spent most of the tour sleeping on the grass, instead of going into the buildings. It was warm and sunny and there were sunbathers on various pieces of grass in various stages of undress. One museum housed three Viking ships, used for burial around 850-900 A.D. Another one had Thor Heyerdahl's rafts: Kon Tiki and Ra II, on which he crossed oceans. Ra I sank in the Atlantic.

*   *   *

We docked at Copenhagen, Denmark, the next morning. Bonny was still weak, but she wanted to get out so we walked to the Rosenborg Castle to see the crown jewels and other royal heirlooms. We also saw the Little Mermaid, perched on her rock by the harbor. It was warm and people were playing in the fountains. Andy took a trip to Europe with his high school class right after he graduated. It is reported that while on this trip he played in the fountains of Paris. Oh well, David Halliburton, who wrote books about his travels around the world in the first half of the 20th century, swam in the pool in front of the Taj Mahal.

After lunch I went out alone, with a vague plan of walking to Tivoli Gardens. It was so warm and I felt so lazy that I didn't get very far. I spent most of the time waiting for the sun to reach the right angle, so that I could take a good photograph of the Little Mermaid. I like to think that we developed a rapport with each other.

*   *   *

After a day at sea our ship wended its way through the 25,000 or so islands in the Stockholm area and arrived at the dock one morning before 8:30 a.m. We took the shuttle bus to the center of town and walked to the Vasa museum. This Swedish fighting ship sank in Stockholm harbor on her maiden voyage in 1628. She was top-heavy and her design was a classic example of a bunch of hands working without a head. Next we walked to the City Hall (Stadshuset), completed in 1923, where the dinner honoring the Nobel Prize winners is held each December. The most impressive room is composed of millions of mosaic tiles of 23.5 K gold. We walked to the old town and ate lunch in a café, sharing a plate of beef, french-fries and salad. Most of the people spoke English and we felt right at home.

*　　*　　*

We were the first people off the ship after it docked in Helsinki, Finland. We set out at a brisk walk, but ended up trapped behind a port building, unable to get through to the city. So much for being pioneers. A man took pity on us and let us into the building. We exited via the entrance, on the other side, and went on into the city. We checked out the open-air market beside the docks and then toured Uspenski Cathedral, with its onion domes. Feeling adventurous, we walked to the Rock Church, a couple of miles away. It is built inside granite. Part of the choir performed as we went through it. The Finnish National Gallery featured local artists and also had one Van Gogh, one Gauguin, etc.

*　　*　　*

Peter the Great founded St. Petersburg, Russia, in the early 1700s because he wanted a seaport on the Baltic. Sweden had other ideas and they fought a war of many years' duration. In recent incarnations, St. Petersburg was also named Leningrad and Petrograd. Our tour guide was named Alla. She spoke very precise English. She took us on a bus tour that made stops along branches of the Neva River and also the numerous other rivers and canals. We saw women sweeping the streets with what looked like tree branches—small branches and twigs at the end of a larger branch. The women were in their 40s and 50s.

One of the most impressive buildings we saw was the Church of the Spilt Blood—also called Church of the Resurrection. The church's design was inspired by St. Basil's in Moscow. Its six onion domes, three of gilt and three composed of vibrant mosaics, give it a fairytale beauty. This church was built on the spot where Alexander II was assassinated on March 1, 1881. We bought two paintings of the church.

Our tour group ate lunch at a new "log cabin" restaurant in the Tsar's Village, now called Pushkin. A group of colorfully dressed musicians played and sang native music. The beautiful singer seduced me into playing a percussion instrument, consisting of sticks that whack each other in time to the music.

We toured Catherine's Palace, built on property given by Peter the Great to his second wife, Catherine I. Elizabeth I, their daughter, built the palace but her daughter-in-law, Catherine the Great, finished it. It is massive (900 feet wide) and beautiful. It was restored starting in the 1960s; restoration work continues. The amber panels from the Amber Room have been missing since their removal during World War II. Nobody has seen them since. Keep an eye out for them. (I recently read that they are being recreated.)

It's not easy to cover the 1,000 rooms of the Hermitage in two hours, but we gave it a try the next morning. Our group charged through the rooms like the Mongol hordes. We saw the works of all the impressionist painters, including Monet, Renoir and Van Gogh, in 12 minutes flat. In many rooms the walls, ceiling and chandeliers are the most impressive part. Some are gold, some are green, with pillars of malachite. The Greek and Roman statues, however, are all copies and we turned up our noses at them, having seen the originals.

Our afternoon tour went through the Yusupov Palace, where Rasputin was murdered. In the actual small room where the dastardly deed was committed, several people, including our guide, Ivan, a graduate student, have passed out. Rasputin was supposed to have magical powers.

During a couple of shopping stops we did our part to revitalize the Russian economy. Dollars were readily accepted, as they are in all third-world and emerging countries. Unfortunately, St. Petersburg looked like a dead city, with its 300 decaying palaces, although some were being restored, but what it needed more than anything else was a healthy injection of capitalism.

*   *   *

Estonia, on the other hand, seemed to be getting that injection. Our guides were young, bright and optimistic. Eva, who led our sub-group on a walking tour of Tallinn, was a bubbly young woman who had studied for several years in Norway and was continuing her studies in Estonia. The cars were newer and the roads were better than those in St. Pete. The prices were the lowest of any place we had been and we seized the opportunity to buy sweaters and amber jewelry.

Eva told us ghost stories about the various buildings in the Old Town, which looked medieval in places. It contained the usual churches and narrow, cobble-stoned streets. The large town square used to be the central marketplace. Eva and her partner told jokes about Lithuanians and admitted that nearby countries told jokes about them. They said Estonian boys were too shy. Eva was wondering what to do with her life. As I gave her a goodbye hug I whispered the magic word in her ear—"computers."

*   *   *

Poland hadn't quite gotten its act together. For example, people were waiting for years with their names on a list to get an apartment. We docked at Gdynia about 10 a.m. and took an afternoon tour. It was almost an hour's drive to nearby Gdansk, through heavy traffic and narrow streets. We walked through the Old Town, with the usual churches, and some houses built in the 15th and 16th centuries, by the rich folks who lived at that time. Almost all had to be restored after World War II. The inhabitants were celebrating the 1,000-year anniversary of Gdansk, once an independent city—997-1997.

*   *   *

When the cruise ended at Dover we took a bus back to London. We spent the next day hunting for ancestors at the Public Records office in Kew Gardens. Two mornings after the cruise ended we found out about Diana's death. Our hotel was close to Harrods Department Store, owned by the father of her boyfriend, Dodi, also killed in the crash, so we walked there before breakfast. Mourners had already attached bouquets of flowers to the entrance doors and video cameramen recorded the scene.

CHAPTER 24 New Zealand and French Polynesia

In 1987, Bonny, Ellen and I toured New Zealand and French Polynesia. We flew into Auckland, the largest city in New Zealand. On our arrival, after we had taken care of some essentials, such as changing money and finding a place to stay, we toured Kelly Tarlton's Underwater World, where the fish swam all around us as we walked through a tunnel. These included some very impressive sharks and stingrays. It was billed as the largest aquarium in the world, and maybe it was, at least at the time.

As we walked the streets of Auckland, we noticed a large American influence. We saw life-size posters of Michael Jackson, and Marilyn Monroe memorabilia were being sold.

We picked up a rental car and I had my first opportunity to drive on the left—with a manual transmission and left-handed gearshift, yet. Just as I was figuring everything out—such as how to shift with my left hand and turn on the turn signals instead of the windshield wipers, a road grader came lumbering down the shoulder toward me—on my left. Talk about panic.

We drove to Rotorua, through green hills dotted with sheep and lambs. As we walked around, looking for a supermarket, a woman not only told us where one was, but walked part of the way with us. This was typical of the hospitality of the New Zealanders, some of the friendliest people in the world. The owner of the motel we stayed at made a sign for us to put in the rear window of our car that read,

"HULLO FROM THE USA." He explained that it would make drivers more considerate of us. It worked, and many drivers waved when they passed us.

We saw a show presented by the Maoris, the New Zealand natives. In song and dance the Maoris told about their trip from Havai'i (now the island of Raitea in French Polynesia) to New Zealand, and other historical events. They also performed traditional war dances and other ceremonies. The women were good at twirling balls on strings and playing catch with sticks. The chants of the men reminded us of the Tiki Room at Disneyland. The men wore flax reed skirts over shorts and were topless. The women wore the reed skirts over regular skirts and wore embroidered tops that glowed in infrared light.

When you visit New Zealand you see a lot of sheep. When we were there the population was 70 million sheep and three million people. In Rotorua we went to the Agrodome, where we saw fine examples of and heard information about the 19 breeds of sheep raised in New Zealand. We also saw a sheep-shearing demonstration and sheep dogs in action. The dogs, some of the smartest in the world, are trained to run over the tops of a closely packed flock to get to the other side.

Wellington, the capital of New Zealand, is at the south end of the North Island. While there we saw parliament in session. It could have been a legislative body, anywhere, as a member was berating the opposition. We took the ferry from Wellington across Cook Strait to Picton, on the south island.

Christchurch is on the east coast of the South Island. While at Christchurch we visited the local natural history museum, which concentrates on the Antarctic collection, with memorabilia from all the expeditions. It is the only collection like it in the world. Along with maps and photographs, the museum contains examples of actual equipment used, including snow vehicles. We also walked through the art museum, reputed to be the best in New Zealand, but it doesn't hold a candle to many in Europe or even Los Angeles. We also took a look at the cathedral, probably out of habit from our European trips, but next to others we have seen it was not remarkable, except for two stuffed penguins.

Twizel is the gateway to the Southern Alps and Mt. Cook. Mt. Cook was covered with snow that looked like whipped cream, good enough to eat. We drove into Mt. Cook National Park and took various walks to scenic vistas of Mt. Cook and the surrounding peaks, some of which are approached via dirt roads. Mt. Cook has an altitude of 3,764 meters and is the highest peak in New Zealand. As in Zermatt, Switzerland, we encountered monuments to people who died trying to climb it. We also saw the terrain covering an underground glacier.

We caught a flock of sheep being driven along the road in the same direction we were going, followed by a truck with six dogs. Only one of the dogs was working; the rest were riding on the back of the truck. The working dog jumped onto the back of the truck when the sheep were all headed in the right direction. We followed them for about 15 minutes, unsure what to do. A woman in a camper overtook us and motioned for us to follow her as she drove right through the flock, parting the sheep the way Moses parted the waters of the Red Sea. On another day we encountered a flock of sheep coming toward us; that one was easier to get through.

From Te Anau, in the southwestern corner of New Zealand, we went by car, boat, bus and then boat again to get to one of the most remote parts of the country, Doubtful Sound. Doubtful Sound was misnamed by Captain Cook, because it is really a fiord. It is a fiord because a glacier formed it; a sound is formed by a river.

When we stopped at Wilmot Pass, overlooking Doubtful Sound, a kea, a green, parrot-like bird, landed on the bus and then bounced around on the ground beside it, giving all of us the eye. After we drove on, it flew beside the bus for a while. During the trip, the bus driver and the boat pilots, long-time residents of the area, gave educated discourses on what we were seeing, filled with dry New Zealand wit. The bus driver claimed it was his first day on the job but, fortunately, because of the challenging drive over the pass, it wasn't. He also entertained us by playing the harmonica.

From Dunedin, we drove across private property, up and down hills, through rain, sleet, hail, snow flurries and gale-force winds, over 40 kilometers, to see penguins, one of Bonny's favorite animals. When we arrived at the penguin place we walked to the edge of the cliff. Far below us on the beach we could see the Yelloweyed Penguins come in from the surf in ones and twos, after a day of fishing. They waddled up the beach and then made their way laboriously up the steep sand hill to their nests, in the bushes above. They were too far away to photograph, but we could see them clearly through the binoculars. We counted ten, altogether. Bonny was ecstatic.

There were three baby goats at the viewing place. One was quite friendly, but another one, who had barbed wire tangled in his hair, was skittish, and retreated to the edge of the cliff when we tried to get close enough to help him. Not wanting to scare him into jumping off, we left him alone.

While in Dunedin we visited the natural history museum, featuring an exhibit of moas. The moa is an extinct bird that was 10 to 12 feet high.

*   *   *

The airport for Tahiti is at Faaa. Faaa is a word typical of Polynesian languages, where vowels seem to predominate. You pronounce each vowel separately (Fah-ah-ah). The same rule applies for the city of Papeete (Pah-peh-eh-teh). On our first night in Tahiti we stayed at an Ibis Hotel, now owned by the same company that owns Motel 6.

Bonny and I walked around the wharf area of Papeete before going to bed. There were many hot food trucks still open for business (it was close to midnight). These look like the lunch trucks in the U.S. A noisy nightclub right outside our room made sleeping difficult. We finally closed the window and turned on the air conditioning. The temperature was in the 70s. The second night we changed hotels and had a quieter and cheaper room overlooking the harbor.

Artistically decorated trucks provided transportation in Tahiti. We figured out how to get around on them, and managed to get ourselves to Point Venus, where Captain Cook observed the transit of the planet Venus in 1769. The black sand on the beach here is crushed lava. Beachwear is very casual, as you might expect if you have seen any of the paintings of Gauguin. We saw two guns that were carried on Magellan's ship. After several hours relaxing, away from the noise and traffic of Papeete, we took a thrilling but inexpensive truck ride back to it.

From Tahiti we flew to Bora Bora. The twin peaks of the island were sticking out of a low-flying cloud as we landed. American Seabees built the runway for Bora Bora during World War II. It is on a *motu*, or small island, a 20-minute launch ride away from the village of Vaitape. From Vaitape, we took a truck to the Hotel Matira, on the southern tip of Bora Bora.

Our bungalow on the beach had a palm-thatched roof and bamboo walls, ending below the roof, with screens above. The primitive lock on the door offered very little security, but a hotel employee informed us that there was no crime on Bora Bora because there was no place to hide. He did mention a small problem with peeping toms, but because of the casual beachwear this wouldn't seem to be a necessary occupation.

The next morning we discovered that we had little food and no transportation to Vaitape, where the food was, four or five miles up the coast. We set out on foot and watched the land crabs scurry into their holes as we passed. They make life interesting for the tent campers. The houses of the local residents were the ultimate in open-air living. Some were even missing walls. We walked about two-thirds of the way before we were able to flag down a truck. Most of the people we dealt with knew some English. They also spoke a combination of French, Polynesian and Chinese.

The beautiful colors of the water in the lagoon beside our hotel varied from green to blue. The crystal-clear water was perfect for swimming. The lagoon is protected from the fury of the Pacific Ocean by a coral reef. The beach is of white, crushed coral. The water remains shallow for a long distance from the shore.

Bonny and I walked up a path to a World War II gun emplacement, overlooking the lagoon. There were two seven-inch guns here and a number of others throughout the island. We saw one on the way to Vaitape. In addition, the hulks of two ships rose above the water in a cove near the road.

The guidebook said that one of the island's twin peaks can be climbed in a couple of hours, but since there was no regular trail and the hills were muddy because of rain, I decided it wasn't worth the effort. Besides, Polynesian paralysis had set in.

We walked around the southern tip of Bora Bora, while Bonny looked for shells. A girl who lived by the shore gave her a couple. We decided this hobby was superior to Andy's hobby of collecting beer cans. Since Andy was in college he didn't go with us on this trip. Cocoanut palm trees were everywhere and cocoanuts covered the ground.

We flew back to Tahiti and rode a ferry on a roller-coaster ride through high seas to Moorea. I braved the deck, but Bonny and Ellen stayed below. On Moorea we stayed at a hotel in Cook's Bay, surrounded by green hills with original shapes. One of the hilltops has a hole through it, put there by an angry god. Bonny and I walked to Pao Pao, at the end of the bay, looking for places to shop. The shops were closed from noon until 1:30 p.m., for the local version of siesta.

We went to Tiki Village to see "authentic Polynesian crafts and dancing." Because of transportation problems we didn't see the crafts. We did see the dancing, and Bonny was volunteered to dance with one of the men. Bonny and I went out in the pirogue to watch the men fish for lunch. The two men used snorkels and a net and gave it their all, but failed to catch anything, except a couple of clams. The wind was blowing and it was raining. We were provided with raincoats, but the divers complained that it was cold in the water. Fortunately, we had ordered chicken for lunch.

During lunch, one of the girls showed us how to wear a pareo (the traditional rectangular cloth garment that Polynesian women wear) 100 different ways. Bonny purchased several pareos, but they were stolen out of our pack on the ferry ride back to Tahiti. Bonny asked one of the girls how to make a flower headdress; the girl gave Bonny the one she was wearing. Bonny also learned how to make a lei.

We rented a car ("very dear," as they say in New Zealand) and drove clockwise around the island to Afareaitu, where Bonny and I walked up a dirt road that later became a trail, until we came to a waterfall with a pool at its base. It was cloudy and windy and we had the place to ourselves.

We then drove to a church in Pao Pao with a Polynesian painting over the altar that depicted the holy family as Polynesians. Next we drove up the dirt road from Pao Pao to Belvedere, where we had an excellent view of Cooks Bay, Opunohu Bay, next to it, and the surrounding peaks, their tops in the clouds. There is an archaeological site here where young girls used to be sacrificed to the gods. However, we had it on good authority that no girls had been sacrificed since the 1950s.

In the evening, our hotel held a Polynesian feast, like a Hawaiian luau, but called a *tamara*. The cooks roasted a pig underground, over hot coals, with vegetables and bananas. The fire pit was right in front of our bungalow and the cooks did an impromptu sing before it was opened. The dinner was excellent. The dessert consisted of cocoanut milk with baked banana and another local fruit. Authentic Polynesian dancing followed. Several different types of drums accompanied the dancers. One of the male dancers ate fire and juggled a sharp knife. One of the girls picked me to dance with her. I can reveal that the secret to the rapid hip movement of the Tahitian Hula is in the knees.

CHAPTER 25 Japan

In 1991, Bonny and I went to Japan. We flew into Tokyo's Narita Airport. From there it took us four hours to go through customs and travel to the apartment of our friends, Marabeth and Bill, in central Tokyo, by train and subway. Fortunately, Marabeth and her daughter, Kirsten, came to the airport and acted as our guides. A walk through their neighborhood revealed some expensive homes, mixed with government housing, commercial establishments and a small park.

The next day we rode the noon *Shinkansen* (bullet train) to Osaka. While we were boarding the train a small child slipped between our car and the platform, and fell down beside the tracks. The mother became hysterical. Since the trains run on time to the minute my first thought was to question whether it would be delayed in order to rescue the child. However, a uniformed Japan Rail employee, carrying a red flag, appeared and performed the rescue very efficiently.

The train, a *Hikari* (super express), made two stops en route to Osaka, and covered the 343 miles in three hours. The ride was so smooth that we consistently underestimated our speed. The route passes Mt. Fuji, the most famous mountain in Japan. My brother, Mike, and his wife, Kim, climbed it in the 1960s soon after they were married in Viet Nam.

Recorded messages were broadcast over the train's public address system, in Japanese and English. At the end of the English version of each message, the female speaker said "thank you" in a voice so melodious that I immediately fell in love with her. I have never heard a thank you like that in the US.

Our niece, Cammie, met us at the station in Osaka, and guided us, using more public transportation, to her apartment in Kawachinagano (Kah-wah-chee-NAH-gah-no), said rapidly. She was living there at the time, teaching English, mostly to bored Japanese housewives. Wherever she went she received a lot of attention because of her long, blond hair.

Her apartment consisted of three rooms, with sliding doors in between, plus a bathroom, and was owned by Cammie's boss. We all slept on futons, on the floor. There were no beds. We also ate sitting on the floor, there and at Japanese residences. The building, which contained eight apartments, was called a mansion. Everything was miniaturized in Japan and I kept hitting my head on doorways and other places. The life expectancy for tall people has to suffer. Of course, now that the young people are growing bigger, the Japanese perspective on size will have to undergo changes.

We climbed Mt. Kongo, a sacred Japanese mountain (because of a battle waged on it in the 14th century), with three Japanese couples, friends of Cammie, who were not traditional urban couples. There was not a salaryman among them. Salarymen are the male workers who work all day in offices and go to bars at night with their coworkers. Cammie lived for three months at the home of one couple. She communicated with all of them in a charming mixture of Japanese and English.

Another man and his wife, the Ozakis, were marathon runners. Mr. Ozaki had been running for 20 years. As he told the story, six or seven years previously, he had advised his wife to start running to stay in shape. The first time she beat him in a race he told her not to run so fast. When we met them he seemed proud of the fact that she was faster than he was. She ran up Mt. Kongo almost every morning, a climb of over 500 meters. She had climbed it about 1,500 times and there was a case near the top containing her trophies.

The trail of the much-climbed mountain had worn down. Many steps had been built to help maintain it. Mr. and Mrs. Ozaki carried long wooden boards, similar to two-by-fours, part way up, to be used for trail repair. In addition, Mrs. Ozaki carried Noi-chan, the two-year-old daughter of one of the other couples, in a backpack. We said *konnichiwa* to everybody we passed on the trail.

There were shops near the top of Mt. Kongo, at an altitude of 1,125 meters. There was also a Buddhist temple, where you could write your wish on a piece of wood and for 100 yen the spirit of the temple would pray for you. We ate a picnic lunch in a shelter (it was raining off and on), including rice balls, seaweed and a small variety of sweet potato.

When Bonny and I went into Osaka alone (Cammie had ridden off on her bicycle to teach) I was gripped by a fear of getting terminally lost, something that had never happened anywhere else. I carefully wrote key place names down and put them in my pocket, to help me if I got separated from Bonny.

Mrs. Izuno, another friend of Cammie, was teaching her the Japanese tea ceremony. We attended one in a special room of her house, decorated like a shrine, featuring a wall hanging with Japanese calligraphy. She wore a beautiful kimono. The ceremony contains a lot of ritual, including much bowing. Bonny and I had difficulty sitting and rising because our calf muscles were sore from our hike. The green tea served at the ceremony is somewhat bitter.

Bonny and I took the train to Nara, by ourselves, and toured the large park there, on a gloomy and drizzly day. A woman volunteer met us at the railroad station and gave us a map and a ten-minute talk on what to see in Nara. The park contains many points of interest and features several thousand deer that have been known to bite.

We saw the five-storied pagoda, and the temple that is the largest wooden structure in the world, although only two-thirds original size. Inside is the largest Buddha in Japan. Outside sits a god who will cure your ills if you rub the afflicted area with your hand, first on his body and then your body. We chose our calves, which were still sore. A Shinto shrine in the park is surrounded by 3,000 stone lanterns, but they are only lit on special days.

We walked through a traditional Japanese garden (all green in October, when we were here), and Bonny fed the koi (giant carp) in the lake, who stuck their heads well of out the water to take the food. We went to the art museum and saw an exhibit of Japanese screens, on loan from the Boston Metropolitan Museum of Art. Thousands of uniformed school children were in Nara on outings. The older ones said hello. One giggling group of girls got up enough nerve to ask me to exchange some American coins for yen, but all I had were yen.

Cammie took us to Himeji, where we toured the big white castle. It is impressive in size and design, but was never involved in a military action. To see the inside we had to substitute sandals for our shoes. I had a hard time keeping my sandals on my feet. It was especially difficult for me to climb the steep flights of wooden stairs to the upper areas, but we had a good view of the surrounding country from the top.

Etsuko, another friend of Cammie, was our tour guide for Kyoto (an anagram of Tokyo). She had attended Kyoto University, majoring in English and Spanish. She said her college days were the happiest of her life because she had no responsibility and could play all the time. After thinking that over for a moment, she said, "I played with the girls, not the boys." However, she did meet her husband at the university.

She spent a lot of time planning the day and brought an elaborately annotated map with her. She also brought two of her friends. All had made special arrangements for childcare so that they could spend the whole day with us. One of them, Yayoi, said her knowledge of the United States came from the movie, *How the West Was Won.* It took us three hours of train, subway and bus rides to arrive at our first destination, the Golden Pavilion. The buses weren't quite as punctual as the subways and trains. The pavilion must be beautiful when the sun is shining.

Parking our umbrellas in a rack at the door (it was raining, as usual), we ate lunch in a typical Japanese restaurant, sitting on the floor. We went to a textile factory and saw some spectacular kimonos being modeled by young Japanese women. Then on to a five-story shop, featuring genuine Kyoto arts and crafts. Bonny bought a wood-block print and some earrings. We also saw an orange shrine, another one of the 2,000 points of interest in Kyoto.

When we returned to Tokyo, Bonny's friend, Marabeth, took us on a tour of Kamakura. The Japan Times predicted a 20 percent chance of rain. It rained steadily all day. Japanese weather forecasters aren't any better than the ones in the US. We hadn't brought umbrellas with us so we bought cheap plastic umbrellas in Kamakura. We saw a number of temples and the Great Buddha. It is the second largest Buddha in Japan, next to the one in Nara. It is also hollow and for 20 yen you can go inside, which we did.

I had two days to myself while Bonny worked at Fuji Xerox. First, I took a walk on the grounds of the Imperial Palace, which was next to the Imperial Hotel, where we were staying in Tokyo, courtesy of Xerox. Uniformed girls stood in front of the hotel elevators and bowed us into them. I visited the National Museum of Western Art, which features the work of many impressionist painters, and sculptures by Rodin, including "The Thinker." The Tokyo National Museum has historical and archaeological exhibits. In the park there is also a temple, a zoo and a five-story pagoda.

A Japanese man waylaid me in the park and talked in passable English about sports in Japan and the US, constantly asking if I understood what he was saying. When it looked as if the conversation might go on forever, I told him I had to go and made my escape.

The Ginza area was also near the hotel. It is a high-class shopping area by day, a high-priced entertainment area at night. The women, if anything, dressed sharper here than elsewhere. Their skirts, which were two to four inches above the knee in most of Tokyo, rose significantly in the Ginza, especially at night. Many of the Japanese women had nice legs and beautiful hair. However, most of them were flat chested and many had crooked teeth.

The next day I took the *Shinkansen* to Odawara, and then a local train that wound up into the mountains, to Hakone-Yumoto. From here I hiked a portion of the Tokaido Highway, to a little past Moto-Hakone on Lake Ashi, more than ten kilometers. This is the road that linked Kyoto and Edo (Tokyo's former name). Nobles from Kyoto had to take this road to Tokyo to pay homage to the emperor. This section goes up through a mountain pass, mostly following a river, and is one of the most challenging parts of the old highway. Some of the road is the original paved stone, but most of it is now the modern road, which is narrow and winding and busy, putting pedestrians in jeopardy. I passed other people hiking the road and said *konnichiwa* to them.

The next day Bonny and I rode the Shinkansen back to Odawara, and rode the local train up the mountain again, this time going all the way to Chokoku-no-Mori. In order to navigate the sharp switchbacks the train changed direction three times. Each time it stopped, the engineer and the conductor walked to the opposite ends of the two-car train, passing each other. The conductor rode in back.

We went to the Hakone Open-Air Museum, set amid scenic mountains, which features outdoor sculptures, many of them striking and unusual. There was also a whole building devoted to Picasso. The collection of his work was so large that the display was rotated each year.

A Japanese friend of Marabeth had lived in Georgia for 32 years and helped Jimmy Carter get elected president. Her home in Tokyo was actually a small apartment, with three rooms and 1.5 bathrooms, which she bought in 1991 for $800,000 cash. Literally. Checks and credit cards were still rare in Japan. She and Marabeth obtained bags full of 10,000-yen notes from the bank (the exchange rate at the time was about 130 yen to the dollar). She did a lot of redecorating and installed a washing machine and dishwasher, which cost about $4,000 apiece. They were miniature versions of the US models, designed to fit into Japanese housing.

Marabeth's friend had liquidated all of her US investments and predicted that the dollar and yen would go to par (100 yen to the dollar). Actually, the dollar bottomed out at about 80 yen, before recovering. What she didn't predict was the crash of the Japanese real estate market, which occurred in the 1990s.

She treated us to an afternoon at her private health club. Men and women had separate facilities. Marabeth's husband, Bill, went with me. The hot tub is very hot, the cold tub is freezing and I only lasted three minutes in the sauna room. Then we had our Japanese massages. Bonny often talks about the little ladies who walked on her back. I don't recall that they actually did that, but I was in a pleasant haze at the time, so who knows. Bill said that with regular massage and sake a wife could become dispensable.

CHAPTER 26 Southeast Asia

In October and November 1998, Bonny and I took our second cruise, in Southeast Asia. We flew from Los Angeles to Beijing and were driven by limousine to the China World Hotel. Since the cruise didn't start until the next day we had to pay for the large suite we were given on the 12th floor, with two bathrooms and five telephones. They saw us and our American dollars coming. The next night we moved to a single room, paid for as part of the cruise.

Like most mega-cities in the third world, Beijing has major smog. Our first daytime look at Beijing, out the window of our hotel, was into a sea of it. After breakfast, we walked several miles west on the main street to Tiananmen Square. Pedicab drivers solicited our business. The multitude of bicycles and pedicabs had their own lanes, on either side of the main thoroughfare, which was alive with modern cars. The road was wide and straight and the traffic moved fairly well. Uniformed officers on platforms directed traffic from the middle of major intersections, even the ones with traffic lights.

Subways helped pedestrians get across the very wide street. At one intersection we crossed a side street on a decorated pedestrian bridge. On our way back to the hotel two Chinese girls walked beside us and talked to us in English. They were studying art history of China and would probably teach it.

The next day we flew inland to Xian (SHEE-on), on China Northwest Airlines. In Xian, local buses took us to the terracotta soldiers. Our guide was funny and interspersed his rapid-fire, accented talk with Americanisms. He repeated words for emphasis. The land was fairly flat, but dotted with large mounds, the tombs of 74 ancient emperors. Xian is the old capital of China. The bus driver continually honked his horn as he passed bicycles, motorbikes, cars, trucks and buses, often in the face of oncoming traffic.

Three pits had been excavated at the site of the life-size soldiers, which were discovered by a farmer in 1974. The farmer no longer farmed. Instead, he apparently was getting paid to autograph books about the soldiers at the visitors' center. He autographed a book for us in Chinese characters.

Huge, roofed buildings covered the digs. Taking pictures inside was forbidden. All the uncovered figures had been damaged, but some of the men and horses had been repaired and put in place. The original wooden roofs were set afire and fell on them soon after the emperor, Qin Shi Huang, died, 2,200 years ago. Another roof collapsed later and smashed the soldiers. Some soldiers were beheaded, which ended their after-lives. It is estimated that a total of 60-70,000 figures exist.

On the grounds, we were besieged by entrepreneurs, mostly young, trying to sell us postcards, terracotta figures, etc. Everything cost "one dollah." We heard the chant, "one dollar" so often while in China that members of our tour group would take it up.

On the bus ride to the hotel, after dark, we were gridlocked at an intersection, where traffic seemed to be heading in all directions. The driver yelled at people through a loudspeaker. The tour guide got off the bus and apparently exercised some symbol of authority, because the other vehicles moved enough to let us through.

Our guides talked about the one-child policy, which had been in effect for 20 years. They didn't admit that more boys than girls survived childbirth. People who had two children were threatened with the loss of their jobs. Farmers appeared to be more equal than others, in regard to enforcement of the policy. Some people "gave away" girl babies, to try to have a boy. However, girls who grew up and went to the city to work were sending back money equivalent to many times what the typical farm earned. The boys who left the farm weren't as reliable about sending money home.

A favorite saying is that the Chinese eat everything with four legs, except tables. We looked carefully at the food we were served, but we never detected anything that we wouldn't have eaten at home.

We were also told that to get ahead in China you had to be a member of the Communist party. One of our guides said she used to worship Mao. Each morning she would bow to his picture and say, "I love you, Chairman Mao." She would confess her transgressions to him and promise to do better. All that has changed. It has been officially established that Mao made many mistakes.

In the morning we walked along the top of Xian's city wall. It is 14 kilometers around, but we only covered a small section of it. People were dancing to western music in the square below.

We saw the Wild Goose pagoda, over 1,300 years old. It was about 13 stories high, but two stories were lost in an ancient earthquake. I paid 20 yuan ($2) to ring the big bell on the grounds, but the sound was disappointing and didn't carry for kilometers, as advertised. It did live up to its other promise, that it would avert calamities.

Back in Beijing, we rode to Badaling in a 12-bus convoy, led by a police car with a flashing red light and priority over other traffic. The Great Wall crosses a pass in the Swallow Mountains at Badaling. A cast of thousands was present on a beautiful but nippy Sunday to walk on the Wall. I climbed to the tower at the 805-meter marker, but couldn't escape the crowds. At one point the climb steepens to high, narrow steps. I took a firm grip on the handrail, but many people were still undaunted.

Bonny accomplished one of her three great desires by walking on the Wall. We had our picture taken, kissing, with the Wall stretching behind us. The Wall goes through some very rugged country and I wondered whether all 4,000 miles of it were necessary to protect China from the Mongolian hordes. (Apparently, it didn't keep them out, anyway.) Begun in 200 B.C., the Wall (actually a series of walls) was worked on into the 17th century.

We toured the Summer Palace, used by the emperors, including empress dowager Cixi (SEE-shee), who ruled for 48 years, ending early in the 20th century. The last emperor was the grandson of her sister, but she sat behind a screen and wielded the power. After a walk on the grounds we took a boat ride on the adjoining lake.

We did a lot of walking to see all of the Forbidden City, home of the emperors. It is much larger than the impression given by watching the movie, *The Last Emperor*, with spacious courtyards and many buildings. A turtle statue in a courtyard stands for longevity. We couldn't go into nearby Tiananmen Square because of construction activity, but we did get a good look at it. It is large enough to hold 500,000 people. Soldiers were drilling in the square, but there weren't any tanks.

While eating lunch I became woozy, possibly because of MSG in the food. Bonny and one of the men we befriended on the tour helped me walk downstairs and outside of the restaurant. I stayed there and breathed fresh air until I felt better. I never did go back into the restaurant.

Our cabin on the Sky Princess was on deck seven, the Aloha Deck. I walked each day for Cruisercise bucks, which I exchanged for caps and T-shirts at the ship's store, but the track, on the Sun Deck, was disappointingly small, 11 laps to a mile. I also received Cruisercise bucks for ascending and descending the stairs that went from the top to the bottom of the ship. From a sample of two, we determined that all the captains of Princess ships were English and were named Michael.

Our entertainment director, Brian, had also been on our other cruise. The entertainers put on excellent shows. Bonny got her 15 seconds of fame when one of the male dancers pulled her up on stage from her front row seat and danced with her. He recognized her from our previous cruise and told her it was nice to see her again. She beamed and thoroughly enjoyed herself while she was on stage. We also played some video poker. Using my super system I won some money during the cruise, but Bonny lost most of it.

*   *   *

Our guide for Seoul, Korea, population 11 million, was a pretty and young looking 35-year-old, who had us call her Sue. She was dressed better than we were. She talked like a feminist, but Bonny doubted that her actions matched her words. Confucianism is the dominant philosophy in Korea. It favors males over females, and young people are rebelling against it.

We walked around the grounds of the Toksu Palace, where a dozen brides-to-be and their grooms were having their pictures taken in full wedding dress at the scenic spots. We were told that they were all getting married the coming weekend. We walked through one of the shopping areas and bought some silk scarves. While we were there, Magic Johnson came loping along the sidewalk with a woman, presumably his wife. It was nice to see a familiar face from home.

*   *   *

Shanghai is one of the world's three largest cities. When we were there it also contained a high percentage of all the construction cranes in the world. From our ship on the waterfront, we walked along the Huangpu River to a state-owned Friendship Store, which sells high-quality goods, manufactured in China. We also went to one in Beijing.

Our afternoon tour took us to see the Jade Buddha, made from white jade, in Burma in 1882. A larger replica, also on display, was made in 1919. There were other Buddhas and gods on display, large statues made of wood, with gilt finish. We went to an arts and crafts center that was sponsored by the government, in an attempt to retain some of the traditional artistic skills, including paper cutting, making dolls out of a dough composed of water and flour, needlepoint pictures, jade cutting, embroidery, lacquer ware and silk lanterns.

From Shanghai we rode a train to Wuxi (WOO-shee), a middled-sized city of four million. Here we took a boat for a cruise on the Grand Canal, which is 1,100 miles long, connecting Beijing and Shanghai. Most of it was built about 600 A.D., to allow goods to be shipped within China. Traffic was heavy on the canal, and included small barges, 60-70 feet long, on which families lived. They hung their washing to dry outside their cabins and when we waved they waved back. Navigation was tricky because of the traffic, and people stood on the prows of some of the barges to signal oncoming vessels.

We went to a pearl center, where oysters were cultivated in fresh water, and bought a pearl necklace for Bonny. Then on to a silk factory, where silk worms were cultivated. The cocoons were harvested and turned into silk. The process was interesting, but difficult to follow. It involved the use of much hot water and heavy machinery. One cocoon produces a considerable quantity of silk thread, which is spun onto large spools. The women workers constantly had their hands in hot water, which damaged the skin on their fingers.

*　　*　　*

Hong Kong has the world's densest population. That was easy to believe as we sailed down the runway just before dawn and saw the hundreds of high-rise buildings on both sides of us. After we docked at Kowloon we took the Star Ferry to Hong Kong Island and rode the tram up Victoria Peak, which overlooks the harbor. We walked to a viewpoint and observed the continuous activity below us, amid moderate smog. An endless procession of boats plied the harbor area: ferries, tugs, barges, dhows, freighters, cruise boats and an occasional harbor patrol craft. In spite of the enormous number of buildings, there were more under construction.

Coming back to Kowloon on the ferry, we rode on the top deck for an extra seven cents apiece. We walked through the fancy shopping area around Nathan Road, where Judy, one of our dinner partners, was out buying "adult jewelry," as she termed it. I don't think her older husband was with her. The double-decker buses driving on the left reminded us of London.

*　　*　　*

When we arrived at Viet Nam I had a rather nasty stomach virus, but I didn't want to be left behind, so I went on the half-day tour of Nha Trang with Bonny. It rained softly most of the time, but the temperature was in the high 70's. The tropical foliage included coconut palms. The 300,000 people lived in narrow houses, which often had stores in front, where everything conceivable was sold.

185

We walked to the Cham Temple, built 800-1200 years ago. It is not Buddhist, but there was incense burning inside. A Buddhist pagoda contained more incense. Most Vietnamese are Buddhist. About 10 percent are Catholic. A large white Buddha sat on top of a nearby hill, but we didn't try to get close to it.

Our bus stopped at a place where we had the opportunity to drink coconut milk on the beach (this was once a resort community), but we passed and stayed in our seats. The local market sold food and souvenirs and smelled. We saw a carwash but few cars. Most people rode bikes or motorbikes. One beggar was missing both hands. He may have been the victim of a land mine. There was a war memorial commemorating the liberation of Nha Trang by the Viet Cong in 1975. The dollar was overvalued, as it is in many third-world countries.

It was probably just as well that tropical storm Chip prevented us from going ashore to tour Ho Chi Minh City (Saigon) because I was still feeling rotten when Captain Mike decided to pull the ship out of the port. He said he had no problem with dropping us off for the long bus ride, but that since he was leaving and taking the ship with him we would be stranded there. I had to get a shot from the ship's doctor and take antibiotics before I felt better.

*   *   *

Singapore is at one-degree north Latitude. We docked there in the evening and watched a thunderstorm through our porthole during the night. The next morning we ventured out into the prosperous city and figured out how to use the bus and subway system. We went to a place where residents took their songbirds to sing on Sunday mornings. The cages were ornate and the small birds had nice voices, but traffic noise partially drowned them out.

Hordes of people had preceded us to Orchard Street, the shopping area. We walked to the Raffles Hotel, made famous by Kipling and Maugham, and visited its museum of photographs and old baggage stickers. We had our picture taken in the Long Bar.

After lunch at a sandwich shop, we walked to the Merlion, half lion and half (lower half) mermaid, a statue on the Singapore River, beside the harbor. We walked along the river on a path muddy from rain. When we returned to the World Trade Centre, where the ship was docked, I took the cable car that went over the ship to Sentosa Island and return. It offered a birds-eye view of the harbor area. A cloud cover kept the temperature down during the day and walking was not unpleasant.

*   *   *

We docked at Kuantan, Malaysia, during breakfast, beside a rust bucket of a freighter that later was loaded from a conveyor belt, perhaps with raw tin. Our tour guide informed us that he was not supposed to talk about politics (there were demonstrations going on in Kuala Lumpur, the capital), but he discoursed in an interesting manner on a number of subjects.

We went to a four-star hotel to watch a monkey climb a palm tree and drop coconuts. Monkeys are much preferred over men because they work cheaper and are more nimble. Some boys did a demonstration of martial arts, and the professional top spinners demonstrated their skills. The record is 72 hours, but most tops spin for fewer than two hours. The secret is a heavy and well-balanced top and a rope-pull start (like starting an outboard engine on a boat). We enjoyed watching a mock wedding, complete with fabulous costumes and fabulous women.

We saw fish drying in the air, including shark fins, used in expensive shark-fin soup. Markets in each country have their own distinctive odors, some repulsive to western noses. This one wasn't bad, compared to markets we encountered in China and Viet Nam.

Palm oil was replacing coconut oil in the Malay diet because of cholesterol concerns. That must be a sign that Malaysia is becoming a first-world country. The palm oil plantations employ cobras to keep the rat population down, since rats love the palm nuts. Fortunately, cobras rear up and hiss before striking, giving the workers an opportunity to avoid them. In addition to snakes and tigers, jungle trekkers must beware of iguanas and leeches, one variety of which is as large as your little finger. Only Germans go jungle trekking, we were told. Americans are smarter.

187

*   *   *

Ours was the first cruise ship to ever dock at Laem Chabang, Thailand. We were told that the ride to the Bangkok Airport would take three hours, but traffic was kind to us and our bus made it in two hours. Bonny and I were staying at the Amari Airport Hotel for a night, so we contracted to take a private tour of downtown Bangkok.

Bangkok has its own brand of air pollution, with a unique and unpleasant smell. "Miss Nancie," our tour guide, took us to the Royal Palace in an old Toyota Crown, complete with driver. The palace was dazzling, and not quite like anything we'd ever seen. Presumably, Anna, from *The King and I*, lived here, back in the days when Thailand was Siam.

We took off our shoes to enter a Buddhist temple, where many people were chanting. The monks can't have anything to do with women. Young men are encouraged to try monkhood for at least several months. I suspect that most of them don't last longer than that. On our way back to the hotel we stopped at a government-owned jewelry shop, and Bonny bought an agate elephant.

Back at the hotel, we took a stroll past a school and another temple. The uniformed children behaved like children everywhere. A boy took the cap off a girl's head and ran away. She looked as if she was going to cry. The robed and shaved monks were closing up shop for the day at their temple. Bangkok is very spread out, like Los Angeles, with large buildings everywhere, and about 12 million people.

The coffee shop at the hotel, named Zeppelin, looked like a coffee shop in any US city, but looks are deceiving. Since I can't eat dairy products I ordered oatmeal, without milk, for breakfast. (I usually put cinnamon and nuts on top to make it palatable.) I was served a bowl of dry oats. When I explained that I would like some hot water added, that's exactly what I got—a soggy mess, not worthy of the name oatmeal.

We flew from Bangkok to Tokyo's Narita Airport and then on to Los Angeles. On our flight from Tokyo to Los Angeles we rode on a hurricane and made the trip in 8.5 hours.

Part III Hiking

Hiking is an important and interesting form of walking for the more adventurous of us. Although some hikes, particularly my east coast hikes, are covered along with more casual walks in other parts of the book, this part concentrates on hiking. And rock climbing, which may be stretching the definition of walking a bit (think of it as vertical walking), but a brief look at it is warranted. Just to keep your attention there are adventures on Mt. San Jacinto and Mt. Whitney, and my most traumatic adventure of all—getting lost in the wilderness of Colorado.

Alan Cook

CHAPTER 27 Hiking and Rock Climbing in California

In September 1957 I flew to Los Angeles to attend UCLA for my junior year of college (my first two were at the University of Michigan). Since I had never been west of Michigan or flown in a plane larger than a Piper Cub, it was an adventure. I flew on a DC-7, a four-engine propeller-driven airplane that made the nonstop flight from Buffalo in about nine and one-half hours. During the flight I played checkers with a stewardess. We split two games. I have never been very good at checkers.

Not knowing my way around Los Angeles, I took a bus to downtown LA and stayed the night at the Biltmore Hotel for $6. I still remember being impressed by the army of palm trees bordering the city streets. I had never seen a live palm tree before. Palm trees equaled paradise to me.

My father had sent me a postcard from UCLA while he was there on a business trip, which made me think. Like him, I suffered from allergies and often became sick during cold weather. If cold weather contributed to my problems, why not go to a warmer climate? It worked so well that I have been a resident of the Los Angeles area since 1960.

At UCLA I met Tom Rohrer, who was an avid rock climber and hiker. I had never done any rock climbing, but I was willing to give it a try, even though I suffered from vertigo at the time. The vertigo, I eventually discovered, was caused by two problems, both related to my eyes. One was low convergences, the ability of my eyes to diverge and to focus, especially on a point close to my nose. An ophthalmologist at the UCLA Medical Center diagnosed that and eye exercises cured it.

My other problem was dilated pupils. It took years for Bonny and me to figure out that I am sensitive (or allergic) to certain foods. Over time we have eliminated the main offenders from my diet. Gone are the dilated pupils and a dozen or more other symptoms, although some of them return like ghosts to haunt me when I stray from my diet. I never had any help from a doctor in diagnosing my food problems.

I went on a number of rock climbing expeditions with Tom and his friends. I learned how to use a rope to belay other climbers, how to tie a bowline, and about the use of pitons, carabiners and other rock climbing paraphernalia. I wasn't very good at it because of my vertigo and because I am naturally cautious. A certain amount of caution is necessary for rock climbing because incautious climbers can get killed, but good climbers are also more adventurous than I was. I had some interesting moments, however. As Marv, one of our rock-climbing companions said, "If you don't get a thrill out of doing a 115-foot, overhanging rappel, there's something wrong with you." I can tell you that I got a thrill out of it so I guess I'm normal.

Tom and I were climbing on a relatively small rock at Stoney Point, Chatsworth, in the San Fernando Valley, one day. We weren't using ropes because we considered it to be an easy climb. Tom was above me and as he started to descend he lost his balance. He ran down the face of the rock, out of control, right past me, and was airborne for the last 10 feet, where the rock is essentially vertical. He landed hard on his feet and collapsed to his knees.

I climbed down as fast as I could. Tom was still on his knees and couldn't talk. The wind had been knocked out of him. When he recovered his breath he said his back hurt. I helped him to his car, an old Chevrolet. He was in no shape to drive so I drove us over the Sepulveda Pass of the Santa Monica Mountains to the UCLA Medical Center. The 405 freeway hadn't been built yet so I had to take Sepulveda Boulevard.

I had the unpleasant duty of calling Tom's mother (his parents lived in Los Angeles) and telling her that he had suffered a cracked vertebra. He had to wear a caste that was wrapped all the way around his torso for a number of weeks. This presented certain hygienic challenges since it was difficult for him to wash. The caste, hidden under his clothes, also made him look like a bodybuilder instead of a person with a slim physique. As I recall, he became impatient with his caste and started rock climbing again before it was removed. He tied the belay rope around the caste.

I attended UCLA for only one year and after I left I didn't do any more technical rock climbing, retiring at the ripe old age of 20.

Tom's fall killed one project we had been thinking about attempting after the school year ended: hiking from Badwater, in Death Valley, the lowest point in the United States, to the top of Mt. Whitney, the highest point in the continental US. Now people run races between the two.

Usually, Tom was cautious, and he was good at the technical aspects of rock climbing. Using slings, pitons and other direct aids, he climbed up the overhang at the top of Eagle Rock, in the community of Eagle Rock, near Glendale, while I took pictures from above. He also had a creative mind. He thought he could run a four-minute mile by running downhill on a mountain road. He was actually on a pace to accomplish this, but after half a mile his feet had lost so much skin that he had to stop.

Another project of Tom's was to climb 11 peaks in the San Gabriel Mountains, north of Los Angeles, in one day. He recruited me to be his partner in this undertaking, and another friend of his provided us with transportation between two of the trails and hiked part of the way with us. It took us 12 hours, altogether. Later, Tom claimed he had duplicated the climbs in six hours, with better planning. Some of the peaks we climbed that day were Occidental, Lowe, Lawlor, Strawberry, Josephine and, I believe, Harvard. We also counted Mt. Wilson, of telescope fame, even though it has a road to the top.

Several years later I was living and working in California, single, lonely and restless. I had one of those crazy desires I get: I wanted to climb a mountain at night. At the time I was dating the beautiful

Cookie, whose parents were from Mexico. Well, dating may overstate the case; she let me escort her while she waited for the guy she loved to come to his senses and marry her. Anyway, she agreed to hike with me.

I chose Josephine Peak because its broad trail—actually a fire road—was easy to follow, even at night. We hadn't gone very far before Cookie started worrying about what we would do if we met a boogieman or some other monster (maybe I should have taken Buffy, the vampire slayer, instead). This fear grew until she started back down the trail by herself. Soon realizing that she was more scared alone than with me she came racing back into my arms. This was all right with me, but I acceded to her wishes and we descended the mountain together. (Historical note: On May 11, 1963 Cookie and I attended the Los Angeles Dodgers baseball game and watched Sandy Koufax pitch a no-hitter against the San Francisco Giants.)

Tom's parents owned a cabin in the mountains at Big Bear, above San Bernardino. I went there with the three of them for a weekend. On the drive up the mountain the ear problems I had suffered as a child came back to haunt me. I couldn't equalize the pressure inside and outside my right ear and suffered excruciating pain. Finally, my eardrum perforated, relieving the pressure. It had perforated many times before, either naturally or because my doctor had pierced it to relieve pressure, so I didn't say anything. It always healed itself, but part of my hearing loss now may be due to this repeated trauma.

Tom and I hiked up Mill Peak in the snow and fog. It was my first experience climbing in the snow, but of course I had walked in the snow in New York and Michigan. And ice. And cold. Hiking in the snow when the footing is good and where you can wear enough clothing to combat the cold is not an unpleasant experience. A pristine world of white, unmarred by the tools of civilization that turn snow into a dirty eyesore after a short period of time, is worth making some effort to see.

Tom's favorite expression, when we were in the middle of an adventure that made us some combination of tired, sore, cold and wet, was "Misery." But he would laugh when he said it and it was evident that he loved misery.

Some years later my brother, Steve, and I took a hike in Sequoia National Park in the snow. It was cold enough to freeze the water in our canteens. However, the advantage of hiking in snow is that you have an unlimited clean water supply because snow is easy to melt. We met another couple who were going much farther than we were, oblivious to the snow and cold. No matter how adventurous you are, there are always others who will outdo you.

Steve seemed to have a liking for hiking in snow. Another time, he and I climbed Mt. San Jacinto together in the snow, around Thanksgiving time. Again the water in our canteens froze. (See chapter 28 for more about Mt. San Jacinto.) He also took his son, Gordon, then nine years old, up a snow-covered Mt. Washington, in New Hampshire, in May. (See chapter 3 for more about Mt. Washington.) Sometimes they sank into the snow up to their hips. For the most part I have avoided hiking in the snow. My motto is that I like adventure as long as it isn't dangerous—or cold.

*   *   *

When I started working in California, fresh out of college, I didn't own a car, which is a mortal sin in Los Angeles. I took the "J" streetcar to my job at a bank, after first walking a mile, and learned the LA bus system, out of necessity. On several weekends I went on hikes with the Sierra Club, in the San Gabriel Mountains. In order to catch a ride to the starting point I had to get up at 3 a.m. and walk eight miles. And then hike. Oh to be young again.

On one of these hikes we encountered a man who had sprained an ankle near Ontario Peak. Somebody had rigged a wooden seat for him that could be carried by two people. We took turns carrying him, but his weight and the awkwardness of holding the seat while hiking down a rough trail made it very difficult. Several members of our group raced down to the bottom of the four-mile Ice House Canyon Trail and brought up a six-person stretcher. It was a lot easier for six people to carry the injured man and we gave him a fast, if somewhat scary, ride. One problem we had was that from time to time members of the team got picked off by trees where the trail narrowed.

I returned to Los Angeles after serving six months of active duty in the Army Reserve, with a brand new car. I moved around a lot, as single people tend to do, and found myself living in Whittier at the time President Kennedy was touting the fitness value of 50-miles hikes. Kennedy was too sick to participate in such a hike, himself, but his brother Robert did.

I decided I would take my own hike. I laid out a 25-mile route, starting at my apartment, intending to walk a roundtrip. I rose before dawn, ready and raring to go. The first few miles featured lots of barking dogs, up before their owners. Near the halfway mark I encountered an unexpected rainstorm that considerably dampened my spirits. Then my feet started to hurt. I was wearing the steel-toed shoes I had worn while working summers in a gypsum warehouse during my college days, and these were definitely not suitable for long-distance walking. After about 27 miles I cried uncle and called Bob, my roommate at the time, to ask him to drive my car out and pick me up. It wasn't until years later than I learned enough about foot care to be able to take long hikes without suffering.

*   *   *

In 1981 and 1982, Andy went on backpacking trips with his Boy Scout troop. On the first trip he was still quite small and had trouble carrying his pack, containing food, clothing and a sleeping bag. In 1982, he had grown bigger and stronger and had no problem. I joined him on the 1982 trip.

Before the long-terms, as they were called, we went on conditioning hikes to get us ready for the big one. One of the hikes, in both 1981 and 1982, was up Mt. San Gorgonio, the highest peak in Southern California, at 11,500 feet. Steve and I had climbed San Gorgonio in one day in the sixties; it was a long day.

On the 1981 hike up San Gorgonio, Andy and I went with a number of scouts and the scoutmaster, John. Our plan was to camp part way up and climb to the summit the next day. Early in the hike John tried to jump over a small stream and hurt his foot. We didn't know it at the time, but he had broken a bone. He told us to continue on, go as far as we could and then to return to the parking area. The campout was scrubbed. He said he could make it back to the parking area by himself.

Mt. San Gorgonio is a long, grueling climb, but most of us made it to the top after lightening our packs. Andy grew tired and we left him sitting in a snowbank. Not literally—I made sure he was warm enough. He was right where we left him when we returned from the top.

We hiked down to a clearing not far from the parking lot and realized that several members of the group weren't with us, including John's son. It was getting dark. As the adult, I decided that we could wait a few minutes and then we would have to go to the parking lot to alert John. We would gather what flashlights we could find and return to search for the errant boys. Fortunately, they came striding out of the woods before we left the clearing. But John's misfortunes were not finished for the day. We had driven to the mountain in two cars. The car John drove suffered a flat tire on the way home.

During our 1982 practice climb of Mt. San Gorgonio we did camp part way up and we tackled the summit the next morning. That worked out fine and, as I recall, everybody made it to the top.

On the long-term in 1982, we hiked into the heart of Sequoia National Park from Mineral King. Our group consisted of six boys and three dads. We carried food for about nine days. Andy and I each carried pieces of our backpacker's tent. We ran into some snow, left over from the winter, right at the start of the trip. The boys slid down snow-covered hillsides, taking the fast way down. The sun was shining so it didn't matter much if we got wet. Our sleeping bags and tents kept us warm at night.

In the evenings the boys had a ball attempting to suspend our food bags from the trees, using ingenious techniques, so that the bears wouldn't get them. Apparently, this worked. We never saw any bears and we didn't lose any food to them. One night we camped in an area that still had snow on the ground. We knew it would become quite cool at night. A young woman ranger was camping there, also, but she took her sleeping bag and went up to the top of a nearby hill. As we watched her through binoculars we found out why. Before she got into her sleeping bag she took off all her clothes. Nature girl.

Another time I went backpacking over a weekend with a male friend from work who did the same thing. On that trip I developed poison oak. I knew I was going to catch it because we crawled through beds of poison oak on a poorly maintained trail. That's like knowing you're drinking poison, but drinking it anyway.

Our group of nine boy scouts and dads walked through some gorgeous country on the long-term. We hiked along cliff tops and above and below overhangs. One of the other dads and I climbed Sawtooth Peak, but we couldn't get any of the boys to go with us. I took a photograph of the peak from below, looking like a tooth projecting from a jaw of snow-covered rocks, with a valley in the foreground, containing cool pools and green vegetation.

I had the picture hanging in my cubicle when I was working at McDonnell Douglas. One time, Karen, a sales rep who was having a bad day, announced she wished she were someplace other than the office. When she was asked where she wanted to be she pointed at my photo and said, "I want to be in that picture."

One of the boys, whose father was the third adult in our party, showed more ambition that any of us, racing up a number of peaks that the rest of us passed on. We all saw scenes you don't see on flat land and had the pleasure of eating freeze-dried food. We learned important things, such as not to pee into the wind. Andy carried a can of coke with him for most of the trip and finally drank it near the end, relishing the taste he missed. When we came out of Sequoia eight days after we went in, we hightailed it to the nearest McDonald's and gorged ourselves on fast food.

*   *   *

Favorite weekend getaways for us in California include Death Valley and Anza-Borrego Desert State Park, near the California-Mexican border. Both offer scenic walking opportunities. In Death Valley, which sane people visit only in the winter, they include sand dunes, Scotty's Castle, Ubehebe Crater, Mosaic Canyon and Badwater. Badwater is the lowest point in the US, at 282 feet below sea level, and abuts miles of salt flats: crunchy white blankets of crystals leading to the foot of Telescope Peak, towering 11,000 feet above.

Sometime after our niece Ellen came out to California to live, in 1987, the three of us were camping at Stovepipe Wells in my backpacker's tent. During the night the wind came over the mountains from the west, bringing with it an unseasonal rainfall. We awoke to find Ellen attempting to hold up the tent, afraid that the wind would blow it down. The next morning we discovered no ill effects from the storm, although we did spot a small rattlesnake beside the creek. Bonny and Ellen refused to spend another night holding up the tent so we retreated to a motel in Baker.

Perhaps the most publicized walk in Anza Borrego is the one up Palm Canyon, aptly named for its hundreds of Palm Trees, growing amid the rocks. However, there are other more remote places to walk, featuring wide valleys of flowering manzanita bushes and other exotic flora, unique to this corner of the world.

CHAPTER 28 Mt. San Jacinto

In 1966, Bonny and I bought a cabin in Idyllwild. Idyllwild is in the San Jacinto Mountains, above Hemet, and on the other side of Mt. San Jacinto from Palm Springs. Idyllwild was our weekend getaway spot when we were young. We often invited other couples to stay with us in the cabin.

Tahquitz Peak, at 8,800 feet, is the closest mountain to Idyllwild. The trail up Tahquitz from Humber Park (6,400 feet), in Idyllwild, is a 10-mile round trip. I often climbed Tahquitz, either alone or with others, when we stayed at our cabin. One weekend we invited a number of people from my office to the cabin and I climbed Tahquitz two days in a row, leading a group of co-workers up each time. I once remarked to someone that I wouldn't mind having a job that required me to climb Tahquitz every day, at least in good weather.

There is a fire-lookout tower on top of Tahquitz, so part of the fun is climbing up the tower and talking to the fire lookout, just as it was at Blue Mountain in the Adirondacks, in New York, the first mountain I ever climbed (see chapter 3). The view from the top of Tahquitz encompasses a wide area, including Idyllwild, Hemet and other peaks, dominated by Mt. San Jacinto.

My mother and father climbed Tahquitz Peak with Bonny and me when they were visiting us one summer. We even took a longer trail down than the one that goes to Humber Park. I believe that was the last mountain I climbed with my father.

My brother, Mike, started up the Tahquitz trail with Bonny and me once in the spring. We didn't get to the top because there was still a lot of snow on the mountain. However, some years later Mike returned with his son, Ben, and this time we made it to the top. Three miles above Humber Park is a saddle. Mike is a marathoner and triathlete. Since we were walking he didn't even have to breathe until we got halfway to the saddle.

Trails go in several directions from the saddle. One trail goes to Tahquitz Peak. Another trail goes up Mt. San Jacinto, which at 10,800 feet is the highest mountain in the San Jacinto range. Mike decided to run up the San Jacinto trail for a while and then to return to the saddle and join Ben and me on Tahquitz. Ben and I climbed to the top of Tahquitz at a slow but steady pace and waited for Mike to join us.

Ben even became concerned about his dad, but not to worry. After some time Mike appeared, sweaty but happy. He had actually made it up the San Jacinto trail to a point higher than Tahquitz. Since he has run up Pikes Peak, a 14,000-foot peak near Colorado Springs, and also completed the Hawaiian Ironman Triathlon (2.4 miles swimming, 112 miles bicycling, 26.2 miles running), this was not surprising.

My favorite peak to climb is Mt. San Jacinto. I have climbed it many times, including nine times in the 1990s. I have climbed it by two different routes from the Idyllwild area, including at least once in the snow, but it is easier and more fun to climb from the top of the Palm Springs tram.

The ride up the tram is the most spectacular ride in California. It starts at 2,643 feet and climbs to 8,516 feet, along 12,800 feet of cable, through five life zones, ranging from Sonoran to Hudsonian-Canadian. In the year 2,000 new round tram cars were installed that rotate twice during the ascent and descent so that no matter where you are in the car you get a 360-degree view. And what a view—from the desert golf courses in Palm Springs to Mt. San Gorgonio, across the Coachella Valley, the highest peak in Southern California.

The climb up Mt. San Jacinto from the top of the tram is an 11-mile roundtrip, with a 2,500-foot gain in altitude. The well-maintained trail rises through groves of stately pine trees, sentinels that have protected the mountain for hundreds of years. Squirrels, chipmunks and lizards dart here and there, and one day a deer briefly walked in front of me on the trail. Near the summit a hawk took off so close to me that I heard the whirr of its wings.

A lot of people have climbed Mt. San Jacinto with me, including Bonny, Andy, two of my brothers and various other relatives and friends. We have a picture on our wall of Andy, perched on top of the mountain, wearing his youthful long hair. Upon seeing this picture, his wife, Melissa, remarked that her father would never have let her date him in his hirsute stage. Fortunately, he cut his hair before he went to graduate school, where he met Melissa.

Our nephew, Art, who went to law school in Los Angeles, has climbed Mt. San Jacinto three times. My cousin, Kimberly, climbed to the top twice and partway another time, as a teenager. The time she didn't make it to the top was in the year 2000 when we were forced to climb from the Idyllwild side because the tramcars were getting replaced. We didn't run out of energy, we ran out of time. I didn't want to risk being on the mountain after dark. When nobody else was available I have climbed it by myself.

Our niece, Ellen, has climbed Mt. San Jacinto twice. Her first climb, in 1988, turned out to be the most exciting one I have been on. Bonny was supposed to go, but she woke up feeling sick and stayed home. The southern California deserts were baking in a July heat wave and it was already hot when Ellen and I arrived in Palm Springs a little after 8:30 a.m. The temperature would climb to 110 degrees F later.

As we prepared our packs Ellen asked if it was really necessary to take her sweatshirt. I said I didn't think so. The temperature was 65 degrees F at the top of the tram. The couple we were climbing with, Rene, a mountain man, and Joanne, half Japanese and half Hungarian and the best half of each, were already at the ranger station when we arrived there, having taken an earlier tram.

We wore T-shirts during the three-hour ascent and drank ice water from Joanne's water bottle, which she had put in the freezer the night before. We rested at a viewpoint, where we could see Tahquitz Peak and its fire-lookout tower. Ellen and I had climbed Tahquitz several weeks before with Bonny and one of Ellen's sisters.

The fleecy clouds grew darker as we approached the peak. It was cool on top. We ate our lunches while gazing down at the desert floor below, which was still basking in the sun. However, we each added a layer or two of clothing, all except for Rene, who remained in his T-shirt. Several of us took aspirin for altitude headaches.

The clouds blocked our view of Mt. San Gorgonio, across the valley. As we ate we heard claps of thunder and after a while we saw flashes of lightning. One or two drops of rain fell on us, but we were not very concerned. It was raining a little when we started down and as we passed the rock shelter house below the summit someone made a joking reference to using it for its intended purpose.

Ten minutes later we wished we had given the shelter more serious consideration. As we continued down the trail the lightning and thunder came closer. Soon the lightning was striking on all sides of us and some of the strikes were uncomfortably close. I told the others that you can tell how close lightning is by counting the seconds between the lightning and thunder and multiplying by 1,100 feet. Ellen immediately asked how far away it was when the lightning and thunder occurred simultaneously.

This was more real than funny, and the thunder was so loud it made me jump on several occasions. The sound of nearby thunder is a sharp crack rather than a rumble. Ellen screamed at least once but nobody heard her.

Meanwhile, the rain increased greatly in force and then turned to hail. The hailstones were cold and painful as they bounced off our heads and backs. Joanne was wearing a light, nylon parka and Rene lent his parka to Ellen. I was wearing a sweatshirt. Rene was still in his T-shirt and claimed he wasn't cold. My sweatshirt quickly became soaked and I shivered uncontrollably.

We stopped under a pine tree for a few minutes, which offered us some protection from the hail, but we wondered about the danger from lightning. However, there were quite a few other trees around and we figured the risk was minimal.

We decided to walk some more and try to get to a lower elevation. Now the trail was a rushing torrent and pockets of hailstones covered the ground, looking like snow. We went as fast as possible, but most of the time we walked through several inches of water. Rene and

Joanne were wearing very light boots with lug soles. Ellen and I were wearing sneakers. None of our footwear was waterproof.

I was now colder than ever from the hail and rain and didn't know how long I could continue. Fortunately, Rene, who was leading, found a rock overhang by the trail and we all crowded into the small space underneath it. There was barely room for the four of us, and Rene's arm stuck out. He was still in his T-shirt and still claiming he wasn't cold. However, I noticed goose bumps on his arm. Joanne explained that he was toughening himself up. I was still shivering.

Water ran down the rock that formed the roof of our small cave, creating an upside-down stream, and some of it dripped onto our heads and backs, but we hardly noticed. We huddled together while nature put on a splendid show. The hail continued to fall fast and furiously and pile up on the ground, lightning continued to strike all around us and thunder rattled the heavens.

This was all great fun for Rene. He advised us to inhale this experience to the fullest extent possible because tomorrow it would be just a fading memory. We told each other stories of nail-biting events from our pasts. I took a picture of the scene before us. It was the end of my roll of film. I couldn't change film because my hands were wet and there was no way to dry them. Besides, they were shaking so much from cold that I wouldn't have been able to perform the necessary operations, anyway.

The sky grew lighter, little by little, the hail turned to rain and then slowed to a drizzle, gradually stopping. We ventured forth from our cave after being there half an hour, and continued down the trail, our feet crunching on the hailstones as we tried to avoid the deeper puddles.

Away from the shelter of the cave and the warmth of the other bodies, my thoroughly soaked sweatshirt made me colder than ever, and I could hardly talk because my jaw muscles weren't working properly. Fortunately, my legs still worked all right. I took off the sweatshirt.

We stopped at the viewpoint and removed the wettest articles of our clothing. As we became warmer and dryer, we felt better about life. We coasted down the rest of the trail to the tram. Rene spotted a coyote and we watched it watch us for several minutes as it worked its way up the hillside above us. We arrived back at the tram in time to catch the 5 o'clock car down. It was wonderfully hot and dry at the bottom.

CHAPTER 29 Mt. Whitney

I have climbed two 14,000-foot peaks under my own power. I have been on top of two others (Pikes Peak and Mt. Evans, in Colorado), but I went up by car. In the case of Mt. Evans, Bonny, one-year-old Andy and I attended a reunion of my mother's family in Evergreen, Colorado in 1969. Uncle Jim drove a group of us up to the top of the mountain, including Bonny and me. Jim had played football at the University of Michigan, but he told us that whenever he had an urge to exercise he laid down until it went away. The rest of us spent several hours hiking back down Mt. Evans, but potential knee problems aside, it is much easier to hike down most trails than up, especially at that altitude.

In 1962, my brother, Steve, and I drove to Denver from Los Angeles, where I was living and where he had been working for the summer. With our cousin, Kay, we set out to climb Grays Peak, a 14,000 footer, also in the Rockies. The climb, itself, is not onerous since the trail starts at 11,000 feet, but on the way down we encountered a sleet storm that thoroughly froze us. I developed a splitting headache from the altitude, but aside from that and getting cold we had no particular problems.

My climb of Mt. Whitney, the highest peak in the continental US, was not carefully planned and is not to be used as a model for any kind of serious expedition. Don't try this in the mountains. In 1989, Andy turned 21 and so Bonny, Andy and I formed a vague plan to drive up Route 395 to Reno or Lake Tahoe so that he could do some gambling. A look at the map reminded me that we would be going through Lone Pine. I suggested that we camp the first night at Whitney Portal.

Whitney Portal is west of Lone Pine, at an altitude of 8,400 feet. I had been to it once before. One day in March 1962, when I was still single, I jumped into my car and, on a whim, headed north from Los Angeles on 395. I got all the way to Lone Pine and decided to drive up to Whitney Portal. The snow stopped me before I reached the Portal, but I was able to hike to it through the white stuff. I returned to my car and drove back down to Lone Pine, but I wasn't ready to head home. I wanted to go through Death Valley (see chapter 27). To get to the floor of the valley I had to drive over a mountain range. Near the top my 1961 Ford Falcon lost power, but I didn't think anything of it.

I had my first look at the starkly beautiful Death Valley, driving from Stovepipe Wells south to the exit that goes out through Jubilee Pass. Then I proceeded south to Baker, which is on what is now I-15, the main route between Los Angeles and Las Vegas.

I started up the Baker grade toward Los Angeles and my car overheated. I stopped and rested it for a while, then tried again. Again it overheated. I made a U-turn and coasted back down to Baker. By now it was evening, but I found a garage that was open and told the mechanic my problem. He checked my sparkplugs and said that two of the four plugs were bad. I asked him how much replacements would cost. He said five dollars. I had just gotten gas and had exactly five dollars on me. In those days I didn't have any credit cards. He replaced the plugs and I drove home, uneventfully, arriving in the wee hours of the morning.

The weather when Bonny, Andy and I arrived at Whitney Portal was clear and beautiful. We slept in our tent and at 8 a.m. the next day we walked up to the Mt. Whitney trailhead, proposing to reconnoiter the trail for a possible future climb of Whitney, something I had never done, to my sorrow. The sign announced that the peak was 11 long miles away and we knew from the map that the net gain in altitude was over 6,100 feet. Accepted climbing time is two or three days.

Steve climbed Mt. Whitney in the 1960s, taking another and more difficult route called the "Mountaineer's Route." The last 2,000 feet involved climbing a long chimney, down which head-sized boulders came bounding from time to time (sounds like a video game, doesn't it?) and then a 500-foot third-class climb up a cliff that, fortunately, had plenty of handholds and ledges. Of course he was young and vigorous then.

Anyway, the three of us started up the trail. Early on, Bonny let Andy and me go on ahead while she strolled up the trail in a leisurely fashion. She eventually reached Mirror Lake, over five miles from the trailhead. There are two backpackers' campgrounds along the trail, but you have to make reservations for them on the first day reservations are open in the spring because they fill up immediately. Andy and I reached the upper camp in good fashion, before noon. My altitude problem usually kicks in around 10,000 feet and we were well above that, so we each took an aspirin with our lunches.

Next came the endless switchbacks, leading up to the notch in the ridge. There was a patch of ice on the trail at one point and a metal railing to keep hikers from falling off the cliff as they walked around it. Andy's hip started bothering him and he had to stop frequently. I slowly pulled ahead and eventually reached the notch, where the trail enters Sequoia National Park and joins a section of the John Muir Trail. I took a picture of two small lakes far below.

Now the trail rollercoastered both up and down as it went along the backsides of the peaks that had been visible to me during the morning. After a while the John Muir Trail branched off and headed down into the spectacular valley while the Whitney trail headed up again. Two miles to the summit.

Up to this point, I had been fooling myself, making myself believe that I was just out for a hike and it didn't matter how far I went. Otherwise, I might never have started such a daunting climb. But now I had an open window and I was determined to go through it. I wished I were wearing boots with lug soles instead of sneakers. The need became increasingly clear as the altitude robbed me of some of my coordination. I stumbled frequently during the last pitch, but I reached the summit at 3 p.m.

I looked smugly down on the rest of the 48 contiguous states and watched the little birds running around me, looking for handouts. A large rodent, probably cousin to the woodchuck, ambled about the summit, clearly his territory. I had my picture taken by a meditating hedonist who had removed his boots, and I registered my name, noting that a number of people in their 70s had preceded me. The Smithsonian Institution built the summit shelter house in 1909.

I waited for half an hour in hopes that Andy would join me, and then started down. The uphill pitches I had to climb to return to the notch were the hardest part of the whole hike. They exacerbated my nausea and I was glad to leave the notch behind me, even though it meant going down the endless switchbacks, which I had to take fairly slowly. I didn't catch Andy until I was within three miles of the bottom. I learned that he had given up trying to make it to the top and had napped in the sun while he waited for me. We didn't reach the trailhead until after 8 p.m. Bonny had thoughtfully left the car for us, but we almost missed it in the dark, even though we were carrying a small flashlight.

Of course, Bonny had become worried about us, but she had been told that the climb was so long that if we had really gone to the top it would take us a long time to make it back down. Those who have to wait for others to return go through their own emotions, and books have been written about them. Bonny could write one of the books.

CHAPTER 30 Lost in the Colorado Wilderness—Poem

COLORADO MYSTERY

When the earth is baked by the heat of the sun
Till one's sweat tastes like salt, then strange things are done.
The weather called for minimum dress
In Colorado's wilderness.
Even at this high altitude
The heat had the mountain goats subdued.
Five intrepid hikers came to clear
A trail in this rarified atmosphere.
They were Adam and Keith and Al and Dan,
And the lady named Chris, who was younger than
The others, her greatest joy was to spend
Her time with nature; it was her friend.
A ranger was Adam, he had in tow
His ranger talk and his radio.
He babbled about each tree and shrub,
And Dan belonged to the Sierra Club.
Both Keith and Al were there for fun,
To do some hiking and get some sun.
They hadn't come just to relax;
Each carried a tool: a shovel or ax
Or saw, and they went to work with a will.

They chopped and sawed and shoveled with skill,
And as they went they left behind
A trail that those who followed would find
Was erosion-proof and free of trees,
A trail that could be hiked with ease.
They stopped at noon to rest and eat,
And get relief from the sun and heat,
And then once more they set to work;
This wasn't the place for those who shirk.
They finished what they had begun,
And felt good about the things they'd done.
It was late afternoon; Adam led them to
Supplies that were dropped for a fire-fighting crew.
Chris protested because to her this cache
Was nothing more than ranger trash.
At least there was water to slake their thirst,
For the work and heat had done their worst.
They were dragging now, both hot and tired,
No longer fresh, no longer inspired,
And all that they wanted within the hour
Was a place to rest and a nice long shower.
The trail went downhill and it wasn't far
To civilization—a waiting car.
A few minutes later they were surprised
When they counted noses and realized
That Al had completely disappeared.
He had vanished; it was really weird.
He'd been lagging behind (he had a sore knee),
But now he was gone; the mystery
Deepened as they retraced their route
And found not a sign of a pack or a boot,
Or a hat, or a shovel (that Al had carried).
He might as well be dead and buried.
They shouted and whistled; the only sound
They heard in return were the worms in the ground.
Adam called for help on his radio,
And then the group set out to go,

Before it got dark, to the parking place,
Where Chris was to meet her fate face to face.
They were joined by the Alpine Rescue Team,
An awesome group that reined supreme
In finding hikers who had lost their way.
They could hunt by night, they could hunt by day.
They brought three dogs that wouldn't fail
To follow by smell a hiker's trail.
So Keith, after consultation, went
To procure some clothing that had the scent
Of Al. The group then made a plan.
They were led by Charley, a capable man.
When Chris first saw him she was impressed.
He was handsome and smart, and he possessed
The attitudes that she somehow knew
Were compatible with her point of view.
And so, although she was dead tired,
She was able, with effort to get herself fired
Up enough to climb slowly back up the trail.
At first her speed was the speed of a snail,
But she was a hiker and disciplined,
And she gradually gathered her second wind.
At a branch in the trail the party split;
Here Charley asked Chris if she wanted to quit.
(It continued hot and the wind was still.)
She refused, and kept on as the trail went downhill.
Then they saw in the path something lodged in the ground,
Sticking up in the air—a pole that was round.
"It's a shovel," said Chris, and so it was.
This caused the little group to pause.
And on the shovel they found a note,
And on the note they found this quote:
"I'm heading downward on this trail."
It was signed by Al. "We cannot fail,"
Said Charley, "We know his direction."
They soon approached an intersection.
"This intersection forms a T,"

Said Charley, "Let us hope that he
Has left more signs of which way he went."
Poor Chris again was almost spent.
And when she learned that from this spot
All three paths went up she cursed a lot.
Her body sank down to the ground,
But then she cried, "Look what I found!
An orange peel—with 'Al' and an arrow."
"It points to a trail that's steep and narrow,"
Said Charley, "and it climbs a mountain."
Though Chris wished she had her own personal fountain
To slake her thirst and a nice soft bed
To rest her muscles, she forged ahead
With the others; once more they started to climb.
It was steep and hard; they took their time.
They continued on all through the night
With flashlights and the moon for light.
They followed that trail for many a mile.
They searched for more clues all the while.
They were thorough, they were diligent;
They brought the dogs, but those lost the scent.
They never found another trace
Of Al, and no one has seen his face
From that day on; this mystery
Is now part of local history.
And what became of Charley and Chris?
Did they say goodbye without even a kiss?
No! They courted in front of a roaring fire
On camel saddles. To stem their desire
The saddles were placed on either side
Of the fireplace, which was tall and wide.
They couldn't touch so they had to talk;
Then sometimes they went out to walk.
They found they had a lot to tell;
Soon they knew each other very well.
They married, lived happily ever after
Through days of joy and days of laughter.

213

But Chris still has that orange peel.
When she looks at it, it makes her feel
Shivers up and down her spine.
She keeps it as a kind of shrine.
And with its help she'll never forget
That night when she and Charley met.

CHAPTER 31 Lost in the Colorado Wilderness—Story

In June 1990, I attended a Lincoln family reunion (my mother's family) in Colorado. Bonny couldn't attend because of business commitments, but my mother was there, along with various uncles, aunts and cousins (by the dozens).

Several of the halest and heartiest reunionists signed up to go for a hike, starting at the 12,400-foot level of Mt. Evans. Perhaps I shouldn't have counted myself a member of this elite group because a painful knee had bothered me for over six months, but I didn't want to admit that anything could slow me down.

This wasn't an ordinary hike. Cousin Dan Lincoln, a member of the Sierra Club, had agreed to clear a trail in the Mt. Evans Wilderness. In addition to Dan and me, the group included Dan's brother-in-law, Keith, Christiane, who lived with Aunt Freddie (Dan's mother), and a Forest Service employee named Adam. Each of us carried a trail-clearing implement, including a bow saw, two axes (called Pawloskis) and two shovels. It was warm; we wore shorts and T-shirts.

A flock of white mountain goats stood on the road near where Beth, Dan's wife, dropped us off. I took close-up pictures of the longhaired beauties as Christiane urged me not to touch them since they were wild. My first official step of the hike, a two-foot drop to the trail from the road, gave my knee a jolt of pain, but I wasn't going to quit before I got started.

After a mile hike in the wrong direction we corrected the error and set about clearing trail: cutting trees that had fallen on the trail, cleaning out water runoff ditches (called water bars), and generally making it hikeable. The weather was warm and sunny, except at lunchtime, when it rained. Adam stopped at every tree to identify it and talked a blue streak, so our progress was not rapid. As long as we didn't go too fast and I was careful of my knee it didn't bother me, excessively.

Finally, Dan had to call a halt to the clearing process so we could hike out of the wilderness in time for a reunion dinner. At 4 o'clock we refilled our water bottles from supplies parachuted in by the Forest Service a week before. They had been used to aid in fighting a forest fire. Christiane, the idealist, called these supplies ranger trash. Adam defended the forest service, a government agency that could do no wrong.

At 4:30 I was lagging behind the others because my knee was hurting. I realized I was off the trail. I walked a zigzag pattern, looking for signs of a trail on the forest floor. I saw a flash of yellow ahead as Adam's jacket disappeared into the woods from a clearing and figured that if I took a course to that spot I would intersect the trail. I did that and searched the edge of the clearing in the immediate vicinity of where I thought I had seen Adam, but I didn't find the trail.

I had to get to the reunion dinner. I couldn't waste time. I was an experienced hiker. If the others could follow the trail, I could too. I plunged into the woods, in the direction I thought I had seen Adam go, sure that I would pick up the trail soon. Unfortunately, I didn't. It was nowhere to be found and by the time I acknowledged that finding it was not going to be easy I was too far away from the clearing to retrace my steps to it. By leaving the clearing I had violated a rule of search that says, "If you are lost and you know people are looking for you, stay in one place, a place where they are likely to look."

I heard the others calling me, faintly, from what sounded like a great distance. Should I return the shouts? If I taxed my voice with shouting, what would it accomplish? Even if I could make the others hear me, I was so far away from them that they wouldn't be able to pinpoint my direction. In addition, it occurred to me that there was no sense in all of us being off the trail. I remained silent.

Since I wasn't in a place where anyone was likely to look, I set a course along the contour line, keeping the setting sun on my left in order to head north. I gradually lost altitude. I needed to find the parking lot, where a car was waiting for us. I had taken a look at Adam's map when we had stopped for water, but not thinking I would have to navigate on my own, I hadn't tried to memorize it. I did have a compass, but as long as the sun was up I didn't need to use it.

Bushwhacking wasn't difficult, but I did lose a couple of items from my pack, including an old parka, as I scrambled through brush and over and around fallen trees. Occasionally, I had to crawl for a few feet. Sometimes I carried my shovel and sometimes I dragged it behind me. Even though I favored my sore knee I made good progress, and I came to a trail within half an hour. This must be the correct trail. I took it in the downhill direction, which I assumed would take me to the parking lot.

Meanwhile, my companions returned to the clearing and searched for me for an hour. When they didn't find me Adam used his radio to call in the Alpine Rescue Team, a trained group of volunteers. They would bring dogs to help in the search: a Husky, a bloodhound and a German shepherd. My companions agreed to meet them at the parking lot.

I soon realized that I had no reason to carry the shovel. It was heavy and slowed me down. I stuck it into the ground in the middle of the trail. I wrote a note on the inside of a cardboard box that had contained sandwich bags and spiked it onto the wooden handle of the shovel. The note stated that I was heading downhill on the trail.

After considerable downhill hiking I came to a trail intersection in the shape of a T. One of the branches of the T was the continuation of the trail I was on, which a rough sign informed me was called the Cub Creek Trail. The other branch didn't have a name. I didn't have any reason to favor one over the other. I felt very discouraged. For the first time I wondered if I might get so lost that I would never be found.

I rested for 15 minutes and pondered what to do. I was out of writing materials so I wrote my name and an arrow on an orange peel and placed it at the trail intersection, inside a small plastic container, pointing to the continuation of the Cub Creek Trail. Sorry about that, Christiane.

I followed this trail for five minutes, until it started uphill. This had to be wrong. I returned to the intersection, turned the orange peel 180 degrees and set off along the other trail. Within 20 minutes it too was going steadily uphill. In addition, it was poorly maintained and was rapidly disappearing. It would soon peter out, altogether. As I headed back to the intersection again I realized that neither of these alternatives was correct. In fact, all three directions from the intersection went uphill. Wherever I was, it wasn't anywhere near the parking lot.

After I reached the intersection for the third time I took off my shorts and put on my jeans, even though it was still warm. I placed my sweatshirt within easy reach at the top of my pack, nibbled on some of my remaining food, checked my water supply (adequate, because I had refilled my canteen at the supply drop) and got out my compass and flashlight. I remembered that by a stroke of good luck I had some new batteries in my pack. I placed them in the flashlight.

My companions arrived at the parking lot and met the members of the Alpine Rescue Team there. Charley, the leader of the Team, dispatched Keith to drive to Dan's house and acquire an item of my clothing for the dogs to sniff. When Keith arrived, relatives asked him how the hike had gone. He said, "Well...Alan has disappeared." That put a damper on the festivities.

Charley put together a profile of me by asking questions of Dan and the others. He was impressed with my experience and decided that I probably wouldn't panic, even alone in the wilderness. Little did he know. In addition, he said most lost hikers stayed close to where they got lost. Sorry about that, Charley.

It was 7:40 p.m. I could bivouac at the intersection and would be found eventually, I was certain, but it was clear that I would still have to hike up one of the three trails to get out. It was better that I do the uphill hiking now while I still had some energy. I didn't want to retrace my steps so I chose to continue in the direction in which I had been headed, on the Cub Creek Trail. Once again I turned the orange peel 180 degrees and set off. I vowed to follow the trail until I got somewhere—wherever that was. The trail went up—and up—and up.

I heard noises of engines in the distance. Maybe the trail was heading up to a road. With renewed hope I plodded onward and upward. The noises continued, intermittently, but after half an hour they didn't seem to be any closer. I finally figured out what caused them. They were the sounds of the airplanes landing at the Denver airport. I must be directly underneath the flight path. No help there.

Resigned to a long hike, I went slowly to conserve my energy and my sore knee. I was continuously thirsty, but I only sipped at my water. I worried about my relatives worrying about me. At dusk I saw a large shape lying in the middle of the trail. I approached it cautiously. It didn't move. I identified it as a bull elk, complete with velvet-covered antlers. That shook me up. Then I saw the large hole in his side and realized he was dead. I walked on by. His pungent animal odor followed me for some distance after I passed him.

Some of the searchers found my shovel on the trail and reported that fact by radio to Charley and the others. There was modest rejoicing. At least I was still alive and on a trail.

I started to use my flashlight, flicking it on and off to save the batteries. The trail was well maintained and I could sometimes follow the cut through the thick growth of evergreen trees, even with the flashlight off. A waxing quarter moon also added light when its rays could penetrate the trees. I got off the trail a few yards and immediately corrected my mistake. I had to be extra careful now.

Then the trail came to a dead end. It disappeared, just like when I had first gotten lost. It occurred to me that although I would probably be found eventually if I was on a trail, my chances deteriorated significantly if I wasn't. I had to get back on the trail, but I had to be extremely careful how I looked for it. Half a dozen times I returned to the spot where I thought I had left the trail and headed in different directions, but the result was always the same. No trail. Finally, I retraced my steps another 15 yards and found that what I had thought was the trail wasn't. Fortunately, the real trail now appeared as a white strip, lit by the flashlight and the moon.

Relief flooded through me. Moving more slowly and cautiously than ever, I continued along the trail. It leveled off and headed downhill. I learned later that I had hiked over Shadow Mountain at 10,500 feet, from a low of 9,000 feet. The moving shadows caused by the flashlight shining on the bushes beside the trail looked like animals slinking through the night. I searched nervously for bears. Why else would this be called the Cub Creek Trail?

Then I received the first really good news since I had found the trail after I became lost. I passed a sign, facing in the opposite direction from where I was heading. I turned around and read it. The sign welcomed hikers to the Mt. Evans wilderness area. I reasoned this meant that I must be *leaving* the Mt. Evans wilderness area—and, hopefully, approaching civilization.

Another sign marked the national forest boundary. This boundary followed the trail in the form of a barbed wire fence. Could those be lights in the distance? They were—more signs of civilization. Should I leave the trail and go cross-country, directly toward the lights? No. I had done enough foolish things for one day. There was no way to judge how far away they were.

At about 11 p.m. I reached a fence that marked the end of the trail. I was never so glad to see a "No Parking" sign. I was now on a dirt road. There were houses along the road. I would go up to one of the houses and ask for help.

Most of the houses were dark. I took the road in the downhill direction, looking for a house with lights on. I spotted one with a relatively short driveway. I shone my flashlight on the porch by the front door and a large dog, stationed there, started barking at me. I decided against this house. It occurred to me that dogs and people made this area more dangerous than the woods.

Another lit house. I walked cautiously up the driveway. No dogs. Onto the front porch. No door. The porch continued around to the side. The door must be there. I peeked around the corner at an uncovered window of a brightly lit room. A bare foot was in evidence. The picture was clear. A man was facing the window, probably watching television. I had to pass the window to get to the door. When I did the man would either have a heart attack or shoot me. I retreated to the road.

The road went steadily downhill, but it seemed to continue forever. I flagged down the first moving car I had seen since coming out of the woods. Blinded by the lights I couldn't see the occupants. I said hello, and from the response I knew there was a teenage girl in the car. After a few seconds I could see that there were two of them. Afraid of scaring them and getting myself into more trouble, I asked them how to find a telephone. They said to go all the way down to the bottom of the road and turn left. I asked them if I was near Conifer (where my cousin Carol lived). They said Conifer was to the right at the bottom of the road.

I finally reached the telephone at 12:30 a.m. I tried to find Carol's number in the phone book, but it wasn't listed. Not wanting to fool around any longer, I dialed 911 and told the operator I had been lost and could she send a sheriff's deputy. She asked if I was at the Brook Forest Inn. I said it sounded logical (I was on Brook Forest Drive and there was an inn across the street). She put me on hold. When she came back on the line she asked me if I needed medical aid. I said no, but I thought people were looking for me and could she call them off? She said she could and she would also send a sheriff's deputy.

While I waited I found Dan's telephone number in the book. Dan lives in Evergreen. I had no change in my pockets so I called collect. My Aunt Kim answered, but didn't immediately accept the call. That was because she thought it was Bonny, calling from California, and Kim didn't know what to tell her. I didn't recognize Kim's voice and told the operator I thought she had dialed the wrong number. She got huffy. Then my mother came on the line and accepted the call. She sounded relieved to hear from me. I told her I would call back with my location.

The deputy arrived and had his dispatcher call Dan's number again to get somebody to pick me up at the Brook Forest Inn. Aunt Freddie, who also lives in Evergreen, knew where the inn was. Of course, Dan was still out looking for me. The deputy gave me the orange from his lunch and said I had walked a long way. I already knew that.

Freddie, my mother and my Uncle Lou arrived a little after 1:30 a.m. The deputy asked Freddie her age so he could fill out his paperwork. Like most women, she was reluctant to give it and asked him why he needed it. Lou chimed in and said, ingenuously, "Don't you remember? You and Joyce (his wife) were born on the same day, bla-bla-bla." I think Freddie wondered why she had bothered to rescue me.

Charley and the Alpine Rescue Team didn't get credit for a "find" because I walked out of the woods before they caught me. Finds are what they live for since they don't get paid. However, Charley found something better—a wife. He and Christiane started dating. Until they got to know each other better they sat on the camel saddles on either side of Freddie's large fireplace, to avoid temptations of the flesh, and talked. After doing this for a while they realized that they were made for each other.

I don't normally like to cause trouble for people. During this escapade I caused trouble for my relatives and the members of the Alpine Rescue Team. I certainly appreciate their concern and their help. Incidentally, if I had taken the Cub Creek Trail upward instead of downward at the time I first found it I would have intersected the correct trail shortly thereafter.

Part IV Long Walks

Even walkers who think nothing of covering several miles every day may consider the idea of completing a marathon as unthinkable. However, what is a long walk but a series of short walks strung together? And what is a multi-day walk but a series of one-day walks strung together? There are both challenges and benefits from long-distance walking that we won't receive by walking around the block.

First, Ethan Loewenthal tells what it's like to walk the Appalachian Trail. Then I tell about my three long walks. I give enough detail so that anybody who hears the call can reproduce them. On the other hand, I try to include enough human-interest stories to keep the attention of the casual reader. Such as the effect the events of 9/11 had on us when we were in Great Britain in September 2001 (see chapter 42).

Alan Cook

CHAPTER 32 Appalachian Trail

The Appalachian Trail winds through 14 states, from Springer Mountain in Georgia to Mt. Katahdin in Maine. It is over 2,000 miles long. Ethan Loewenthal walked the Trail, starting on April 4, 1999 and ending on October 8, 1999. He was just 20 years old when he started and celebrated his 21st birthday on the Trail. The following are his own words about walking the Trail.

My parents like to tell the story, grinning, of the first time I saw the ocean. They say that I took one long look and then raising my arms, I roared at it like a lion. Granted, I was only a year old at the time, but I like to think that was the beginning of the feeling that brought me to the Appalachian Trail. And it wasn't until I hiked the entire thing 20 years later that I began to understand that feeling.

That feeling, it turns out, is my desire to be in the presence of bigness. And it's why when my family goes to the beach now, my favorite thing to do is get crushed by breaking waves. I mean this literally, which is why my family is never very happy about it. I like to fight my way out to the breakers, wait for a good one, suck in some air and then get flipped over and tossed and slammed against the bottom. And it's all I can do to keep my mouth shut until I make my way to the surface again, because when I do I'm gasping and sputtering and laughing hysterically, and thinking to myself, "God, ocean, you're so strong." And then I limp back up to the house, hip bruised and back scraped up by seashells.

When I pass my sister, she turns to see the blood. "Great. Good job, Ethan," she says, in total disapproval, knowing exactly what I've done. But I'm still smiling and feeling that energy and knowing again why I roared at the ocean: It wasn't a challenge or a desire to compete with it. It wasn't aggression and it wasn't testosterone; it wasn't a stunt and it wasn't ego. It was a provocation. I wanted it to come and get me, swallow me up and show me its power. It was appreciation.

For me, the Trail was just another wave I was stepping in front of. It was another provocation, another deal I had made with the world: I would put in the miles, and it would deliver me to a new place, one of heightened emotions and grand aspirations. That's why I felt humbled and privileged to be out there experiencing it, even after epic 24-mile days over several mountains, on days when my body had performed so beautifully. Even though I was the one who hiked it, it was about so much more than my personal effort. Yes, the doing came from me, but the reward did not. The reward was everything that I could not control; the reward was what it felt like. The walking was just the tool to make it happen.

And this was nothing new to the human experience—doing something hard and not quitting. It's just that it was the first time for me, and I was getting a glimpse of it. Like seeing my first tornado or falling in love for the first time, this was just something huge I was crossing paths with, something huge I had worked hard to put myself in the path of.

This theme of experiencing the bigness of the physical world was there on the Trail all the time and was the source of both inspiration and fear for me—fear when I was shown how big it really was, and inspiration when I kept going despite that fear. I won't say I bit off more than I could chew, but hiking the Appalachian Trail was biting off a lot, and I first realized that when, three weeks into the hike, the day after we walked into Great Smoky Mountains National Park, I ended up in the hospital, vomiting and dehydrated, and convinced I was going home.

For a lot of reasons, including having eaten too much greasy food in the last town, I woke up that first morning in the Park, throwing up and feeling miserable. Before my friends and other hikers realized how sick I was, they were gone, on to the next shelter, and I was already getting dehydrated. My limbs tingled, I was dizzy, I couldn't sleep and I couldn't stop puking. It was the kind of feeling that makes the world seem viciously large, the kind of feeling that makes you promise you'll never again do anything to make yourself feel this way, certainly not try to walk from Georgia to Maine. I cursed myself. What was I thinking to take on something so big?

I began dreading what I would have to do: strap on my 50-pound pack, hike several miles back out of the park and call an ambulance. I lay there in the shelter as the day warmed up, putting off what was inevitable, looking out at the trees, which were getting blurry now, and thinking the wave I had picked was too big. I was going to get crushed for real this time.

I stumbled and moaned my way down the mountain. I would walk until I couldn't stand it anymore, and then find a downed tree and lean over it and get up what I could, a small puddle of yellow bile maybe—a little reward, I thought; a little prize for my efforts. And then I would feel better for another mile or so. "So this is quitting," I thought. I wasn't thinking about what I would do when I got home, and I wasn't thinking about the life that my friends would have on the Trail without me after I was gone, and I wasn't disappointed. I wasn't anything, really, just a bumbling, vomiting, barely conscious mess that was done with the Trail. No decision had been made—it just was. My hike was over. The wave was rising up, peaking, and about to break, and I wasn't about to let it fall on me this time. I had to turn around.

Crossing Fontana Dam (in North Carolina), I could see the payphone, but I wouldn't make it. "All right, one more time." I leaned over the edge of the dam, looked down at the expanse of concrete flaring out hundreds of feet below me, and spinning now, I produced a few green globs that floated down and then disappeared. I choked on the burn in the back of my throat. "So, this is what it is," I thought. "It's concrete and dirt and water, and none of it cares that I'm here." Earth, the ultimate strong and silent type, was letting out a great silent roar right back at me, and I couldn't hold up to it. "I won't provoke you anymore. I promise."

The next day, I broke that promise. I had been taken to the hospital by ambulance, filled with saline, given anti-nausea drugs, and driven to a motel by a policeman. And when I woke up I was on a new planet. I was better, my head was clear and I had the same feeling that I would later have every morning after I swore I would quit: "I can't quit. I don't know how. Maybe tomorrow, but today I don't know how."

The surprising thing was, it felt like a betrayal to get back out there, like I was being a fair-weather friend to myself, and I felt disappointed for not carrying out my plan to quit. But the draw was too great. Taking just one more step was always easier than the mechanics of getting myself off the Trail and home. It became what seemed like an evil temptation—just one more step, just one more mile and then I'll go home. To some, it must seem like masochism; I've even heard that A.T. stands for Addictive Torture. But I believe it's possible to see it in a different light. I believe that to understand why I got back on the Trail, repeatedly, is to see fear as a portal to greatness, and from there to know the exhilaration of running straight towards it when you have the option of running in any other direction.

So I was back on the Trail, but that episode scared me. There was no telling if it would happen again, and if so, where I would be. I had been lucky to be camped only a few miles into the woods that time, but in Maine there would be a stretch of forest with no help available for a hundred miles. Would I be alone by then? And that was months away; could I even make it that far?

Three weeks later, in Damascus, Virginia, it did happen again. And I recovered again and got back on the Trail, but it was different after that. The possibility of illness hung over me all the time, especially during those first few months when my body was adjusting and exhaustion made me emotionally fragile. In six weeks the hike had switched from a physical journey to a walk inside of my own heart. The walking was still hard, always an incredible labor, always epic days, but overcoming the fear became the focus for me, and the fantasy of reaching that wooden sign on top of Mt. Katahdin and collapsing and having a good cry for all the effort I had put in became a recurring daydream when the trail was steep.

I didn't start to put this into words until we met a woman later in the summer who told us, "The ones who make it are the ones with the biggest hearts." And this was good to hear, and I wanted to believe it was this simple, and this flattering, but it was only part of what I was learning. The full truth was that staying out there came not from finding the will, but from not allowing the fatigue to steal the will I already had. And that could happen no matter how big my heart was. It had happened in the Smokies—I broke like a toothpick that time— and it could easily happen again. All it would take was that miserable exhaustion ratcheted up enough to take my mental edge for good. So I decided that doubt and hopelessness were precisely my cues to keep going, maybe even go harder, and from then on all negatives had been turned back on themselves, and I knew my mission: defy. Ultimately, it was that defiance that inspired even myself.

But until then, searching for inspiration elsewhere was important in the continual efforts to fend off the quitting. I found a lot of that in stories of others who had done hard things and not quit, many of them athletes, and especially Lance Armstrong. The year I hiked was the year he came back from cancer to win the Tour de France for the first time. He had survived testicular cancer that had spread to his lungs and brain, and yet here he was winning the 2000-mile bike race. "You're blowing up the Tour de France!" his coach had yelled into his earpiece when he was winning one of the time trials.

It was so easy to imagine us covering those 2000 miles—him pedaling, me walking. I thought of his chemotherapy and the feeling of puking off Fontana Dam, multiplied a thousand times, and on top of that the very real possibility of falling off, of floating down and then disappearing. For the first time in my life I had chills thinking about great triumphs, and I had an answer to them; I was walking to Maine.

And to make it there, I also learned, I needed other hikers. I had planned the hike, thinking I would be alone for weeks at a time and had mentally prepared myself for that. But I realized I couldn't afford to be out there alone, partly for safety reasons, but also because sharing our experience became the experience. These were all people who had spent hours and hours waiting in line at the grocery store, sitting in class, struggling through seminars, and waiting at stoplights, daydreaming about hiking 2000 miles through 14 states, just like I had.

That was a guarantee with all other thru-hikers before I even met them, that they shared that exact same feeling. Just showing up at Springer Mountain was proof enough that they believed in making the romance a reality. Having been away from it a few years now, I think it can be very difficult for people to return to life away from the Trail, because it's so hard to find such an immediate and true connection anywhere else in this society. There's rarely a reason for it.

It wasn't until closer to the end of my hike, when I had learned enough about my body to avoid illness that I was able to focus more on the walking, itself. I had started out thinking nothing of walking and nothing of backpacking. Even though I had always been into endurance sports like running and biking and rowing, that laboring was just going to be a tool for me, a tool to get me out in front of that breaking wave. But once I felt more confident that I wouldn't get sick again, I started to think more about the act of walking. Trying to keep my center of gravity at the same level as I stepped over rocks and dips and trying to move as efficiently as possible became a fun challenge. Walking became a simple way to seek grace.

CHAPTER 33 California Coast—Poem

CALIFORNIA COASTWALK

A jagged line from Oregon to Mexico
drawn long ago
by a child too young to get it straight.
It calls the restless to their fate.
It sings a song of crashing waves
and squawking birds and sailors' graves;
a route of sea-worn rocks and silky sand
and crumbling cliffs on unstable land.
Follow the roads and the railroad tracks;
walk across the fields where the woodsman's ax
once rang; but now they're full
of sheep and cows—keep an eye out for a bull!
The stately Redwoods touch the sky,
too old to play, too young to die.
But play do dolphins, seals and whales;
the otters and the elk tell tales
of crunching abalone shells
and locking horns and smelling smells
of shipwrecks, wafted on the breeze,
and exotic islands in exotic seas.

So come to the shore of which we boast
and walk with me on the sunset coast.

From Mexico embark
on this journey at Border Field State Park.
Head north along the Silver Strand—
between bodies of water a needle of land;
across the Coronado Bridge,
(only on special days is this pilgrimage
allowed for walkers) through bustling San Diego.
After Mission Bay go
along Pacific Beach, La Jolla, Torrey Pines,
Del Mar, Solana Beach; the sun shines
on those who live here; there's Cardiff By the Sea,
Encinitas, Leucadia (a jug of wine and thee);
on to Carlsbad and Oceanside;
across Camp Pendleton on a surging tide;
San Onofre,
San Clemente, Doheny.
Dana Point reflects the past
in this seaman's book, *Two Years Before the Mast*.
Laguna, Emerald Bay, Crystal Cove, Corona del Mar,
Balboa, Newport—home to many a tar;
Huntington, Bolsa Chica, Sunset, Seal;
and Long Beach—its expanses reveal
that it's well named; the harbors of Long Beach and LA
beside San Pedro—on San Pedro Bay;
across the Vincent Thomas Bridge;
again, walkers may make this pilgrimage
only when gods and civic leaders smile;
Palos Verdes Peninsula is worth the while
of the traveler; then on to Torrance, Redondo,
Hermosa, Manhattan and El Segundo;
Dockweiler, Playa del Rey
and Marina del Rey on a summer day;
then Venice (but not Italy),
Will Rogers, Topanga, Las Tunas, the sea;

the siren call of Malibu,
Corral, Point Dume, Zuma, Carrillo and Point Mugu;
Point Hueneme and Oxnard Beach;
McGrath and Ventura within easy reach;
Emma Wood, Seacliff and Carpinteria;
and on to Santa Barbara to see a
view of the students at Isla Vista;
El Capitan, and who can resist a
closer look at Refugio
and Gaviota, but on we go
to Point Conception and Vandenberg AFB;
to Surf, Point Sal and history.
Pismo Beach—vroom! vroom!
Grover City and Shell have plenty of room;
Avila, Point San Luis, Montana de Oro,
and on to the Rock and Bay known as Morro;
Atascadero and then Cayucos,
Harmony, Cambria, San Simeon and glucose;
the Big Sur digs of W. R. Hearst,
with zebras and such—but who was here first?
Piedras Blancas and Ragged Point;
Gorda, Point Lucia, fountains to anoint
the intrepid walker; John Little, Burns, Molera, Point Sur,
Point Lobos, Carmel, Pebble Beach go by in a blur;
Pacific Grove via Seventeen Mile Drive;
Monterey, Sand City, Marina, then arrive
via Moss Landing and Sunset at old Santa Cruz;
to Davenport and Año Nuevo to lose the blues;
Pigeon Point, Bean Hollow and Pescadero;
Pomponio and San Gregorio;
Tunitas and on to Half Moon Bay;
Montara, Gray Whale Cove, San Pedro Point and Rockaway;
Pacifica and San Francisco;
and across the Golden Gate we go
to Stinson, Bolinas and Point Reyes;
Dillon and Bodega Bay, it says;
Salmon, Shell, Sonoma, Armstrong, Jenner, Fort Ross;

233

Salt Point, Sea Ranch, Gualala know who's boss;
Anchor Bay and Point Arena.
Have you seen a
nicer place than Elk or Mendocino?
On to Jug Handle, Fort Bragg and we know
to MacKerricher, Westport, Cape Vizcaino we'll rove;
the Lost Coast to Sinkyone and Shelter Cove;
Honeydew, Petrolia, Capetown, Ferndale;
Eureka and Arcata faster than airmail;
McKinleyville, Little River and Trinidad;
Patrick's Point and Big Lagoon (it's bad);
Humboldt Lagoon, Klamath and Redwood Park;
Crescent City and Smith River on a lark;
to Pelican Beach and the Oregon border;
then back to a life of schedules and order.

CHAPTER 34 California Coast—Mexican Border through Los Angeles County

I started walking the California coast by accident. Bonny, Andy and I moved to the Palos Verdes Peninsula, which is on the coast 10 miles south of the Los Angeles Airport, in June 1971. The peninsula rises to an altitude of 1,500 feet and has many scenic walks. Most of these walks have a view of the ocean.

During the first few years we lived here I took walks on and around the peninsula. In addition, I walked the beaches directly to the north. By 1974, I had walked the section of the coast from San Pedro to Santa Monica, a distance of about 30 miles. I kept reading about a local family whose members were walking the California coast a little bit at a time. That sounded like fun, and I enjoyed walking on the beach so much I decided to attempt to walk the whole coast.

I enlisted Bonny and Andy to be my support team. Bonny said she would take the job on condition that no vacation time would be used for walking (we were both working full time). Vacations were reserved for real trips. She also made the stipulation that I couldn't go on any overnight trips without her. She was afraid I would get lost or otherwise get into trouble. Her fears were justified. Because of these restrictions, on my coastwalk I never walked for more than three days in a row.

To give myself a chance to actually complete the walk I had to be opportunistic. I made a rule that I could walk the sections of the coast in any order and in either direction. No day's walk was too short. I walked pieces on more than 64 different days. After I officially declared I was walking the coast my first day's walk occurred on April 28, 1974. I completed the walk on March 4, 1984.

To be honest (and when I met Bonny I told her I was a pathological truth-teller) I completed all but one small section—over the Coronado Bridge in San Diego, because no foot traffic was allowed on the bridge. When I learned that there were officially sanctioned run/walks over the bridge I signed up for one and actually walked across it in October 1994.

In spite of my walking and hiking experience, I was a novice at long, multi-day walks. The farthest I ever went in three days when I was walking the coast was 70 miles. I hadn't yet learned how to take care of my feet and avoid getting blisters. In comparison, when I was walking from Los Angeles to Denver I once walked 43 miles in one day and another time I walked 108 miles in three days.

One morning, during my coast walk, I was tired and sore from the previous day's efforts. I could hardly move. The only reason I kept going was because I was in the middle of nowhere and I had nothing else to do. I had come a long way to walk so I had to at least make an effort. Gradually, my muscles became more flexible and my speed picked up. I ended up walking 30 miles that day.

Knowing that I could keep going when I wasn't at my best helped me on my other long walks. Until I got close to finishing the whole coast, I couldn't use that goal to spur me on because it seemed unreachable. Instead, I had to concentrate on getting to the next milepost, and sometimes just the next rock or tree.

In order for the story of the walk to make sense I am telling it in geographical sequence, from south to north, starting at the Mexican border and heading north to the Oregon border. Since I didn't actually walk it in this order the story will jump backward and forward in time, but I will try to make it as seamless as possible.

I did start at the Mexican border, in San Diego County, on my first official walking day, April 28, 1974. There is a park at the border named, appropriately enough, Border Field State Park. A monument here is named the Mexican Border Monument. As I walked north I took the isthmus to Coronado to avoid the industrial area east of San Diego Bay.

I was cruising along the beach in an area called the Silver Strand when a naval officer came cruising along in his jeep. He warned me that there might be unexploded shells on the beach. Heeding his words, I took Route 75 the rest of the way to the Coronado Bridge. As I mentioned before, the Coronado Bridge, which goes over the bay to the mainland, is usually not open to foot traffic. I didn't actually cross it until 20 years later.

It wasn't until August 16, 1975 that I walked the next stretch, from the east end of the Coronado Bridge to Torrey Pines Beach State Park (I walked it north to south). From the bridge the route goes north on Harbor Drive, Lowell Street, Nimitz Boulevard, Sunset Cliffs Boulevard and West Mission Bay Drive. Mission Bay and Pacific Beach both have scrumptious beaches, with easy walking.

Sea World is located on Mission Bay. I don't go to Sea World anymore. Some years ago Marineland of the Pacific was located on the Palos Verdes Peninsula. The owners of Sea World bought Marineland and in the middle of the night (this is a true story) they took the killer whales from Marineland and transported them to Sea World in San Diego. The next morning residents of Palos Verdes whose homes overlooked Marineland scanned the pools for their beloved orcas, but they were gone. Marineland was closed in 1987. Self-respecting residents of Palos Verdes no longer patronize Sea World.

La Jolla is north of Pacific Beach, with its expensive homes and rocky beach. There are much-used paths on the cliffs above the beach that also give a good view of the La Jolla caves. North of La Jolla there is good beach walking through the Torrey Pines area. Blacks Beach is located here, one of the most famous clothing-optional beaches in California. Unfortunately, the day I walked along this beach all the optionals were men.

The stretch north from Torrey Pines to Oceanside is easy beach walking most of the way. In places the going gets stony at high tide, but you can always leave the beach temporarily. For a list of the names of beaches along this and other parts of the California coast, see my poem, "California Coastwalk," in chapter 33. The only problem I had was getting down the cliff to the beach at Torrey Pines. I finally found a steep path opposite the golf course.

The next part of the walk goes through Camp Pendleton. I don't know whether walkers can get official permission to go through Camp Pendleton. I didn't. I have a book showing the California coast bicycle route. It states that bicycle travel within Camp Pendleton is restricted to daylight hours. I walked through Camp Pendleton from north to south, starting at San Clemente State Beach.

This is how I did it. I had to leave the beach to detour around the San Onofre Atomic Power Station, but I was able to walk on the sand the length of San Onofre State Beach, a secluded area with access only by half a dozen footpaths. I was breezing merrily along the beach on Camp Pendleton when Bonny drove down to the beach and intercepted me. She told me there was a secure area ahead. She had obtained a car pass for Camp Pendleton. I walked the rest of the way to the south entrance of Camp Pendleton on the road, with Bonny driving beside me. I hopped into the camper for the last few feet before the guard shack so the guard wouldn't get suspicious. We came out of Camp Pendleton at Harbor Drive, Oceanside, near the multi-story condominium building.

North of San Clemente State Beach, in Orange County, is an area with private homes on the beach. Although by law all the land below the mean high tide line is public property, I had to skirt these homes the day I passed them because the tide was in. I walked past them on the railroad tracks. North of here is Doheny State Beach and Dana Point, named after Richard Henry Dana, who wrote about his sailing expedition along the California coast during the 1830s in the book, *Two Years Before the Mast*.

My log states that I walked the two miles south from Crown Valley Parkway to Dana Point with Andy and that Bonny rode back to meet us on her new bicycle (after parking the car at Dana Point).

I walked the section from Crown Valley Parkway north to Seal Beach on four consecutive Wednesday evenings, after work. Because I was alone I walked a roundtrip each time. North of Crown Valley Parkway is the artsy-craftsy city of Laguna Beach. Each year the residents present the Pageant of the Masters, a show in which real people take the places of figures in paintings and sculptures. When a tableau is properly lit the actors disappear into the background of the painting and become part of it. The only deviation from reality I've seen is that in the nude scenes male actors wear loincloths.

The coast at Laguna is broken up by rocks and cliffs, which form many small and secluded coves and bays. The bad news is that it is impossible to walk on the sand for long distances without coming up to the road to avoid a cliff. Public access paths between the houses that line the beach make the job of the walker easier, however. In the center of town there is a small park, with paths and picnic tables.

At low tide it is possible to walk on the sand from the north end of Laguna Beach to Corona Del Mar State Beach. It is necessary to walk on Route 1 (Pacific Coast Highway) through parts of Newport Beach, but Huntington Beach is a long and wide and lovely beach, with easy walking on the sand.

North of the Huntington Beach pier there is a rocky area on the beach that is impassable at high tide. However, from here it is smooth walking on the sand all the way to Surfside, north of Sunset Beach. Surfside is a private community and I wasn't able to walk on the beach here. North of Surfside the beach walking is good through Seal Beach. The evening I did this part of the walk I received a $5 parking ticket from the Seal Beach police. That was in 1975. I'm sure the ticket would cost more now.

North of Seal Beach is Los Angeles County. A combination of street and sand walking takes one through aptly named Long Beach to the Gerald Desmond Bridge, which goes to Terminal Island and the Long Beach Harbor. One of the ships visible here is the permanently docked Queen Mary. It is legal to walk across the Gerald Desmond Bridge, but not the Vincent Thomas Bridge at the other end of Terminal Island. On the day I did this part of the walk I made a long detour north, across another bridge, then came back around to Western Avenue and 25th Street in San Pedro. Much later, in November 1993, I walked across the Vincent Thomas Bridge on an officially sanctioned walk/run, even though I didn't need to do it to make a connection.

25th Street becomes Palos Verdes Drive South, which follows the coast all the way around the Palos Verdes Peninsula, becoming Palos Verdes Drive West when the coast turns north. In places it is possible to get to the beach, with difficulty, but there are many cliffs and rocks and coves. Donald Trump owns the Ocean Trails golf course on Palos Verdes Drive South.

My city, Rancho Palos Verdes, used to have its very own secluded nude beach at Portuguese Cove, somewhat bohemian for a conservative middle-class area, but the city fathers and mothers eventually made nudity illegal, apparently because of reports of illicit sexual activity (homo, not hetero). See chapter 8 for more on this. There is a permanent landslide in this area, which swept away several hundred houses in the late 1950s. The utility pipes are kept above ground and Palos Verdes Drive South has alarming dips and undergoes more or less continuous repairs.

As the coast turns north you pass the Point Vicente lighthouse and whale-watching center. After crossing into Palos Verdes Estates you pass a prime surfing cove, much prized by the locals. So prized that in the past they have gone to great lengths to keep other surfers out. There have been reports of slashed tires and even fights. On a cliff near here my half-uncle Karl got married at sunset.

The beach at Malaga Cove, on the north side of Palos Verdes Peninsula, is called Rat Beach by the locals. Supposedly, this means, "right after Torrance," since Torrance Beach is immediately north of it. It is possible to walk on the sand from here all the way north to Marina Del Rey, with only a short detour to get by the Redondo Beach Pier and King Harbor Marina. After Torrance and Redondo come Hermosa Beach and Manhattan Beach and then the open area behind the Los Angeles Airport. A lot of two-person beach volleyball is played here, and both Hermosa and Manhattan host major professional tournaments.

You never know what you might run into on the beach. One day I was walking along Redondo Beach in a high wind when a large beach umbrella came cartwheeling across the sand. Thinking that it could hurt somebody, I stepped in front of it and was able to grab the handle. A panting man came running up to recover it.

You can take the bike path around Marina Del Rey and then there are more good beaches through Venice and Santa Monica. Venice Beach is known for its interesting characters, such as the street performers who juggle chainsaws, among other things. Colorfully dressed in-line skaters dance near the bike path and all kinds of souvenirs are sold.

When niece Ellen first moved to California she lived in an old apartment building on Venice Beach, quaint but impractical. One of the best pictures I have ever taken is of Ellen sitting on the railing of the fourth floor balcony of the building, at sunset. In the background you can see dozens of people below, walking along the beach.

I was able to walk from Will Rogers State Beach in Santa Monica north to Corral Beach, completely on the beach. The significance is that this route goes through Malibu, where the rich and famous have tried to block access to the beach. Although there are some public-access paths to the beach in Malibu, the locals have put up a strong and long fight against opening more. In addition, some houses are built so close to the high-tide line that I found myself walking between support pillars once in a while. I walked a roundtrip on this day and at high tide parts of the route were impassable without actually walking through houses. I was chicken to try this, but with more guts I might have met a celebrity or two. Or their bodyguards.

The coast runs mostly east and west from Santa Monica to Point Conception, which is west of Santa Barbara. Heading west from Corral Beach, the beach is passable at low tide to Leo Carrillo State Beach, beyond Point Dume and Zuma Beach. I did some climbing and scrambling to get around Point Dume. The beach ran out at a point between Zuma Beach and Leo Carrillo State Beach because I arrived exactly at high tide. After waiting for some time for the tide to subside I grew impatient and waded through the surf to the next walkable section of beach.

CHAPTER 35 California Coast—Ventura County through San Francisco

In Ventura County I walked on the local streets to get around Point Mugu and the Naval Air Station. This is an agricultural area, with lots of vegetables (lettuce, cabbage, spinach, tomatoes) and fruit trees, especially lemon. From the Point Mugu missile display at Wood Road and Route 1 I walked north on Navalair Road and west on Hueneme Road. I went north on Ventura Road through the city of Port Hueneme and past the Navy Seabee headquarters and museum. I trudged west on Channel Islands Boulevard, past the Channel Islands Harbor and north on Harbor Boulevard in the city of Oxnard.

I rejoined the coast and saw houses on the beach that were built on stilts. High tide the morning I was there had washed past these houses and across the road behind them. The porch of one house had been damaged several weeks earlier. What did the Bible say about building your house on the sand? Maybe it was talking about sand near water. I walked on the sand through part of Ventura. One stretch was too rocky to walk on. It was low tide and hundreds of clam diggers were on the beach digging up hundreds of clams.

West of Ventura, I walked into Santa Barbara County on the sand. After I passed Carpenteria I had to walk on the road and railroad tracks for a while. I also had to wade across a lagoon in a swampy area called El Estero to avoid taking a detour. I hate taking detours and have gotten into trouble upon occasion for trying to always go in

242

a straight line. Some houses are built on the rocks beside the water, making it very difficult to pass them on the beach. No trespassing signs are everywhere. On the day I walked this stretch (April 3, 1976) it rained hard in the afternoon.

The beach area is very walkable through Santa Barbara. West of Santa Barbara, a bike path and road cross Goleta Slough to Goleta Beach County Park, just east of Isla Vista, where the campus of the University of California at Santa Barbara is located. On the sand dunes near Isla Vista the dress code on the beach was very relaxed and many of the beachgoers were students.

I stayed on the beach between there and El Capitan State Beach. I had to walk on the railroad tracks above the beach most of the way between El Capitan and Gaviota State Beach, except for a brief section at Refugio State Beach. Part of the reason may have been because there was a full moon and resulting high tide on the day I walked this stretch.

Between Gaviota State Beach and Jalama Beach the coast starts heading north again. Just west of Gaviota the beach is impassable and it is necessary to walk on the road, but after a bit it is possible to descend the cliff and walk on the sand. I found many abalone shells on the beach east of Government Point. I collected a bunch of them; they are still sitting on our back patio.

I also encountered some surfers who had driven down private roads through Hollister Ranch to the beach. One challenged me, although of course it is legal to walk on the beach. He suspected that I had gone through private property to get there. I didn't feel I had to answer to him because it was obvious that was exactly what he had done (he claimed he had permission).

Between Government Point and Point Conception, the cliffs make the beach impassable again. I climbed the cliff and walked around the offending area. I may have trespassed on government property going past the Point Conception lighthouse (but I'm a taxpayer, right?).

On the walk from Jalama Beach north to Surf (at the end of Route 246, west of Lompoc) the beach is impassable most of the way. I walked on the railroad tracks above the beach. On the day I did this stretch four trains passed, two freight and two Amtrak. Miles and miles of pastureland bordered the ocean, with hundreds of cows. I saw many other animals, including rabbits, squirrels, snakes, hawks and pigeons. My log also notes strange cactus-like plants and pretty wildflowers. I passed the Point Arguello Coast Guard Station, but I saw very few people the whole day.

I actually walked this bit from north to south. I started out from Surf at low tide and walked on the sand for several miles. The cliffs came ever closer to the ocean. I waded through shallow water at one point and began to get claustrophobia. When I arrived at a cliff that was impassable I wisely (for once) retraced my steps to an abandoned stairway going to the top of the cliff. A concrete dock was at the bottom of the stairs. I climbed the stairs very carefully (they were not in good repair) and that's when I took to the railroad tracks.

I walked through Vandenberg Air Force Base with my coworker, Don, his teenage daughter, Jennifer and her friend, Beth. Perhaps I figured that since I was probably breaking the law I wanted company. I had written to the Commanding General of Vandenberg, asking for permission to walk across the base, but he didn't condescend to answer me.

We actually covered the distance from Surf north to Point Sal, but in reverse order, since we walked from north to south. We saw a few people on the base, but they didn't bother us. It is possible to walk on the beach near Surf. Then there are dirt roads to follow. At Purisima Point we climbed up sand dunes and joyously slid down them. There is a wide and beautiful beach north of Purisima Point. Near Point Sal we walked on a paved road because, as we found out, it isn't possible to get around the cliff south of Point Sal on the beach.

The walk from Point Sal to Oso Flaco Lake, in San Luis Obispo County, was an interesting one. I hiked two hair-raising trails, one on the hill going around Point Sal and another going around Mussel Rock. What made them hair-raising was the exposure; they went right along the edge of the cliff. On the secluded beach between Point Sal and Mussel Rock I saw a shack with a sign that read "Hotel California."

There is a wide beach north of Mussel Rock. Motor vehicles such as dune buggies are permitted here. I had to wade across the Santa Maria River and the creek from Oso Flaco Lake to the ocean. Neither one was more than a foot deep. I followed the creek from the lake through the sand dunes to the beach (I walked north to south) and then followed the beach to Mussel Rock. I saw many birds during the day, including pelicans. I also saw seals, both living and dead.

I had a miserable experience walking on Pismo State Beach, north of Oso Flaco Lake, which also allows all terrain vehicles and dune buggies. The problem wasn't just the noise and confusion of the vehicles. Fortunately, I was walking north to south, which actually meant in a somewhat easterly direction, because there was a strong wind blowing constantly from the west. It did act as a sort of sail for me and I was glad I wasn't walking the other way.

North of Pismo Beach the coast is so jagged that it is impossible to walk on the beach for very long at a time. Houses are built on the cliffs above the beach. I walked through the residential areas of metropolises such as Oceano, Grover City, Pismo Beach, Shell Beach and Avila Beach.

Starting from the bridge in Avila Beach at 9 a.m., I took the road west to Port San Luis. Then the fun began. The beach was impassable so I walked up the hill to a road that led around a curve of the coast to the lighthouse. I bushwhacked past the lighthouse and got on a dirt road. From there I walked alternately on dirt roads, through cow pastures (keeping an eye out for bulls) and on the beach, itself, when possible. I passed the Diablo Canyon Nuclear Power Plant near Lion Rock (this was in 1978 when the plant was under construction) before it was fashionable for protestors to attempt to gain access to it. There were no guards in sight.

I arrived at the beach at Point Buchon at 4 p.m., too late to make a connection with Bonny. I walked on to Los Osos and met Bonny there about 7:40 p.m. The animal report in my log for that day states that I saw seals, birds, crabs and cows.

From here it is an easy six-mile walk to Morro Bay and the famous Morro Rock, following South Bay Boulevard and going through part of Morro Bay State Park to Main Street in Morro Bay.

I did the stretch from Morro Bay north to Cambria on July 5, 1974. This was one of the first sections I did after deciding to walk the coast. I remember setting out from Morro Bay at 9 a.m. in dreary weather and Bonny telling me I didn't have to do this. I figured that if I chickened out when I had barely gotten started I had no business attempting to walk the coast. The weather got better as the day went on.

I walked north, starting on Main Street. At Atascadero Beach State Park I took to the sand and stayed on it to the north end of Cayucos. There are many beachfront houses, and rocks come out to the water in places. I followed Route 1 north to Cambria.

I was able to do the short walk from Cambria County Park to San Simeon State Beach on the sand. But now I was in the Big Sur, with its jagged coast and unwalkable beaches, and I was destined to stay on Route 1 for many a mile. North of here the road goes beneath the Hearst San Simeon State Historical Monument, built on the hillside, more familiar as Hearst Castle. Then comes the Piedras Blancas Light Station. I passed a house on the beach side of the road with a sign that read, "This place dangerous to dogs, children and reasonable people." The yard was strewn with junk.

Then come the hills, where the road goes up to over 700 feet after Ragged Point and near the San Luis Obispo/Monterey County line. There are a couple of drinking fountains alongside the road. I used one of them as a starting point for a day's walk. In places Route 1 is narrow, with no good shoulder to walk on. I spent all my time watching the oncoming traffic. The RVs, with their long outside mirrors, like the horns of a bull, made me feel like a matador without a cape as their drivers often decided I wasn't worth leaving any room for.

North of here is a nothing place called Gorda, although it was supposed to have a restroom, telephone and food (note the use of the singular form throughout). I passed sections of the road that had been washed out and replaced. In one location part of a stone wall had fallen over the cliff. Washouts and landslides have closed Route 1 for weeks at a time during some years. Bonny refuses to drive on it anymore.

North of Gorda there is a campground at Kirk Creek. Then the road rises to 800 feet at Lucia before taking an easy downhill to Lime Creek. It was at Lime Creek on November 26, 1976, the day after Thanksgiving, that I had to stop after walking 19 miles because of pain in my right leg, between my knee and my foot. I have never had pain exactly like that before or since, thank goodness. From time to time my body finds new places to hurt, however.

Next comes Julia Pfeiffer Burns State Park. The road rises to over 900 feet between the Castro Canyon Bridge and the Pfeiffer Canyon Bridge and then falls to 200 feet at Pfeiffer State Park. The views of the coast are spectacular from the bridges. In places the road wends its way inland to find the easiest route among the cliffs that crowd the ocean. On a summer day in 1979 I got the black flag from Bonny near the Point Sur Light Station because I was walking too slowly. I had gone 23 miles and had sore feet and ankles. In those days I made a big deal about walking in pain. The next morning I walked to the top of the hill that I had started from in March 1978.

At the end of February 1978, I flew to Carmel with coworkers for a business meeting. As our United flight waited for takeoff at Los Angeles, a Continental DC-10 failed in a takeoff attempt and cracked up on the runway. Several passengers were killed. When we returned from Carmel the damaged plane was still sitting there.

On March 1 my coworker, Al Werker (the name fits), drove me 15 miles south of the intersection of Route 1 and Carmel Valley Road and I walked back to the intersection. I still hadn't learned that it is better to wear sneakers than stiff hiking boots for walking on roads. I developed a huge blister that I sported throughout the multi-day meeting that followed. I must have been too proud of the blister to pop it.

On a gorgeous day I walked side roads from Route 1 (Rio Road, left on Santa Lucia, right on Scenic Road). I followed the Beach to San Antonio and then walked to the Carmel Gate of the private Seventeen Mile Drive. I was allowed in free; cars were charged four dollars at that time. Here are located the magnificent golf courses of Pebble Beach where, if you lose your ball the fish are likely to claim it. I walked on the ocean side of the Drive around the Monterey Peninsula to the Lighthouse Gate at Pacific Grove. Bonny and Andy joined me for lunch near some tide pools along the Drive.

I took walking paths that follow the beach through Pacific Grove and into Monterey. I followed an old railroad track part of the time and walked through Cannery Row, made famous by John Steinbeck.

The canneries were gone in 1980, replaced by shops, and later the Monterey Aquarium was built in the area.

A beautiful, curving beach extends for several miles along Monterey Bay to the north. I walked past Fort Ord, where I went through basic training in 1960 and lost part of my hearing. It has since been closed. I reached the mouth of the Salinas River within an hour of high tide and was afraid to cross it. I followed the river through marshland to Route 1. I took Molera Road around Castroville and came back to Route 1 again near Moss Landing.

I walked the stretch from Moss Landing to Santa Cruz (which is in Santa Cruz County) north to south on a day when my plans went awry. From Santa Cruz I took San Andreas Road south, took a jog over to McGowan on Beach Road and then followed a bike path from McGowan toward the beach. The path ended and I couldn't get either across the Pajaro River or to the beach, because of Harkins Slough. I tried crossing the slough, but its mud was reminiscent of quicksand and I finally retraced my steps to McGowan and took Trafton Road back to Route 1. This little adventure cost me about four miles and some muddy shoes.

Walking through the laid-back city of Santa Cruz (there was even an overlook above a beach with a sign designating it as Peepers' Point) involves walking on a combination of beaches, roads and railroad tracks. From San Andreas Road you can follow the railroad track to La Selva Beach. There is good sand walking through Seacliff State Beach and New Brighton State Beach, around the curve to Soquel Creek.

From here, follow the Esplanade and the Cliff Drives (Cliff Drive, East Cliff Drive, Opal Cliff Drive), but jog up to Murray Street on Lake Avenue to cross Woods Lagoon. Cross the San Lorenzo River on the railroad track (a walkway is provided) and then follow Beach Street and West Cliff Drive to Natural Bridges State Beach. As you exit the beach on Natural Bridges Drive you have your choice of following the railroad track or Route 1 to Bonny Doon Road.

The coast directly north of here is too jagged to allow beach walking. Route 1 is the only game in town. As I walked north from Bonny Doon Road into San Mateo County in May 1981 I encountered a headwind that at one point blew sand into my face. Aided by low tide, I was able to walk on the sand from Pescadero State Beach to San Gregorio State Beach, and then back to Route 1 for the run into San Francisco.

I followed Route 1 through Half Moon Bay and past a series of beaches and marine reserves to near Pacifica, where Route 1 becomes a freeway. Then I walked on the Bicentennial Bicycle Path to Route 35, also known as Skyline Boulevard. I walked on 35 into the city and county of San Francisco (they have the same boundaries) and took the Great Highway north, past the famous Cliff House. I did some improvising to get through Lincoln Park and connect with a walk I had done earlier in San Francisco. I was able to walk on the western (ocean-facing) beaches part of the time. I passed a dead, 25-foot whale that was attracting attention. It was probably a Gray Whale.

The earlier walk I had done was during a business trip I took to San Francisco a month before, in April 1981. I walked in a business suit because I had no other clothes with me. I followed Camino del Mar from Lincoln Park and then went north on Lincoln Boulevard, Bowley Street and Merchant Road to the Golden Gate Bridge. I walked across the bridge into Marin County to the Vista Point at the north end and then back to the car. The weather was typical for San Francisco: cool and breezy. However, it was clear, with no fog. See chapter 11 for more on walking in San Francisco.

CHAPTER 36 California Coast—Marin County to the Oregon Border

On the day I walked north from the Golden Gate Bridge (May 29, 1982) I left my brain somewhere else. I headed north from the bridge, exited 101 as soon as I could (101 is the route that goes over the bridge) and followed a surface street into Sausalito. I crossed under 101, but missed the turn onto Route 1 and walked through Mill Valley and then sharply uphill (this should have been a clue that I was on the wrong road) to Panoramic Highway in Mt. Tamalpais State Park, overlooking the coast. Using a map I received from a helpful homeowner who probably wondered about my sanity, I was able to get back down to Route 1. However, I wasn't through acting foolish.

At Stinson Beach I walked on the sand to a point that ended at Bolinas Lagoon. I suspect that when I looked at the map I thought I could connect to the mysterious city of Bolinas. Actually, Bolinas is only accessible from Route 1, on a road with no sign, and that is the way the residents want it. They would prefer that nobody knew how to get there. Cartoons about them have been published in the San Francisco newspapers. In any case, I had to retrace my steps to Route 1 and finally stopped for the day at Milepost 17.

Milepost 17 is significant because this is where I finished my coastwalk on March 4, 1984. I walked to this point from about 15 miles north of here, all on Route 1. Bonny and Andy were supporting me and we drank champagne at the finish. (I don't remember whether Andy drank champagne. He was only 15 at the time.)

North of Point Reyes Station, Route 1 goes alongside Tomales Bay. The bay has mud flats and shallow water. While I ate lunch there I watched ducks fishing for a meal. Point Reyes National Seashore is on the ocean side of the bay, but it doesn't connect to the mainland at the north end so I couldn't walk through it. I was smart enough to figure that out. Route 1 curves inland at the north end of Tomales Bay and then back to the coast near the city of Bodega Bay, in Sonoma County, but there is no alternative so I had I had to follow it.

Route 1 is so narrow going through the city of Bodega Bay that I thought I was on one of the many European streets left over from 17th century. However, the danger wasn't from horses but from cars. Ten miles north of Bodega Bay is Jenner, another quaint little village near the mouth of the Russian River. When I walked this area there were many rock and mud slides from recent heavy rains. Sonoma County has sheep on an open range (much like New Zealand), which means that sometimes you meet them on the road.

Ten miles or so north of Jenner is Fort Ross, which consisted of the Fort Ross General Store. On one trip, Bonny, Andy and I were heading north in our Volkswagen camper when it died at Fort Ross. We had it towed to a Volkswagen dealer in Guerneville, on the Russian River, where we left it while we caught a bus to Oakland and then flew back to LA. The following weekend I flew to Oakland, where the camper had been driven by a friend of ours, and drove it home. Unfortunately, the battery was continuously discharging and I had to get it charged several times on the way. After that, on our northern trips we flew to San Francisco or Eureka and rented a car.

North of Fort Ross, Route 1 is still the only possibility for walking. It rolls gently, with no big ups and downs, and sometimes goes straight for extended stretches. There are no large centers of population, but houses are common on both sides of the road. This situation continues as you enter Mendocino County, upon crossing the Gualala River.

South of Point Arena the coast becomes rocky and spectacular, much like that in the Big Sur. North of Point Arena Route 1 goes through villages such as Elk and Little River. The picturesque city of Mendocino sits on a cliff to the west of Route 1. It makes a perfect postcard and I can see why people want to live there. In places the narrow road twists and turns. On one curve I literally had to hug the rock wall while a camper and a pickup truck passed me.

Fort Bragg is north of Mendocino and is the only other population center of any magnitude along this part of the California coast. Just north of Fort Bragg it is possible to walk on the beach past the impressive sand dunes of MacKerricher State Park for several miles. I stayed on Route 1 because on the day I walked this section it was raining. People were living in old buses and odd-looking vehicles at parks along the way.

I was walking along the Mendocino coast one day when a pickup truck passed me, going perhaps 50 miles-per-hour. As I watched in horror, a dog fell out of the back of the truck and rolled over and over, its momentum carrying it along in the direction in which the truck had been going. It finally stopped rolling and came to a stop in a heap. To my surprise and relief, the dog got up and trotted back to the truck, which had stopped some distance down the road.

Twenty-some miles north of Fort Bragg, Route 1 climbs to 700 feet and then drops to 40 feet at Rockport. Thirty miles north of Fort Bragg my walking route entered the aptly named Lost Coast of California. I turned left (north) on Usal Road (also called Mendocino County Route 431), a dirt road that starts at Mendocino County Milepost 90.87 on Route 1.

Usal Road is rough and unpaved, with many severe ups and downs. Much of the land it winds through is forested, and views of the coast are restricted. The road goes down to sea level at Usal Creek, six miles north of Route 1. There is a nice campground here with wildflowers on green slopes (in May when I walked this area). I also encountered mosquitoes, unusual for California.

Approximately 25 miles north of where it starts, Usal Road crosses another unpaved road called Briceland Road. This intersection is grandly called the Four Corners. It is a number of miles and about a century southwest of Garberville, which is inland on 101.

Usal Road becomes Chemise Mountain Road in Humboldt County. My route jogged from Chemise Mountain Road to Shelter Cove Road and then to Kings Peak Road. While on the short stretch of Shelter Cove Road I obtained a splendid view of Shelter Cove itself, nestled under the cliffs. Although dirt, the roads were in good condition and the ups and downs were somewhat diminished in this area. The traffic was minimal. Aside from Shelter Cove, there wasn't much to see except trees.

Bonny and Andy were driving ahead of me when I walked this stretch (I walked north to south). They took a wrong turn and ended up in an even more remote area. They came upon a large hex or voodoo sign that scared the bejeebers out of them. They raced back to me and refused to drive along the road any more in that direction. They took a long detour and finally met me at the intersection of Usal and Briceland Roads. When Andy drew a picture of the sign for me he showed a skull mounted above a scary brown face, above purple and yellow leaves or feathers, sitting on a pole. Perhaps marijuana growers put the sign there.

From Kings Peak Road I jogged onto Wilder Ridge Road, heading north. On the day I walked this stretch it rained alternately hard and harder for the first eight miles. I changed socks twice, repowdered my feet with cornstarch and changed from boots to sneakers when the rain stopped for a while. In those days I was still subject to blisters. Wilder Ridge Road was partly paved. It climbs down the ridge, with steep switchbacks in places.

I turned left on Mattole Road, which follows the Mattole River to near the ocean. Recent rains had washed out sections of the road, and in fact it poured part of the time I was on it (this was in November 1983). I walked through the pretty village of Petrolia, one of the few signs of civilization in the Lost Coast. North of Petrolia, Mattole Road goes to the ocean and then climbs a steep hill. It goes all the way down again to cross the Bear River. Then it climbs a small mountain, although it doesn't feel so small.

After climbing the mountain, Mattole Road cruises downhill into Ferndale, the largest center of population on this route since Fort Bragg. In Ferndale I turned left on Main Street and continued on to Fernbridge. I crossed the Eel River on a narrow bridge and turned left on Eel River Drive, taking it to the Loleta exit from 101 at Hookton Road. I saw many deer, sheep and cows. The rivers and streams were high and rushing and I encountered more road washouts.

I took 101 north to Eureka, the really big city in northwestern California. Although 101 is a freeway, bicycles were allowed on it (it was part of the Pacific Coast Bicentennial bicycle route) and so I assumed that walkers were too. California Highway Patrol cars passed me and didn't stop. In any case, there was no practical alternative. The road comes to the coast and goes alongside Humboldt Bay.

To get through Eureka, which is peppered with Victorian houses, I roughly followed the Bicentennial route. Signs were posted for bicyclists. I followed 101 north from Eureka, alongside Arcata Bay to Arcata. I jogged onto Central Avenue, which goes through McKinleyville and past the Arcata Airport. North of the airport I walked on 101.

On October 22, 1983 I was walking north on 101 on a sunny morning, beside a body of water called Big Lagoon. Everything was quiet and peaceful. I saw some beautiful water birds, including a white bird, standing motionless in the still water, which reflected it, perfectly. It may have been an ibis. I took a picture of the pastoral scene and walked down beside the lagoon, where I photographed several sea otters. The map showed a connecting strip of beach along the ocean side of Stone Lagoon, which was coming up shortly. I decided to walk on the beach so that I could stay off the road for a while.

What the map didn't show was the cliff that soon blocked my way. At this point I could have easily retraced my steps and taken Route 101. Something there is in me, however, that doesn't like to retrace steps. Instead, I decided to bushwhack over a hill straight to 101. Bushwhack turned out to be an understatement. The farther I went into the bushes, which were taller than I was, the less freely I was able to move.

Finally, I stopped being able to move, altogether. In any direction. I now know what it's like to be in an impenetrable jungle. I longed for a machete. I longed to be somewhere else. Anywhere else. I worried about Bonny worrying when I didn't show up at our meeting place.

I panicked. My heart hammered as though it were trying to break out of my chest. I doubted that even a helicopter crew could spot me in these bushes. Years from now someone would find my skeleton and wonder how it got there.

Gradually, however, I worked out a system. Sometimes I was able to crawl a few inches. At other times I fell forward onto the bushes and the weight of my body broke them down. That gained me several feet. I lost my water bottle doing this.

Entwined among the stiff bushes that held me in place were blackberry plants with thorns and thin tentacle-like branches, 20 feet long. When I passed them they wrapped themselves around my body, like thin boa constrictors. Since they were almost impossible to break I had to unwind them. Slowly. One at a time. It was an interminable process.

Eventually, I worked clear of the bushes and found my way back to the beach on the far side of the cliff. I still had to walk around Stone Lagoon to get to 101. I arrived at my rendezvous with Bonny three hours late. My face was covered with scratches and I looked like one of the living dead. Bonny had been driving back and forth, frantically looking for me, and was just about to call the police. When she drove up and saw me you can imagine what she said.

North of the lagoons 101 goes inland and climbs to over 800 feet just before the Del Norte County line. It passes through the largest stand of redwood trees in the US. These coast redwoods include the tallest trees in the world. Walking among them evokes feelings of awe in me similar to being in one of the huge European cathedrals. The road also passes through an elk preserve where I saw a number of elk.

Route 1 goes over the Klamath River Bridge at close to sea level and into the village of Klamath. I saw more redwoods north of Klamath as 101 climbed from sea level to 1,200 feet and then back down to sea level a little before Crescent City, which is on the coast.

At the end of our honeymoon, in September 1964, Bonny and I drove south along this part of the California coast. We stopped at the Crescent City beach, where we saw giant pieces of driftwood on the

255

sand. They were redwood trees, apparently washed out to sea by tidal waves caused by an Alaskan earthquake that had occurred a short time before. We took pictures of ourselves with the trees. We looked like midgets beside the huge gray tree trunks.

North of Crescent City I followed Lake Earl Drive, which runs parallel to 101. There are other opportunities to walk on side streets north of Smith River. Smith River is the northern-most village on the California coast. Route 101 crosses into Oregon at the coast, near Pelican State Beach.

I walked the stretch between the Oregon border and Klamath in December 1979. Bonny, Andy and I had spent Christmas with friends in Seattle and were on our way home. We stayed in a motel in Crescent city, where there wasn't a lot to do. Bonny and Andy spent so much time in the Ben Franklin store in Crescent City that they could have done the stocking and inventory control.

CHAPTER 37 Los Angeles to Denver—California

I started walking from Los Angeles to Denver on Sunday, October 8, 1978. On the cover of my logbook I optimistically wrote, "Coast to Coast Walk." At some point I modified my aspirations, largely because of the 800 miles of flat nothingness east of Denver (apologies to eastern Colorado, Kansas and Missouri).

I think the reason I started this walk was because I was getting bogged down on my California coast walk. We had to travel many miles to reach the places I hadn't walked yet. I wanted a goal that I could work on closer to home, at least in the beginning.

I started from our home in Rancho Palos Verdes, at the 700-foot level, and walked down to the beach at Malaga Cove, accompanied by Andy, following the route that he had just started using to walk to the Malaga Cove Intermediate School (see chapter 4). Then we walked north through Torrance Beach to near Redondo Beach, which became my official starting point. When I tell southern Californians about my walk I say I walked from Redondo Beach (rather than Torrance Beach) to Denver because the locals have all heard of Redondo Beach, but few people know that Torrance even has a beach, since most of the city is inland.

It was a muggy and smoggy autumn day, with the temperature in the 80s, F. Nowadays, smog that bad is a rarity. I headed east on Pacific Coast Highway (at that point PCH runs east and west) and followed it to Long Beach Boulevard in Long Beach. The next week

257

I continued my walk eastward during four of my lunch hours. I was working in Long Beach at the time, which was very convenient. On each of these days I progressed about two miles and then had to walk the return trip back to my car.

A large traffic circle at Pacific Coast Highway and Lakewood Boulevard looks completely out of place. Since there are very few traffic circles in the United States (as opposed to zillions of roundabouts in the United Kingdom—see Chapters 40-43) people here don't know how to drive on them. The story is told that the designer of the circle died in an accident while driving on it. This is probably apocryphal, but it would have served him right.

When I reached the traffic circle on my walk I jogged left or northeast on Los Coyotes Diagonal, cleverly saving myself a few feet, since this was taking the hypotenuse of a right triangle, the length of which, as we all know, is less than the total of the lengths of the other two sides. I jogged right on Willow Street, heading east again.

Willow becomes Katella Avenue when it enters Orange County. On Saturday, October 14 and for two lunch hours the following week I continued east on Katella and made it to Harbor Boulevard, not far from Disneyland. All this time the weather continued to be hot and smoggy. Fires were burning in Malibu, but, fortunately, not where I was. I made a note in my log that when I walked slower I had fewer problems with blisters.

On Saturday, November 25, 1978 I continued east on Katella in cooler weather, until it became Villa Park Road and then Santiago Canyon Road. The bridge over Santiago Creek was washed out and the road came to a dead end. In front of me was a cliff going down to the creek bed. What to do? I was in the wilds of Orange County by this time and there was no good alternate route. Utilizing my rock climbing training from my youth I carefully climbed down the embankment and then up the other side. Fortunately, I didn't slip because there was nobody around to hear my screams.

I turned left on Silverado Canyon Road and went to Black Star Canyon Road. The area was dirt-bike heaven and the bikers were out in force. The next day I walked perhaps the most rugged section of the whole trip. The shortest way to get to Corona is to cross the Santa Ana Mountains, so this is what I did. I followed Black Star Canyon

Road over the mountains, climbing to an altitude of 3,000 feet or higher. In Riverside County the name of the road changes to Skyline Drive.

There was a locked gate at both ends of the road and, in addition, obstacles on the road made it impossible to drive a vehicle all the way through. The road climbs to a ridge in the mountains and then goes down into a valley where Hidden Ranch is located. It climbs again past several houses (whose antennas are visible from Corona) and then descends rapidly into Corona, via many switchbacks. The only access to the houses and the ranch by road is from the Corona side. I stopped in Corona at the corner of Ontario Avenue and Main Street.

Corona, like many cities at the intersection of major highways (I-15 and 91), gives the impression of being all motels and fast-food restaurants, sprinkled with car dealerships. It was not always thus. Early in the 20th century, when Bonny's grandfather, Frank, came out to California from Connecticut on the train to stay with his aunt on a ranch in Corona, it was rural and unpopulated. The story is that Frank's aunt died when her voluminous clothing caught fire. He returned home to Connecticut after several months because his mother was ill. He was also a walker and there is more about him in chapter 6.

On Sunday, February 4, 1979 I followed Ontario Avenue and Temescal Canyon Road east to Cajalco Road. Cajalco Road goes along the south shore of Lake Mathews and eventually crosses I-215 (it was still called Route 395 when I did the walk). The pretty lake had boats but no fishing. The road name changed to Morgan Avenue and became dirt, but I soon turned north on Perris Boulevard and east on the Ramona Expressway, stopping at the Lake Perris turnoff.

This was a day that poets sing about, with air as clear as a vacuum and the three premier peaks of Southern California—Mt. San Gorgonio, Mt. San Jacinto and Mt. Baldy—all visible at the same time. The snow level was down to 3,000 feet and the mountains hovered over the landscape like white ghosts.

Two weeks later, by the grace of Bonny, I was able to continue east on the Ramona Expressway. I followed this and Route 79 to the five corners in downtown San Jacinto, where the well-known Vosburg Hotel is located. This relatively flat area is used for hot-air ballooning. A balloon landed beside the road while I was walking. In addition, many of the dairy farms that had been located in Orange County when we moved there in 1965 had relocated to this part of Riverside County.

On Friday, April 20, 1979 I walked from the village of San Jacinto up into the San Jacinto Mountains. I went via Mountain Avenue to Hemet and then continued on Route 74. Each year Hemet sponsors the "Ramona Pageant," an outdoor play based on the novel, *Ramona*, written by Helen Hunt Jackson. It is produced and acted by the local residents, in a beautiful, rocky setting, and features a large cast, complete with galloping horses.

We have attended and enjoyed the pageant several times. During one performance I witnessed one of the most amazing things I have ever seen an actor do. A young woman in the cast managed to put on her shoes while running at full speed.

I ended the day at Mountain Center, after a climb of several thousand feet. Mountain Center is a few miles from Idyllwild, where Bonny and I owned a cabin during the first years we were married. Route 74 is narrow and twisting heading up the mountain and I had to keep a sharp lookout for cars.

One week later, on April 27, I continued east on Route 74 on a beautiful spring day. The road climbs from Mountain Center to Keen Camp Summit, at an altitude of about 4,900 feet. After that, it drops into Garner Valley, passes Lake Hemet, returns to 4,900 feet at Santa Rosa Summit and eventually starts to drop into the Coachella Valley.

On June 23 I made it down to the valley floor on a hot summer day. Route 74 descends steeply in a series of switchbacks, called Seven-Level Hill. I cut several of the switchbacks and averaged over four miles-per-hour for the first 8.5 miles. As I entered Palm Desert a cool breeze from the sprinkler systems of the condominiums beside the road helped me.

I headed east on Route 111 to Indio, along the desert floor. The temperature rose to over 100 degrees F, and I had to stop in the shade and drink liquids often. At one point I drank a quart of Gatorade before I gave up walking for the day.

It wasn't until almost a year later, on Sunday, May 4, 1980 that I was able to continue my walk. I walked partly in reverse order for

Bonny's convenience. When you are dependent on the goodwill of your driver you have to do things for her convenience. My route started on 111, crossed bridges over Interstate 10, railroad tracks and a river (if you can believe that a river exists in the desert) on Van Buren, followed Avenue 44 to Dillon Road and then Dillon Road north to San Berdoo Canyon Road. The temperature was in the 90s, but a breeze helped keep me cool part of the time.

Now comes a gap of almost two years, until Sunday, February 14, 1982 (Valentine's Day). This day must have been a Valentine's present from Bonny. I walked through one of the most scenic areas I have ever seen in my life, in Joshua Tree National Monument. I walked south on the Geology Tour Road, which begins inside the Monument near Jumbo Rocks Campground, to Dillon Road. The Geology Tour Road becomes San Berdoo Canyon Road outside the Monument.

The road went gently uphill at first and then descended into a large and beautiful valley, full of nicely spaced Joshua Trees, for as far as I could see. Joshua Trees don't look like any other trees. They are small and odd-shaped, with sawed-off branches and spiky leaves. Since Joshua Trees only grow in a limited area this was a unique scene. I might as well have been alone on another planet. The feeling of aloneness was intensified because I saw only a couple of vehicles the whole day (Bonny did not drive on this road). In addition, I saw almost no animals, but the desert vegetation was plentiful.

After descending for some distance, the road climbs steadily over a ridge of the Little San Bernardino Mountains. Then it goes downhill the rest of the way. For the most part the road was dirt. Pieces of it were paved near the south end. My skin burned some in the sun and a gusty wind boxed the compass, coming at me from all directions.

Next we have a gap of almost three years, to Saturday, November 24, 1984. By this time I had finished my walk of the California coast and could concentrate on getting to Denver. I started at the beginning of the Geology Tour Road in Joshua Tree National Monument and walked mostly north through the Monument to Route 62, entering San Bernardino County, the largest county in California. The first six miles were rolling, with strong and cold gusty winds. I headed east

261

on Route 62 and went to milepost 48, going about 28 miles for the day.

Route 62 goes gently downhill to Twentynine Palms and is perfectly straight for long distances. There are many small houses and shacks along the road, some inhabited, some not. It rained gently for over an hour. Don't let anybody tell you it doesn't rain in the desert. The afternoon was quite dark. Somewhere along here I saw a sign that read, "Next gas, 106 miles."

The following day I was able to walk another 22 miles on Route 62, to milepost 70. The road went straight for a while and then wound around a series of hills. The scenery looks a lot like the stark beauty of Death Valley. All the rocks were in razor sharp focus in the pristine air, even those many miles away.

Another year went by before Bonny and I made it out here again. On Saturday, December 28, 1985 I started at milepost 70 on Route 62 and walked east to milepost 102, for a total of 32 miles. It was T-shirt weather most of the day. Five people stopped to ask if I needed assistance and two asked Bonny the same question when she stopped the car. Traffic was light. People look out for each other in remote regions.

In this part of the country you feel as if you can see forever, especially where the road goes straight for many miles. My log states, "The road went gently downhill for a long way, then gently uphill for a long way, then gently…" I crossed Route 177 at milepost 85. This was significant because it was the only major crossroad since Twentynine Palms. I saw a hawk, a rabbit and a tarantula, lean desert vegetation and lots of sand. I passed Iron Mountain, where a million armored personnel were trained during World War II. I believe General Patton was involved.

I walked the next 11 miles on Route 62, to milepost 113, on Sunday, March 23, 1986. My log reports that the cloud cover helped to cool the air and that a breeze blew off and on. The road was fairly flat, with dips, and the traffic was moderate.

On December 29, 1985, the day after I walked 32 miles, I walked another 30 miles, from Parker, Arizona west to milepost 113 on Route 62. The 62 total miles was a two-day distance record for me at the time (later to be broken). I crossed the Colorado River into California immediately after starting out. The weather continued to be perfect. There were many dips in the road, especially near the beginning. In some places the shoulder was navigable; in other places it was too soft or stony.

Route 62 crosses US 95 at milepost 126. The biggest problem I encountered was cars passing other cars while overtaking me from behind, because they came into the lane on my side of the road and scared me. I continued my ongoing battle with the drivers of large RVs, with mirrors that stuck way out to the side, who wouldn't move over to give me room. Near the end of the day I got shooting pains and cramping in my calves. At lunch I popped a blood blister on the ball of my left foot and put mole foam on it.

CHAPTER 38 Los Angeles to Denver—Arizona

I walked the first part of Arizona on Saturday and Sunday, March 22 and 23, 1986. I went southeast on Arizona Route 95 from Parker and then on Route 72 to the intersection of 72 and US 60, a total of 49 miles. (On Sunday afternoon I finished the 11-mile section of Route 62 in California that I hadn't completed—see previous chapter.) I started from Parker on Sunday morning while it was still dark, and had the privilege of watching the sunrise. The road was rolling, with some curves. The traffic on 95 was heavier than that on 72.

On Saturday I started at the other end, at the intersection of 60 and 72, and walked northwest on 72 for 34 miles. This part of the road was straight and flat. It became hot and Bonny and I both suffered from the heat. We wore shorts and T-shirts and drank water constantly. Wildflowers dotted the edge of the road, mostly yellow, with some orange and violet. On the southernmost stretch a few majestic saguaro cactus plants grew.

The narrowness of the road was made up for by the lightness of the traffic. The animal life consisted mostly of lizards—alive and dead. The population is sparse and the only village has the unlikely name of Bouse.

I went to the other end of my route and started walking toward Los Angeles from Denver in July 1986, when Bonny and I were in Colorado for a family reunion. Then in December 1986 we made it back to Arizona. On Friday, December 5 I headed east on US 60, from its intersection with Route 72, and walked 30.5 miles to milepost 80. The weather was ideal, with high clouds and occasional sun. Traffic was light and the road had a wide shoulder. After some climbing and a few curves the road went straight and flat for many miles.

Saguaro cacti highlighted the desert foliage. Gourds grew alongside the road. They look like small pumpkins or melons. I saw three jackrabbits, but not many people. Small piles of dung were spaced at regular intervals. Was this the work of coyotes? Cotton trucks drive this route and there was enough cotton on the side of the road to supply a clothing factory.

On Saturday, December 6 I walked another 29.5 miles—east on US 60 to Route 71, then north on 71 to where it ends at Route 89. It rained almost continuously for many hours. I wore a parka and a hooded sweatshirt. Route 71 runs almost straight and almost level for many miles, after going over a low pass. The part of 71 south of US 93 was uninhabited. Literally. I mean, there was nobody there. And we think the earth is overpopulated.

There were beehives, however, and a coyote ran across the road in front of me. I saw some Joshua Trees, reminiscent of my walk through Joshua Tree National Monument. I finished near the village of Congress, which lies underneath the mountains to the north.

The next day I walked another 16 miles, north to south on Route 89, from milepost 284 to milepost 268. It was pouring when I started and I stopped at our motel in Yarnell to change shoes and socks and repowder my feet (I use cornstarch or baby powder) after walking only 2.5 miles. Gaining courage, I walked another four-mile section north of the motel. Yarnell is at 4,800 feet and on the final stretch I coasted down the mountain from Yarnell back to the previous day's finish. The sun finally came out and with it a never-ending view.

Purists will say, no fair; I walked down the mountain instead of up because it was easier. Guilty as charged (although it was also shortening our drive home), but, as you will see, I climbed a lot of mountains before I completed this walk. So I don't feel guilty about skipping this one.

During a four-day period starting Friday, April 29, 1988, I set personal distance records for walking two days, three days and four days. On the first day I walked north on Route 89 from milepost 284, through Prescott, and then jogged onto 89A and continued to milepost 320, for a total distance of 36 miles. The weather was beautiful and I got sunburned on my arms and neck.

The start of the walk, Peeples Valley, is over 4,000 feet high. From here the road goes downhill to a much larger valley, with typical desert brush and not much else. After crossing this valley the road winds uphill for a considerable distance, through the mountains and an evergreen forest, before dropping into mile-high Prescott. There are massive granite boulders north of the city.

On Saturday, I continued north on Route 89A for almost 35 miles, to Cottonwood, stopping at a motel just shy of milepost 355. From Prescott Valley, where I started, I could see the snow-capped San Francisco Peaks north of Flagstaff, over 80 miles away, including Humphreys Peak, the highest mountain in Arizona at 12,663 feet. Since my goal for this trip was to reach Flagstaff, the sight was supposed to spur me on, but the mountains looked too far away to reach. They might as well have been on the moon.

The weather remained good, with gusty winds that made me hang on to my visor. I wore a long-sleeved shirt with the collar up to prevent more sunburn. Out of Prescott Valley the road climbs from 4,000 feet to 7,000 feet (I told you I did a lot of climbing). It became very narrow and I walked on the right some of the time because there was a cliff on the left, which left me no escape when I met a car coming around a left-hand curve. That was more excitement than I craved.

I went through Jerome, a former copper-mining town that hugs the side of the mountain in vertical layers. The road goes through it in switchbacks, each one considerably lower than the last. I cut two of the switchbacks, one by descending a stairway and the other by scrambling down a steep and rocky path.

My feet were in good shape, partly thanks to a suggestion from my brother, Mike, marathoner and triathlete, to wear two-ply socks. The idea is that one ply sticks to your shoes while the other ply sticks to your feet, but it prevents moisture from getting to them.

On Sunday I continued north on Route 89A to milepost 392, another 37 miles. I had my two-day record of 72 miles and my three-day record of 108 miles. I encountered many different kinds of weather: sun, clouds, wind, rain, sleet and even snow flurries. I wore a parka and leggings to ward off the weather. The road climbs from 3,000 feet to 7,000 feet. I went through the picturesque village of Sedona, with its red-rock formations that look very much like the rocks in Monument Valley, Utah.

After Sedona, the road goes through Oak Creek Canyon, which follows Oak Creek upstream. Rushing rapids helped to create more towering cliffs, by cutting through the rock for millions of years. The road climbs straight up to get out of the canyon and then starts rolling its way toward Flagstaff.

I came to two bridges in the canyon that had "No Walking" signs because they were narrow and attractive to the many sightseers that flock to the area. Since I wasn't a sightseer I figured the signs didn't apply to me so I scooted across the bridges when cars weren't coming.

On Monday, May 2, 1988 I walked from Flagstaff south on Route 89A to milepost 392, an additional 11+ miles. I closed a gap that I had created by walking north from Flagstaff in 1987 (see below). I felt very proud of myself for walking 120 miles in four days. The final stretch was anticlimactic, with some up and down. There was ice on the windshield of the car in the morning when we got up.

The walk I took in 1987 was on Saturday, May 16 and Sunday, May 17. I walked north from Flagstaff on Saturday, following US 89 to milepost 457 at Gray Mountain. The distance of over 43 miles is my single day personal best for "official" walking (I have done a couple of long unofficial walks). A light cloud cover kept the sun at bay and made the temperature perfect for walking. Some wind blew and a light rain fell in the afternoon. I passed the San Francisco Peaks in the Coconino National Forest, the same peaks I was to use as guiding stars in my walk north to Flagstaff (see above).

The road was about 7,000 feet high at first (the highest point is 7,282 feet), with some ups and downs. Later it dropped below 6,000 feet. The area north of Flagstaff is mostly uninhabited, but I passed several Navajo trading posts in the valleys. Traffic was moderately heavy. Evergreen trees grow at 7,000 feet, but vegetation is sparse lower down. The local lizards look like horned toads. I passed two natives digging up flat red rocks and putting them in a truck.

In addition to Bonny, our nieces, Ellen and Heather, accompanied us because we were on our way to the Grand Canyon. They did some sightseeing during the day, including a visit to Sunset Crater National Monument. At lunchtime, Ellen massaged my shoulders, which were stiff from carrying a pack, giving me welcome relief.

The next morning I was able to walk another eight miles on US 89, to the intersection of Route 64, which goes west to the Grand Canyon. It was sunny and warm. The road dipped below 5,000 feet just past Gray Mountain and entered a series of valleys, with escarpments of red rock and dirt. I was now in the huge Navajo reservation and a number of jewelry stands lined the road. They were made of wood and had roofs to protect their wares from the elements. I also saw several bicyclists and some Navajo hitchhikers, including a woman.

At this point there is a gap of almost six years in my walk. I was still considering walking all the way across the country during this time because my logbook shows two days of walking in Massachusetts, on and near Cape Cod (originally, the idea was to end the walk at Cape Cod), and another two days in western New York, near my parents' farm, for a total of a little over 100 miles. Not enough to tempt me to do the rest, however.

Finally, on Saturday, February 19, 1994 I started at the intersection of Route 64 and US 89 in Arizona and headed north in a snowstorm. I turned right (east) on US 160 and continued northeast to milepost 331, covering 35 miles for the day. In the next two years I would get to know US 160 very well.

It was snowing when I started, hard at times. I wore boots and four layers on top, including thermal underwear. I walked through an inch of slush and snow in places, but the temperature was above freezing and snow wasn't sticking to the road. Cameron, at the intersection of Routes 89 and 64, consists of a few Navajo houses. I didn't see the motel Bonny and I had stayed at in 1967, after we hiked to the bottom of the Grand Canyon.

Almost immediately, I crossed the Little Colorado River, which escapes from the big Colorado River in the Grand Canyon, west of there. It had a nice gorge, but hardly any water. All the roadside Navajo trading posts were closed. I passed many mesas made out of red rocks—the mesas that you see pictures of in magazines like *Arizona Highways*.

In this wide-open country I could see the snow squalls coming. I would look at the ominous black clouds bearing down on me and know that in 15 minutes I would be in a snowstorm. Sure enough, within 15 minutes it would start snowing. It would snow for a while and then the squall would pass and I would start looking for the next ominous cloud.

US 89 heads mostly downhill to US 160. US 160 heads up a hill and rolls after that, with more down than up. Tuba City, located near where 160 begins, was bustling—it even had a movie theater. I saw nine horses and one cow. The horses ran from me. Most Navajos lived in trailers and small houses, few in the traditional round hogans.

Bonny's mother, Ellen, accompanied us on this trip because we were taking her to Monument Valley, in southern Utah, to visit it again as we all had done in 1970 (see chapter 12). This was one of the last of the many trips that Ellen went on with us.

Bonny and Ellen were in Tuba City while I was walking. They followed the sounds of drums to a coming-of-age ceremony for Hopi children, taking place in an open area. The Hopi reservation is contained within the Navajo reservation. The children—both boys and girls—wore brightly colored blankets with one arm sticking out—despite the cold. Many of them were barefoot. They danced and marched in a long line and finally descended a ladder into a large kiva, where private initiation ceremonies took place.

The Navajos and Hopis drove pickup trucks and vans. In 1967 they drove slowly, apparently to conserve fuel. In 1994 they drove faster. Perhaps they had become more affluent. However, they sometimes squeezed as many as six people into the front seat. At least four people, including two women, asked me if I wanted a ride. They sometimes hauled large chunks of coal in the backs of their pickups.

On Sunday, February 20, 1994 I walked northeast on US 160 from milepost 331 to milepost 348, short of Cow Springs. The temperature was below freezing when I started and the wind (from my front right) provided an additional chill. The patches of snow beside the road didn't start melting for the first two hours. The road went uphill for the first five miles and then rolled, with the emphasis on downhill. Vegetation consisted of low bushes, but no trees. At least the road was dry. A Navajo police officer stopped his SUV and asked me whether I needed help.

We purposely left a 30-mile gap here so that we could get closer to Kayenta, where we planned to stay the night. There aren't a lot of motels in Navajo country. I continued my walk on February 20, 1994 from milepost 378 on US 160 (see below).

On Friday, November 11, 1994 I filled 23 miles of the gap. I walked northeast from milepost 348 to milepost 371 on US 160, where Bonny made me stop because it became dark. The temperature was in the 50s, with gusty southerly winds, which buffeted me and sometimes gave me a push. The wind must have strengthened the effect of the slipstreams of the semis going by because when one hit me it was like being hit by a football linebacker. However, the traffic was fairly light and the road has a broad shoulder.

I wore my new silk long underwear to keep my legs warm, and four layers on top. The road parallels a major rail line. Even in the space age I still get a thrill watching the trains rumble by. The few houses were a mile or more from the road. The red-rock mesas continued; some extended for many miles. The vegetation was sparse. I saw some sheep and goats. The road was a recycler's dream. An enterprising youngster could have made a fortune from the aluminum cans on the shoulders.

The next day I filled the other seven miles of the gap I had left, to milepost 378 on US 160, in the rain. I passed a pipeline that snaked over the hills, over the road and into a large tank. Then I continued walking from milepost 409 (see below).

Now we go back to February 20, 1994. In the afternoon I continued northeast on US 160 from milepost 378 to milepost 388. Three dogs came from a house and chased me. I crossed the road, hoping they wouldn't follow. They didn't. A red-rock gorge I passed had a little water at the bottom. A few evergreen trees grew in this area. I stopped five miles short of Kayenta, where we stayed the night. Kayenta was the largest center of population around. It even had one of the big chain motels.

On Monday, February 21, 1994 I continued east on US 160. US 163 goes north from Kayenta to Monument Valley and, not surprisingly, the rock formations near Kayenta are similar to the spectacular formations in Monument Valley. After passing Kayenta, US 160 goes straight and level for a bit and then ascends a mesa. In the morning it was foggy, and slippery on the shoulder of the road because of overnight snow. As the road warmed, that problem disappeared. The temperature remained in the 30s, however, with some sun and occasional snow flurries.

Not long after lunch I was walking ahead of Bonny and Ellen and our car, when another car stopped beside me. The occupants asked me if I was Alan. They informed me that the battery in our car had died and Bonny had frantically flagged them down. The family drove me eight miles back to Kayenta, where I borrowed jumper cables from a gas station. Then they drove me back to the car. We started the car and I drove it back to Kayenta and purchased a new battery. Then we drove back to where I was walking.

This took a lot of time and I only walked 21 miles for the day, to milepost 409. When I finished walking we drove back to Kayenta to spend the night. We gave a ride to two Navajo high school boys who had run out of gas. They got a can of gas and we drove them back to their car. Tit for Tat.

On Saturday, November 12, 1994 I continued walking from milepost 409 to milepost 432 after I finished filling in the 30-mile gap (see above). It rained off and on. The sun came out late in the afternoon, enabling me to walk a mile after sunset. The road is mostly between 5,000 and 6,000 feet, with beautiful red-rock mesas (this is getting redundant, as my grandson would say).

I wore up to six layers on top: T-shirt, silk underwear top, thermal top, two sweatshirts and a rain top. I wore three layers over my legs: silk underwear bottom, pants and rain pants. The temperature was in the 40s, with some wind.

A small village, Tes Nez Iah, sits in a gully at milepost 429. It had a motel, but no restaurant. And, as I found out in 1996, it also didn't have any telephone service at that time.

The next day I continued east from milepost 432 to milepost 464, at Teec Nos Pos, about six miles short of the Four Corners. It started out sunny, then clouded over and snowed. After that it was intermittently cloudy and sunny. I went through Mexican Water and the aptly named Red Mesa, which has a high school. I saw two horses on the road. There was also a cow on the road and people were chasing it.

CHAPTER 39 Los Angeles to Denver—Colorado

I walked the remaining few miles of Arizona on one of nine consecutive days of walking, during which I completed the final 182 miles of my Los Angeles to Denver walk. On Thursday, May 2, 1996 I walked east from Arizona milepost 464 on US 160 to Colorado milepost 15. The Four Corners (where Arizona, Colorado, New Mexico and Utah meet) are past Arizona milepost 470. It was T-shirt weather. A warm tailwind blew me the last five miles.

Bonny and I paid $1.50 to drive a half-mile off 160 to the actual place where the four corners meet, commemorated by a plaque. One-quarter of the plaque is in each state, so the thing to do is to have your picture taken with a hand or foot in each state. The Navajos sell jewelry at stalls here. They also sell Indian fry bread, a chewy kind of bread that can be addictive.

After leaving Arizona, US 160 takes a very short jaunt through New Mexico before it heads into Colorado. In Colorado, it almost immediately crosses the San Juan River. This is the country where you can see forever, or am I being redundant again? Brown flattop mesas line both sides of the road. They are composed of many round mesas, linked together. Can anybody explain why the mesas are red in Arizona, but brown in Colorado? Or gray—see below.

On Thursday, April 25, 1996 I walked on US 160 from milepost 15 to the El Capri Motel in Cortez, Colorado. I bucked a headwind at first, which later backed around to the west, off my beam, since I was

273

heading north. I wore a sweatshirt, usually with the sleeves rolled up. The road has a wide shoulder here.

I crossed US Route 666, which heads south into New Mexico. Its name has recently been changed to Route 491. The original number's "negative connotation" is one that officials don't want associated with New Mexico because it discourages tourism and area economic development.

I used a rearview mirror, attached to my glasses, for the first time, to watch for cars passing in the left lane behind me. It worked well when I remembered to look at it. There is a Ute gambling casino between milepost 26 and 27. Cortez is at 6,200 feet. Long, flat, gray mesas extended for miles. I saw snow-capped peaks on the horizon to the north and east—a foreshadowing of days to come.

Irrigation sprinklers shot water out of long pipes attached to large wheels that gradually rolled across the fields. The landscape is dry and the natural vegetation is mostly sagebrush.

My log states: "Ball of my left foot is a little sore (normal), left hip is sore (chronic). Problems I have had recently with my left ankle and foot have not recurred." This information is important because it was the first of my nine consecutive days of walking.

I should explain how this trip came about. I estimated that I had 180 miles remaining to walk between Los Angeles and Denver, in a single stretch on US 160. Bonny agreed to take some vacation time so that I could finish in one trip. Previously, I had never walked for more than four consecutive days.

I drove to Colorado alone from Los Angeles. Before I got to Colorado I stopped in Tes Nez Iah, Arizona, hoping to spend the night in the one motel there. I wanted to call Bonny and tell here where I was, but the clerk at the motel told me they had no regular phone service. They only had a radio for emergencies. I wasn't carrying a cell phone and I don't know whether a cell phone would have worked there.

Not wanting to be out of touch with Bonny, I drove on to Cortez and stayed at the El Capri Motel. The next morning (April 25) I hired a taxi to drive me approximately 21 miles south to milepost 15 on US 160 and I walked back to the motel (the walk described above). I stayed at the motel a second night and then drove east on 160 to Durango to pick up Bonny, who was flying into the Durango Airport.

I walked the stretch of US 160 east from Cortez on the last day of my walk, Friday, May 3, 1996. Bonny and I stayed at the El Capri Motel again the night before. I started walking east from the motel, which is near milepost 36, and finished my walk (having walked every inch between Los Angeles and Denver) at milepost 54. The road climbed about 800 feet, from 6,200 feet to 7,000 feet, but I still finished before noon. I passed the entrance to Mesa Verde National Park at milepost 48, and also saw a newborn colt.

To celebrate finishing the walk, Bonny and I toured Mesa Verde and the cliff dwellings. We had visited the park before, in 1967. It wasn't as exciting the second time.

On May 1, two days before, I walked east on US 160 from milepost 54 to milepost 73. I actually started walking west from milepost 73, but I was bucking cold headwinds of 20-30 miles-per-hour. After walking fewer than four miles I said "uncle" and had Bonny drive me to the western end of the walk, which is near Mancos at 7,000 feet. The road has long ups and downs. Traffic was moderate to light. The wind kept it from becoming too warm. And it blew me the last few miles when I was slowing down.

Which takes us back to April 26. After I drove our car from Cortez to Durango in the morning I took another taxi west about ten miles, to milepost 73. I walked back to the car, at the intersection of US 550, stopping to reserve a room at the Wapiti Lodge. A sign on the lodge stated: "Only nice folks stay here and I grouch." The woman who was presumably the grouch was very nice, however. I picked up Bonny at the Durango Airport and continued walking east to milepost 91.

The temperature was close to 80. US 160 heads steadily uphill east of Durango, which is at an altitude of 6,500 feet. Because of road construction, traffic was restricted to two lanes (instead of three), but I had a lane all to myself, protected by the traffic cones of the construction crew. I had a tailwind part of the time, when the wind wasn't swirling or blowing from other directions.

On April 27 I walked east on US 160 from milepost 91 to milepost 113. The sun warmed the air up to T-shirt weather. The shoulder was plenty wide for walking. Traffic was moderate, but later became lighter. For a walker this was heaven. The road went up, then down, and then was remarkably level for Colorado until a long, gentle uphill stretch. Bayfield is at 6,900 feet. The wind became gusty and strong, but since it was a tailwind it carried me along right smartly.

I crossed the Los Pinos River. The countryside does have pine trees, but most of it is open, with more chaparral and sagebrush than trees. Horses abounded in the fields. I saw at least three dead deer on the road.

On April 28 I walked east on US 160 from milepost 113 to milepost 135. It was cold at the start and remained cool. I wore gloves off and on. An erratic wind blew from all directions and carried significant chill with it. I walked through the village of Chimney Rock. The rock itself is on a ridge, visible for several miles. Alongside it is another rock that looks like Stirling Castle, in Scotland, because it is castle-shaped and sits on top of a cliff, as does Stirling Castle.

On April 29 I walked east on US 160 from milepost 135 to milepost 157, another 22 miles. I wasn't pushing myself because, having never walked more than 120 miles on a single trip, I didn't want to wear out my feet or the rest of me. It was about 20 degrees F when I started at 8 a.m. I wore six layers on top and two on my legs. The sun warmed me and I eventually took off three layers.

My left hip ached like a sore tooth. I did some stretching and felt a lot better. I walked through Pagosa Springs at 7,100 feet, which boasts the hottest hot springs in the world, beside the San Juan River. The night before, Bonny and I had soaked in one of several pools of various temperatures, which helped to restore my body. Bonny also treated me to an early birthday present—a massage from a local masseuse.

The road continued to be easy for walking, with wide shoulders. As I neared the approach to Wolf Creek Pass, which is on the Continental Divide, snow-capped mountains loomed dead ahead. My previous association with Wolf Creek Pass occurred in 1964. I decided to drive to Denver to visit my cousin Kay at Easter time. I started out in my Volkswagen Beetle, but quickly ran into trouble when a cylinder went out several hundred miles short of Flagstaff. I continued on to Flagstaff, climbing the hills at 20 miles-per-hour, and limped into town in the wee hours of the morning.

After a few hours sleep at a motel, I arrived at the local Volkswagen dealer when it opened. Fortunately, a good mechanic was on hand and he did an efficient valve job. I drove on, stopping in Farmington, New Mexico to have the valves adjusted. It was dark when I approached Wolf Creek Pass on US 160. As I started up the mountain I realized that the road was glare ice so I slowed to 20 miles-per-hour.

Even so, I went into a skid. On one side of me was a cliff. On the other side was a rock wall. I frantically turned the steering wheel, but it had no effect. I locked the brakes, hoping that the wheels would find some traction if I went toward the cliff. The car spun around in slow motion one and one-half times and finally came to a stop—in a snow bank against the rock.

As I breathed for a minute, thankful that I still could, another car passed me. It didn't stop. I shifted into first gear and slowly turned the VW around. I headed up the mountain again—at ten miles-per-hour. I didn't shift out of first gear until I was down the mountain an hour later.

That wasn't the only excitement I had on the motor trip to Denver. On my way home I was winging my way through northeastern Arizona at 1:30 in the morning without a care in the world—previewing the route of my walk, although I didn't know it—when I ran out of gas. As you might guess, there was no open gas station within 50 miles. I had stopped beside a village, possibly Cameron on Route 89—I don't remember—so I walked into it. I was greeted by a pack of barking dogs, but no people were in evidence. I retreated to my car and tried to keep warm. I napped until morning.

At about 7 a.m. another car stopped beside me. The driver was carrying a five-gallon gasoline can. He poured enough into my tank to get me to a gas station. He said he always carried extra gasoline with him and rejected my offer to pay him a bonus for helping me.

Tuesday, April 30, 1996 was a beautiful day to walk over Wolf Creek Pass and revisit the scene of my near-disaster. I walked east on US 160 from milepost 157 to milepost 174. The 10,857-foot summit is between mileposts 166 and 167. The road has three lanes most of the way and sometimes four. There are now guardrails on the cliff side, something I would have given a lot for in 1964.

Deep snow covered the ground at higher elevations, but the road was completely clear. In places, continuous avalanches fell down the rock wall, consisting of snow, ice, water and rocks. A number of good-sized rocks landed on the road. I thought it was only fair that I clear some of the larger ones off the road. I took two aspirin at the top of the pass to sooth the pain in my left hip.

Previously, on June 22, 1995 I had walked the area east of Wolf Creek Pass, from US 160, milepost 174, to the intersection of 160 and Route 112 at Del Norte (elevation 7,800 feet). I walked it partly east to west, from the intersection of 112 and 160 to South Fork (8,200 feet). Then I started at milepost 174 and walked back to South Fork. For four miles west of South Fork roadwork was in progress, with the attendant dust and confusion.

I changed to newer shoes when I developed a shin problem and a sore right hip. The day was warm and breezy and I became sunburned in spite of generous applications of SPF 30 sun block.

On June 21, 1995 I walked south on US 285 from milepost 83 to Route 112, and then west on 112 to US 160, at Del Norte, over 33 miles. Del Norte is the eastern-most point of my trek along US 160, which had encompassed parts of both Colorado and Arizona. This day's route was all on a level and this part of 285 is straight. The shoulders were wide and flat on 285, but sometimes nonexistent on 112.

I saw yellow-headed birds, red-winged blackbirds and beef cattle. I startled one calf into running a mile down the road before it found an opening in a fence and went back into a field. It was warm but I encountered a brisk headwind on 112.

On Tuesday, June 20, 1995 I walked south on US 285 from milepost 98 to milepost 83, starting at 3:10 p.m. The road rolled gently in shirtsleeve weather, between 7,500 and 8,000 feet. The traffic was very light to practically nonexistent. When the breeze stilled, the loudest sound was the hissing (tinnitus) in my ears, acquired during basic training in the army in 1960.

The Continental Divide parallels 285, not far to the west. Snow-capped peaks of mountains in the Sangre de Cristo Range and others were always in view. I walked through Saguache, which is a nothing village. Even the old hotel was closed.

Going back further, on Saturday, August 6, 1994, I walked from the intersection of US 285 and US 50 south on 285 to milepost 98, over 28 miles. Poncha Pass crests at 9,000 feet. There was a grove of white-barked birch or aspen trees near the summit. South of there is a long walk through a treeless valley, with mountains on either side. The village of Villa Grove is very small and has a river running through it. The warmth of the sun was made bearable by a cloud cover.

One night, Bonny and I stayed in a motel in Salida, which is on US 50, east of 285. I guess we weren't in the best part of town because during the night we heard shouting going on outside our room. We double-checked the locks on our door and huddled together in the bed.

The next morning I walked to the café/night club next door to have breakfast. I heard that a member of a band that had played there the previous night had been killed in a knife fight and his body had been discovered in the bushes beside the building a few minutes before. Had I ventured out sooner I might have been the one to discover it.

On August 7, 1994 I walked just under eight miles on US 285, south from the junction with Route 291 to the junction with US 50, to close a gap I had on 285. The road had an uphill climb of several miles. The day was sunny and warm.

Now we go back in time eight years to Saturday, July 5, 1986. I had one of my most interesting walks on this day. Bonny and I were at a reunion of my mother's family in Evergreen, Colorado. A group of relatives decided to go rafting on the Arkansas River for the day. I went along, not to raft but to walk. I started at the intersection of US 285 and county road 301, near the intersection of US 24 and 285, which is near Buena Vista.

I walked south on 301, a dirt road, to the railroad track. I followed the railroad track south along the Arkansas River to Route 291 and then backtracked slightly on 291 to 285. I walked approximately 16 miles, crossing the river twice on the track, from the east side to the west side and back again. Two trains passed, one going in either direction.

Hundreds of rafters floated down the river, but I was ahead of the reunion party of rafters and never saw them. I did get some good pictures of the other rafters, in their bright orange, rubber rafts, that even show their expressions of delight as they get buffeted by the rapids. The river was high and running fast, beneath the picturesque rock formations. The weather was warm but overcast, and it rained some in the afternoon.

I walked the stretch immediately to the north on July 7-8, 1986. The first 2.8 miles I walked the afternoon of July 7, after having been stopped earlier, north of there, by strong winds and heavy rain. I left a gap of 7.5 miles, which I closed on July 8, during which I walked downhill, with great views of the 14,000 foot "Ivy League" peaks behind Buena Visa: Mt. Princeton, Mt. Yale and Mt. Harvard.

The rest of my walk on July 7 started at milepost 182 on US 285, just south of Fairplay, and went south from there. I walked through a long and relatively level valley. The weather gradually changed from partly cloudy and cool to heavy clouds and then rain. After milepost 162, heading south, the road goes up over a pass and then down the rest of the way to county road 301. I popped a blood blister on my left foot at lunchtime.

On July 8, after closing the gap mentioned above, I walked north on US 285 from milepost 182 to milepost 203, near the top of Kenosha Pass, at 10,000 feet. I also walked over Red Hill Pass, at 9,993 feet. In between the passes is a very long and beautiful valley, dotted with cattle ranches. The weather grew increasingly cloudy as the day progressed and it rained on both sides of us. It didn't hit us until I started up the road toward Kenosha Pass. Because of unlimited visibility I was able to track the progress of the rainsqualls, just as I was able to track the snow squalls in Arizona.

Returning to August 1994, on Friday, August 5 I walked south on US 285 from Rosalie Road, near milepost 225, to milepost 203, just beyond the summit of Kenosha Pass. The route was mostly uphill and there was a headwind much of the time. The shoulders were mostly adequate, either asphalt or packed dirt and gravel. Traffic was moderately heavy.

On August 3, 1994 I walked south from the intersection of Foxton Road and US 285, near Conifer and milepost 235, to Rosalie Road, about 10 miles, on up-and-down terrain. It rained BIG drops for over half an hour. I had driven myself to the starting point and planned to walk back to the car, but after retracing my steps for three miles I was caught in a thunder-and-sleet storm. Scared (of the lightning), cold and wet, I was looking for shelter when a passing roofer (not a dog but a person who installs roofs on buildings) took pity on me and gave me a ride in his truck back to my car.

Returning to July 1986 and the family reunion, on July 4 (Independence Day) I walked from the intersection of Route 74 and Route 73 in Evergreen, south on 73 to 285 and then south on 285 to Foxton Road. I walked the 9.5 miles in two sections, with a break for lunch at the home of my cousin Carol in Conifer. The road ascends steadily for several miles out of Evergreen and quickly goes above 8,000 feet. Even at this altitude the weather was hot. Evergreen forests cover the hills. I had been walking for three days and the ball of my left foot was quite sore and somewhat swollen.

The day before, on July 3rd, I walked from the corner of Colfax Avenue and Wadsworth Boulevard in Lakewood, or west Denver, south on Wadsworth to Morrison Road (Route 8), then west on Morrison Road, through red-rock country to the village of Morrison. From here I took Route 74 up the hill to the appropriately named Evergreen, stopping at the intersection of Route 73, for a total of about 22 miles.

Morrison is at 5,800 feet and Evergreen is at about 7,800 feet, at Aloha, the "cabin" of my Aunt Freddie, which is higher than downtown Evergreen. (The two buildings called cabins on the family property are large, multi-storied houses, erected many years ago.) The altitude where I started is about 5,400 feet. Route 74 ascends steadily, but not steeply. The road follows Bear Creek. Although the creek lends mountain atmosphere to the walk, the foothills block a view of the high peaks. Many of the houses built along the creek have driveways with bridges that go over it. A thermometer in Evergreen registered 87 degrees F, but intermittent clouds helped to moderate the effect of the heat.

On August 1, 1994 I walked from Wadsworth Boulevard east on Colfax Avenue through downtown Denver, which includes the civic center and the tall buildings that are supposed to mark the heart of a big city. This became the official end of my walk, in location if not time. The good thing about walking in this part of the city was that there were plenty of McDonald's restaurants and other fast-food places with available restrooms. When you're walking in an urban area you have to think about these things.

CHAPTER 40 UK End-to-End—Northern Scotland

The famous End-to-End walk in the United Kingdom is also known by other names: John O'Groats to Land's End (JOGLE) and Land's End to John O'Groats (LEJOG). And it is not only walkers who cover this distance. I have a sweatshirt that purports to list the End-to-End records for, among other modes of transportation: running, backwards running, roller-skating, bicycling and even flying (46 minutes, 44 seconds).

Signs at Land's End, which is at the rocky tip of Cornwall, in southwestern England, and John O'Groats, in northern Scotland, state the distance between them as 874 miles. However, there are many routes between Land's End and John O'Groats, most of which are longer. As nearly as Bonny and I could calculate the length of the route I took, using maps and the odometers of rental cars, I walked about 867 miles, fewer miles than the sign says. This could be attributable to the fact that I was able to walk across a bridge over Dornoch Firth, in northern Scotland, that was dedicated by the Queen Mum in 1991. The bridge cuts off a number of miles since the previous route required walking around most of the firth.

After completing my Los Angeles-to-Denver walk in 1996 I had run out of worlds that I wanted to conquer within the United States. Logical walks such as the Appalachian Trail were unattainable by me because Bonny won't let me go where she can't get to me for more than a few hours at a time. But I needed another goal. Will Durant said that we need "...someone to love, something to do and something to look forward to." I had someone to love; I needed to renew the other two. And have a reason to stay in shape.

We had traveled extensively in the UK, Bonny more than I, because she had flown there on business for Xerox many times. A multitude of our ancestors came from those parts and we had done genealogy research in London and vicinity.

It wasn't difficult to list the reasons why I couldn't complete the End-to-End. I was 61 years old in 1999, when I started the walk, and we knew it would take several trips (which meant several years) for me to complete it. The farthest I had walked on one trip before was 182 miles in nine days in 1996, when I completed Los Angeles-to-Denver. Bonny was still working so we had to use her vacation time, something we had rarely done on my previous walks. And oh yes, Bonny had never driven on what she calls the wrong side of the road before. But if something isn't a challenge, what's the fun in doing it?

Before we started, I scoured the Internet, looking for facts about the End-to-End. The most useful information I found was in a book by Noel Blackham. Noel made the walk in 1988 and wrote about it in *One Man and His Dog Go Walkies*, which he published using his own publishing company, World Musicals, of Birmingham, England. Noel's route is entirely on roads and is one of the shortest. It suited my purposes. We used the Ordnance Survey maps with a 1:250,000 scale and the *Ordnance Survey Motoring Atlas*, which in addition to area maps contains street maps of the larger cities in the UK. When I walked I carried a copy of the map page I was on in a sealed plastic holder, to keep it dry.

I will write about my End-to-End walk in the order I walked it, which is like two swipes of a paintbrush: from the northern end south to Loch Lomond and then from the southern end north to the same point.

On June 30 and July 1, 1999 Bonny and I flew to London and then on to Glasgow, Scotland, where we rented a red Nissan Primera with automatic transmission. Bonny was not about to drive on the wrong side of the road and shift left-handed at the same time. Although our first hotel was literally across the street from the Glasgow Airport we had to negotiate three roundabouts to get to it (traffic on the roundabout has the right of way, even if it is only a circle painted in the center of a small intersection).

The next morning I drove us out of the congested area and then turned the car over to Bonny for her driving lesson. The hardest test came immediately as she drove on Route A82 along the western bank of Loch Lomond, on seven miles of road so narrow that two cars could barely pass each other, let alone a car and a truck. From the passenger seat I kept yelling that we were going to hit the rock wall on our left. At one point there are two sets of traffic lights that allow vehicles to go in only one direction at a time, because the engineers admit that the road is too narrow for more than one lane of traffic.

After we passed Loch Lomond the driving became easier, but when we were near Rannoch Moor a gigantic roar convinced Bonny that we were about to get creamed. It turned out to be the sound of freedom, a Royal Air Force fighter plane screaming low overhead. The same thing happened to her again later when I was walking and she was alone in the car.

Nevertheless, Bonny passed her driving test with flying colors, covering almost 290 miles to Wick, in northern Scotland. She wore a big yellow ribbon on a bracelet on her left wrist to remind her of the mantra, "Keep to the left."

Sat., July 3; Wick to John O'Groats (south to north) on A99—17 miles. The first day of my walk was cool and dreary, with some wind and sprinkles (it would get worse). I walked south to north for our convenience, since we were staying at Mackay's Hotel (pronounced Mack-EYES) in Wick. I was still jet-lagged and as I walked I waited for my endorphins to kick in—and waited.

I passed farmland, with some cows and more sheep. The red Highland Cattle, with wide horns and shaggy hair covering their eyes, are photogenic, but apparently not cost-effective because they aren't raised in large numbers. The lambs sucked milk from their ewes with great gusto and wagged their short tails furiously. The sheep are painted on the side with their owner's colors. Near John O'Groats, the barren landscape was brown-green, with some delicate white flowers. A number of *brochs* are in the area—three or four-story cylindrical towers, tapered at the top, that date from between 100 B.C. and 100 A.D. They were used as fortresses.

We took pictures at the John O'Groats Hotel, my official starting place. We could see the bleak Orkney Islands, farther north, across Pentland Firth. John O'Groats is not the northernmost point on the Scottish mainland, a fact that was pointed out to me on the Internet by a business owner from Dunnet Head, which claims this honor and is a few miles away. Unfortunately for him, nobody has ever heard of Dunnet Head.

After dinner, we watched the members of the Wick Pipe Band (with bagpipes and drums) parade through town in their kilts, playing stirring numbers. Several girls danced the Highland fling. Later, at Mackay's Hotel, we watched a musical performance, featuring an accordion, keyboard and drums, with local singers, including Leslie Mackay (is it true that half the residents of Wick are named Mackay?) and the pipe band again. The audience danced two-steps and waltzes. The local citizens looked well fed.

<u>Sun., July 4; Wick to Barriedale on A99 and A9—26 miles</u>. I walked south from Wick in weather that was "miserable," to quote the BBC. It never stopped raining. Thank goodness for my North Face rain top, purchased for me by Bonny and Andy. I also wore rain pants and rain gloves, but my feet remained wet, even after I changed shoes and socks. My brother, Mike, the marathoner and triathlete, scoffed when I complained about my wet feet and said this was a given in his endeavors. The only good news was a tailwind, which made me wish I had a sail. Spectacular green hillsides and cliffs that plunged into the North Sea kept me in awe. The road was narrow, with occasional walking paths beside it, but traffic was light. We stayed at a bed and breakfast in Helmsdale.

My medical report states that I was doing waist bends for my back and taking an aspirin each morning, as well as some ibuprofen. I sanded a callous on my left foot and put a pad on it. I also placed inserts in my Reebok sneakers for arch support. I used pain salve for bursitis in my right shoulder and Vaseline for anal irritation. Whew.

<u>Mon., July 5; Barriedale to Dunrobin Castle, south of Brora, on A9—26 miles</u>. I walked in fog and rain and wore my reflective spots, fearful that cars wouldn't see me. There were lots of ups and downs early—including 13% grades, reminiscent of the Big Sur on the California coast. At Helmsdale the road falls to the water. I was

heard to say, "Tell me again why people like to visit here." We stayed at a B&B in Brora.

Tues., July 6; Dunrobin Castle to near Alness on A9 and local roads—26 miles. The rain stopped but low clouds remained. A cow jam on A9 stopped traffic. I gave thanks to the Queen Mum for the distance-saving bridge over Dornoch Firth. Noel Blackham had to walk around most of the firth in 1988. I took a local road from Tain to Alness, getting away from the traffic. The favorite Scottish saying seems to be, "If it isn't raining now, it will rain soon," but the Scots optimistically leave their clothes out on the line even in the rain, and most of them wouldn't consider using a clothes dryer. Tall evergreen trees flourished, in addition to moors and farmland. The trees were being clear-cut in some places. The scenery looks a lot like that of central New York State. The sun rose soon after 4 a.m. and set after 10 p.m., but we never saw it. We stayed at small hotel in Alness.

Wed., July 7; near Alness to Beauly on local roads, B817 (through Alness), A9, A862—26 miles. The sun almost came out and I wore a T-shirt for the first time. In general, I walked on the right side of the road, facing traffic, but for a while on A862 I had to hug the left side because of a cliff and stone wall on the right. If there was a sidewalk (walking path) I used it. The extra two feet it gave me made an enormous difference in my stress level as I could almost ignore traffic altogether on a walking path.

In the usual case, when I had to walk on the white line marking the edge of the narrow road, I looked every vehicle past me to make sure it was giving me enough room. After a vehicle passed I invoked the ten-second rule: While the noise still drowned out that of other approaching vehicles, I assumed they were coming in both lanes, especially from behind. That way I didn't get careless and stroll out into the road. The scariest scenario was a vehicle passing another from behind me. I don't like drivers who risk my life to save a few seconds.

At one point I needed something from the car. I saw a red car parked ahead (you wouldn't believe how many red cars there are in Scotland) and went up to the passenger side. The door was locked so I knocked on the window. The window was lowered and I looked in, expecting to see Bonny. However, a man was sitting there, instead.

Embarrassed, I apologized. The man said he had broken down. I tried to recover by asking if he needed help. Thankfully, he said no, because I don't know how I could have helped him. We stayed at a B&B in Beauly.

Thu., July 8; Beauly to near Invermoriston on A862, A833, A831, A82—24 miles. Bonny drove off in the car after I started walking, saying that she was going to do some shopping or something, and would meet me in a little while. I wasn't carrying any water or food so when a little while stretched into a couple of hours I started to worry about her. Maybe she had been in an accident. I had time to invent an elaborate scenario about what had happened to her and what I needed to do to find her. I was ready to contact the police at the next center of population when she showed up, perfectly happy. Of course this irritated me, after all the mental anguish I had been through.

Some rain fell in late morning, as I walked through the hills north of Drumnadrochit, but then the day became sunny and warm. There is a 14 percent downgrade to Loch Ness, where I joined A82. I walked southwest along the north shore of Loch Ness, but there were not enough viewpoints of the beautiful loch, the largest and deepest in Scotland. I saw no sign of the monster. We stayed at a B&B in Invermoriston.

Fri., July 9; near Invermoriston to past Invergarry (southwest) on A82—21 miles. I walked southwest to the end of Loch Ness and then six miles past Invergarry, along Loch Lochy. It was warm and sunny all day and I wore shorts for the first time. My walking pants converted to shorts by unzipping the bottoms.

We had a two-hour pit stop in Fort Augustus because the electronic windows in the car stopped working. That reminded me of something satirist Mort Sahl said back in the 1950s, when American automobile manufacturers weren't known for building racing cars. He told about a Ford Thunderbird that had been entered in a race. He said the radio and air conditioner went out, but somehow the car still managed to finish the race. Nowadays, when we expect absolute luxury in all cars, including the Japanese Nissan we were driving, that may not be so funny. Our call to Avis brought a British AA technician from Inverness, but he couldn't fix the problem. He was able to close the front windows (the rear windows were manual).

From Loch Lochy we had impressive views of the Ben Nevis range. Ben Nevis, at 4,406 feet, is the highest peak in the UK, and always has snow on it. A legend states that when the snow melts, Scotland will be independent. At one B&B we met a couple from Austria. The man said he was a mountain runner and had just run up Ben Nevis. He also smoked.

Some heather had started to bloom—small, delicate, purple flowers. Whole hillsides burst into bloom in August. The official flower of Scotland is the thistle—also purple—but don't touch! All the B&B's we stayed at were clean, nicely furnished, with some newly remodeled, especially their bathrooms. The owners were friendly and helpful. Scottish breakfasts (toast, eggs, sausage, bacon—our ham, tomato, sometimes black pudding) are filling. We also were served orange juice and tea or coffee. On this day we stayed at a B&B in Spean Bridge.

Sat., July 10; past Invergarry to past Fort William on A82—26 miles. It rained a couple of times and was cloudy the rest of the time. The Ben Nevis range was lost in clouds. I walked right beside the south shore of Loch Lochy. The hills rising out of the opposite shore of the loch created the postcard picture of Scotland that the Scottish tourist office wants you to see. Fort William is the largest city we had been in so far on the walk. I had crossed over from the east side of Scotland to the west side. We stayed at a B&B in Fort William.

Sun, July 11; past Fort William to Rannoch Moor Summit on A82—26 miles. At 1,141 feet, Rannoch Moor Summit is the highest point on this part of the walk. The road starts to climb past Ballachulish and goes through Glencoe, scene of the historic massacre of the Macdonalds by the Campbells, in 1692. The climb up Glencoe pass is steady and goes on for miles, which led me to believe I was higher than I actually was. The wildness of the surrounding peaks, with their steep rocky cliffs, contributed to this sensation. Greenish brown heather grew everywhere, and was starting to bloom in the more sheltered areas. We stayed at a B&B at Achallader, three miles north of Bridge of Orchy.

Mon., July 12; Rannoch Moor Summit to past Crianlarich on
A82—24 miles. The road goes downhill to Bridge of Orchy and then
four miles uphill, close to the railroad track and one of Scotland's
favorite walking paths. I saw a host of walkers on the path, but the
major walking paths go in the wrong direction for End-to-End
walkers. It was shorts and T-shirt weather, and a thin cloud cover in
the afternoon was actually welcome, keeping the temperature
bearable. The midges (no-see-ems) came out and we sprayed
ourselves with Off. Bonny was scared out of her wits a second time
by a low-flying RAF fighter plane. We stayed at a B&B in
Crianlarich.

Tue., July 13; past Crianlarich to Balloch on A82, A811—32
miles. I walked eight miles before breakfast, starting at 6 a.m. at
Tarbet. I walked south to north along the narrowest part of A82 on
the west bank of Loch Lomond, to beat the traffic. This is the stretch
where Bonny was initiated into driving on the left and we figured it
would be just as difficult to walk it, as it was to drive it. Traffic was
light. Only once did a truck and car pass me simultaneously. I
pressed myself against the stone wall on the loch side of the road,
wishing I were even skinnier than I am. Fortunately, Scottish people
sleep in during the summer because it stays light so late.

After breakfast I closed the gap from Crianlarich south to Loch
Lomond, and then walked south from Tarbet along the rest of Loch
Lomond. I finished the day by making an easy jog east to Balloch,
which is right at the southern tip of Loch Lomond. My Buchanan
ancestors lived along the shores of Loch Lomond and there is even a
Buchanan castle on the east side of the loch. In 2002, three years
later, I finished my End-to-End walk here. We stayed at a B&B in
Balloch.

I had walked 274 miles in 11 consecutive days, a personal record.
And I felt great. Who says you don't get better as you get older? As
Bonny says, we are aging like fine wine.

CHAPTER 41 UK End-to-End—Southwestern England

Bonny's frequent-flyer miles enabled us to fly first class from Los Angeles to London in August 2000. The 11 first-class seats on our United 777 became beds and we slept some on our overnight flight that landed at Heathrow Airport at 7 a.m.

In addition, Bonny's genealogy research paid off, enabling her to find cousins in England from a branch of her family that had been separated from the American side for 120 years. We visited some of these cousins, in two locations on the south coast of England, before driving on toward Land's End, the southern end of the End-to-End.

Sun., Aug. 27; Camborne to Land's End on A30—26 miles. I walked southwest on A30 from Camborne (instead of starting at Land's End) because we had driven west from near Plymouth that morning, fighting the traffic caused by a bank-holiday (three-day) weekend. It was already 10 a.m. and I wanted to get started without the additional delay of driving another 26 miles. At first, the road was a dual carriageway, with a nice shoulder for walking. As the road narrowed it had walking paths—asphalt or grass.

But beyond Penzance (home of Gilbert and Sullivan's pirates), for most of the final 10 miles, the narrow road had no shoulder or walking path. In order to avoid oncoming traffic I pressed myself into the wild blackberry bushes that grow for miles along the stone walls lining the road. I became well acquainted with the prickly bushes and ended the walk with stinging legs and a rash.

The weather was pleasant, with one rain shower and a moderate headwind at times. Clouds kept the heat down. I had occasional views of rolling farmland, and ocean near the end. Land's End was a tourist trap, with a two-pound charge to park, a few attractions and a hotel. Rocky cliffs keep people away from the water. Some bicyclists were on the road, perhaps doing the End-to-End. I'm convinced that bicycling the route is more dangerous than walking it.

Distance signs are misleading; e.g. within 50 yards of each other one sign says, "Land's End 6 miles" and another, "Land's End 9 miles." An English walker informed me that they are the result of different ways of measuring distance at different periods in history. They were placed there many years apart. We stayed at the Mt. Royal Hotel in Penzance, once the mayor's house.

Mon., Aug. 28; Camborne to Victoria on A30—26 miles. I walked northeast to the Victoria Inn and Lodge (where we stayed), at Victoria. One rain shower interrupted an otherwise nice day, which was partly cloudy and warm, with an occasional tailwind. The traffic was very heavy at times as people returned home from the three-day weekend (equivalent to our Labor Day?), anxious, I'm sure, to get back to work and school.

Sometimes the road was a dual carriageway with a good shoulder or walking path, sometimes two lanes with a shoulder, but sometimes two lanes with no shoulder. I passed large windmills, used to generate electric power, similar to those near Palm Springs, California. I also passed the Jamaica Inn at Bolventer, used as the name of a Daphne du Maurier novel.

The area is thinly populated, with much farmland in shades of brown and green. There are many cows and sheep, and occasional pigs. I was relieved to see the pigs since a traditional English breakfast contains bacon (like our ham), and I had not seen many before in the UK. I took ibuprofen for chronic lower back pain. I also had some pain above my left knee for the first time ever. I suspect it was radiating from my back. We ate dinner at a pub named the Eliot Arms, opened in 1625.

Tue., Aug. 29 (our 36th wedding anniversary); Victoria to south of Launceton on A30—26 miles. The weather, cool and cloudy in the morning, warmed up in the afternoon, but the sun was never bright. I walked through Bodmin Moor, which has stone formations like those at Stonehenge, and group graves, called barrows. I tried a shortcut, taking a local road to Temple, but chickened out at a confusing sign and took a side road back to A30. However, the route would have worked. The rolling hills are primarily used for farmland. The moor looks a lot like the land around it, but rises to 1,377 feet at a hill called Brown Willy. The problems with my left knee became worse and I contemplated taking the next day off, something I have rarely done.

Wed., Aug. 30; south of Launceton to near Meldon on A30 and old A30—19 miles. I walked north on A30 around the south end of Launceston. At Lifton I changed to old A30 and peace and quiet, since all the traffic is on new A30. Not only did the noise level drop, but also the buffeting by the slipstreams of big trucks, or lorries. I took old A30 to where it ends, back at new A30, a short distance from Meldon. This was the first day warm enough for shorts and a T-shirt all day. We ate sandwiches for lunch at the Harris Arms on old A30, dating from the 16th century.

In addition to farmland, I had views of Dartmoor, on our right, with its famous prison, and hills rising to 2,000 feet. My left knee gave me major problems. The pain limited me to a slow pace and I stopped several times to rest it. We purchased a knee brace at a pharmacy in Okehampton. Bonny said she was astounded I could walk at all. I was too. During the day I left Cornwall and crossed the Tamar River into Devon.

Thu., Aug. 31; near Meldon to 8 miles south of Tiverton on a combination of A30, side roads and A3072—24 miles. The easiest way to describe my route on paper is to say I walked north on A30, took B3260 through the village of Okehampton (which has the remains of a Norman and Saxon castle), left on B3215, right on A3072, right on A377, and left on A3072 to an intersection eight miles south of Tiverton. The actual route I took was somewhat different. I turned right from the first A3072 segment onto a side road at Bow and walked through Coleford. At the intersection with A377 I walked a few feet on A377 to a continuation of the side road, continued left on the side road and finally turned left on A3072 at Crediton.

I jumped at the chance to take the side roads because, although they are narrow, they have much less traffic than the A roads. Even the A roads can get very narrow, with stonewalls and/or hedges on both sides rising to ten feet. Some of the old houses had thatched roofs; newer ones had slate roofs; some of the newest houses had tile roofs. In contrast to the sometimes-ancient buildings, the farmers use the latest equipment, including state-of-the-art tractors. John Deere is not a stranger to the UK.

I use the RICE approach on my knee: Rest (when possible), Ice (from sympathetic B&B owners), Compression (knee brace), Elevation (in the evening). It seemed to help. We stayed at an inn at the intersection of A3072 and A396 on the Exe River. A stone bridge over the river, used by A396, was built in the 13th century. Our room had spiders on the walls, ceilings and bathtub, but we learned to coexist with them. They had been there longer than we had. At night we kept the window open and listened to the river.

Fri., Sept. 1; south of Tiverton to south of Taunton on A3072, A396, A361 and A38—26 miles. At Tiverton I turned right on A361 (a dual carriageway) to A38, then walked north to near Taunton. I crossed the M5 twice. M roads are motorways, which are equivalent to American Interstates. Dual carriageways are also divided highways, but access to them isn't always limited and they sometimes have cross streets. I occasionally walked on a dual carriageway, but I stayed off the M roads altogether. An accident on the M5 in Bristol, north of us, backed up traffic all day and a mess of displaced cars almost caused gridlock as the drivers tried to get through Taunton.

Periodic showers fell, followed by a steady rain later in the afternoon. I was helped by a tailwind part of the time. Many people name their houses and farms. The names are often meaningful: Watersmeet, Hilltop. We stayed at a B&B in Taunton.

Sat., Sept. 2; south of Taunton to Rooks Bridge on A38—26 miles. I walked through Taunton, the largest city we've seen so far, North Petherston, Bridgwater and several smaller places. Showers fell in the morning. Traffic on the A38 was still backed up for miles from Bridgwater north because of yesterday's bad accident on the M5 in Bristol. At least one lane had to be repaved. At times I moved almost as fast as the northbound traffic, which couldn't have delighted the passengers in the cars.

I crossed the M5 once and saw brake lights on the northbound traffic. A38 has a walking path most of the way, which made it easier to contend with the heavy traffic. We stayed at a hotel in downtown Axbridge, an old village. We ate dinner in the hotel bar and befriended two men, both of whom had traveled in the US. One was a professional soccer (football) player. I left our camera in the hotel bar, but some kind soul turned it in and it was there in the morning.

Sun., Sept. 3; Rooks Bridge to Filton, north of Bristol, on A38— 26 miles. I walked through several villages, and then came the city of Bristol, for which we were totally unprepared. Bonny and I became separated upon entering Bristol, and neither of us had a street map (this was before we purchased a copy of the *Ordnance Survey Motoring Atlas*, which contains detailed street maps of major UK cities). I tried to get information at a police station, but it was closed. Apparently, Bristol has no crime on Sunday. Next I found a fire station and looked at a street map on the wall. A fireman showed me my location on the map and then had to dash off to a fire. I had a few seconds to memorize the map and wished I could take it with me. From there I navigated from memory and the position of the sun, which fortunately, was shining. I also used a very sketchy map on an advertising flyer.

Meanwhile, Bonny, who was driving the car, bought a street map at a petrol station, but because the route signs in Bristol are almost nonexistent and the street signs are problematic, it took her an hour and a half to get to the north side of the city, after many wrong turns and some tears. Bristol is a major city and the populated area continues north on A38 for miles. We finally met on A38, north of Bristol, and breathed sighs of relief. This was perhaps the deciding argument for me to carry a cell phone. We stayed at a small hotel in Filton.

Mon., Sept. 4; north of Bristol to north of Newport on A38—15 miles. I walked until noon to just north of Newport, an intersection with signs pointing east to Hogsdown, 1 mile; Lower Wick, 1-1/2 miles; Upper Wick, 2-1/2 miles. This is several miles north of the A38-B4509 intersection, with access to the M5. After lunch we drove the M5 south to the M4 and back to Heathrow (and home). The day started out as the coolest so far: 52 degrees F, but quickly warmed up to T-shirt weather as the sun came out. The walking was easy, with walking paths all the way. We ate lunch at a pub that featured a good dish of chili.

In 8.5 days I walked a total of 215 miles, maintaining my average of 25 miles/day for Phases 1 and 2. The UK has many official footpaths, covering thousands of miles, and signs for these lined the roads I walked. In spite of the footpaths, it is not a walker-friendly country for people who want to walk on the roads. Roundabouts are very walker-unfriendly and many narrow roads are lined with stone walls and high hedges, with no escape route for walkers. Bicyclists face an even greater peril since they take up more room and ride with the traffic. However, there are many miles of walking paths along the roads, also, and the lesser roads without walking paths have the advantage of less traffic.

Bonny provided wonderful support and became very competent at left-side driving. We stayed in a series of nice B&Bs and hotels, even with the spiders in one of the hotel rooms. The full English breakfast is suspiciously like the Scottish breakfast: eggs, bacon (our ham), sausage, beans, mushrooms, tomatoes, toast, juice, coffee or tea. Only the name has been changed. We became accustomed to having our pint of lager at dinner.

The English have now learned how to prepare vegetables without overcooking them and celebrated by giving us enormous helpings of cauliflower, carrots and broccoli. They now know how to put ice in a glass of water, also. We asked for tap water, as opposed to bottled water, so we wouldn't get charged for it. And nothing beats English chips (French fries).

CHAPTER 42 UK End-to-End—Western England to Scotland

AMERICA LIVES

I had feared for America.
Had we lost the inner fire
that brought ancestors to these shores?
Had we lost the hot desire,
each to choose a fulfilling path
and set our aspirations higher?

I had feared for liberty.
The fragile dream must be protected.
When everyone's a victim, then
responsibility's rejected.
When we suck the common teat
the dream grows dim and sits neglected.

Others saw the softness here
and sought to decimate a foe.
Tyrants cannot stand the thought
that some are free to come and go.
So on a dark September day
the wings of death delivered their blow.

But then a phenomenon occurred.
Heroic tales from the ruins were told.
The people spoke with one clear voice:
"We will never be controlled."
And I saw with thankful heart
the fire within had not grown cold.

I no longer fear for America.
I no longer fear for liberty.
We have awakened, but the dream
is bright for all the world to see.
When we unite to keep it so
it's a path we choose because we're free.

The third phase of my UK End-to-End walk took place in September 2001 against a background of calamitous events. These events make the walk pale into insignificance, but pursuing it even as the world turned upside down helped Bonny and me retain our sanity, especially during a time when we couldn't have gone home even if we had wanted to.

Foot notes: I wore one pair of Reebok shoes for the entire distance this year. I wore the same pair for almost the entire walk last year (and rested the shoes in between). Even though I owned five or six pairs of the same model Reebok shoes, this pair was the most comfortable. After almost 500 official walking miles in them and an indeterminate number of unofficial miles, I retired them. I wore two-ply socks (available at running stores) and powdered my feet with baby powder or cornstarch each morning.

<u>Tues., Sept. 4: near Newport on A38—2 miles</u>. Bonny and I arrived at London Heathrow Tuesday morning at 7 a.m., after a direct flight from Los Angeles on United, and picked up our gold Rover from Europcar. Gold is an easy color to spot. After driving west we had lunch with some high school buddies of Bonny's, Brooks and Sandy, who she hadn't seen for 43 years. They live in a quaint stone house on a narrow road next to a church.

They lived in Africa for several years and told fascinating stories about life there. At night, hippos would come into their yard and trample their bushes. Sandy constructed a narrow path for them. After that, the hippos would follow the path, placing one foot carefully in front of the other. Brooks told of standing near a well when a camel driver came racing up. A woman handed him a gourd of water, from which he drank deeply. Then he raced off and disappeared.

After lunch we took a room at a bed and breakfast on the A38, two miles north of where I stopped at Newport (north of Bristol) in 2000. The B&B was a good example of a building that has been added on to and/or partially restored on several occasions. We counted at least four different kinds of brick and stone that had been used for its various incarnations. We found that many of the older buildings had been transformed in this manner.

It seemed logical to walk the two miles I needed south of the B&B, because then the next morning I could sail out the door and head north. This was the only B&B we stayed at that didn't have a toilet in the room (room toilets are called en suite in the advertising). We also toured Berkeley Castle, where King Edward II was assassinated by his wife and others in a particularly gruesome manner.

Wed., Sept. 5; A38 Newport north to Tewksbury—26 miles. During the day I passed the 500-mile mark of my End-to-End walk. A38 follows a Roman road south of Gloucester. The Romans were known for building straight and well-engineered roads that stood the test of time, wheels and feet. I left the A38 to walk through the center of Gloucester, where the old Roman roads, Northgate, Southgate Eastgate and Westgate Streets meet in a pedestrian-only area. The lack of cars was refreshing in a country where there are no Stop signs and traffic tends to move continuously, with drivers yielding to pedestrians only grudgingly.

We ate lunch in Gloucester in a café near the Gloucester and Sharpness Canal. Several rain showers dampened the morning, but in spite of an overcast sky it warmed up to T-shirt weather in the afternoon. Miles of blackberry bushes lined the roads. Some of the berries were ripe and delicious, so I picked and ate a handful whenever I could.

I remember a nursery rhyme that goes:

> Dr. Foster went to Gloucester
> In a shower of rain.
> He stepped in a puddle
> Up to his middle
> And never went there again.

I left the A38 again to walk into Tewksbury, where we stayed at the Jessop House Hotel, built about 1600. Traffic was moderately heavy, but not troublesome. There are walking paths and/or bike paths almost all the way on this part of A38. This year I wore reflective spots all the time I was walking, at the urging of Bonny. I noticed that almost all truck drivers and road workers wore reflective vests (called waistcoats here), apparently by law.

We ate dinner at a family-owned restaurant, housed in a building also built about 1600. The only other customers were a husband and wife, slightly older than we were, who lived near London. They had been everywhere and done everything at least twice. They told about the time the wife had her purse stripped from her by thieves on motor scooters in southern France. The husband raced after them in a Jaguar, following them down one-way streets the wrong way, until they dropped the purse. When he spotted the same guys another day they beat it.

Thu., Sept. 6; Tewksbury to south of Kidderminster on A38 and A449—25 miles. I walked on walking paths all the way. I picked up the A449 north of Worcester. The A449 is a divided highway, but not limited access. It didn't warm up to T-shirt weather until the late afternoon, when a significant headwind appeared.

Bonny toured the Royal Worcester china factory in Worcester and we ate lunch at a pub there. The UK is much like the US in many ways, but at about three-fourths scale: in cars, roads, driveways, garages and houses. But not people. This can make driving and parking tricky. However, the restaurant servings tend to be large, like those in the US. And many of the people outside of London, who aren't always racing to catch Underground trains, look very well fed. We stayed at a B&B in Kidderminster.

Fri., Sept. 7; south of Kidderminster through Wolverhampton on A449—25 miles. In the morning I walked north to south from Kidderminster to yesterday's finish. Then Bonny ferried me back to Kidderminster and I walked north from there. There are walking paths most of the way, with a few exceptions. Walking through Wolverhampton is tricky since the downtown roundabouts exclude pedestrians. At first encounter, the subways that allow walkers to go under these intersections appear to either go nowhere or everywhere. One branches in at least six directions, with minimal signs. I felt like Theseus in the Labyrinth and hoped there wasn't a Minotaur stalking me. In some populated areas, badly needed pedestrian crosswalks have been created, with stoplights for vehicle traffic. Stoplights are a rarity in the UK.

The weather stayed cloudy and became windy—with mostly a tailwind. I saw several warning signs at the entrances to farms, urging people to stay out because they might be carrying Foot and Mouth Disease on their shoes or car tires. We stayed at a B&B in Penkridge.

Sat., Sept. 8; north of Wolverhampton to Newcastle-Under-Lyme on A449 and A34—25 miles. The good news is that I walked on walking paths all day. I walked through Penkridge, where we stayed the night before, and then through Stafford, which is a challenge, just as all significant centers of population are. Stafford has a series of roundabouts, arranged in a giant circle, in the center of town. I cursed roundabouts because there is no elegant way to walk around them. The traffic never stops and walkers on a roundabout don't have the right-of-way, as vehicles do. Occasionally, it is possible to cut through the center, but it is usually necessary to walk around the roundabout, losing time, while attempting to pick the shortest direction, with the least number of roads to cross.

At Stafford I switched to the A34 and continued to a Michelin plant in Newcastle-Under-Lyme. I walked a short distance north to south right after lunch, primarily to get some relief from the headwind. It was cool and breezy and the headwind was gusty at times. The traffic was heavy and loud. The terrain in this part of England is mostly flat, with occasional rolls. Much of the countryside is the English green, inhabited by cows and sheep. Farmers drive big, green, air-conditioned John Deere tractors and slow up traffic when they drive on the roads. We stayed at a hotel in Newcastle-Under-Lyme.

Sun., Sept. 9; Newcastle-Under-Lyme to near Northwich on A34, A533 and A530 to A559—26 miles. Before breakfast I walked two miles south to north to Kings Road in downtown Newcastle-Under-Lyme, where we stayed last night, because breakfast was served late on Sundays. My hands got cold. I speeded up to get by a group of loitering young men, not knowing why they were out so early on a Sunday morning, but they paid no attention to me. After breakfast I continued north on the A34, the A533 through Sandbach, the A530 at Middlewich, to the A559, east of Northwich.

The weather was clear but blustery, with a significant headwind at times. The route follows the Trent and Mersey Canal for quite a distance. The pencil-thin canal boats are often used as houseboats. There are no walking paths for several miles on the A530 and A533. Walking paths are made of asphalt (no concrete), sometimes with a grass strip between them and the road. Occasionally, when there is no asphalt path there is a grass strip that is walkable. I encountered a few walking paths that were overgrown with bushes or had crumbled to gravel. Many of the roads have curbs, which add a degree of security if you can walk on a path and not on the road. When there was no path I walked on the right side of the road, facing traffic.

I was carrying a cell phone (called a mobile phone in the UK) for the first time. We rented it along with the car. In the afternoon I received a phone call from my sister-in-law, Judy. She had flown into the Manchester airport and awaited us at the Holiday Inn there. We drove to meet her after I finished walking and stayed at the Inn for the night.

During the day I got what we used to call a "shin splint" on my left leg, although I suspect my medical diagnosis is faulty. I treated it with ice and a hot bath and it was gone by morning.

Tues., Sept. 11; near Northwich north to Wigan on A559 and A49—25 miles. On September 10, Bonny, Judy and I took a planned day off from walking, for sightseeing and genealogy research in Manchester. Then we drove to Hartford (near Northwich) and stayed at the Stables B&B, behind a church, which once had a stable on the site, but is now a thoroughly modern house inside, with a spiral wooden staircase and prints by impressionist artists on the walls. It is owned by Dee and Edwin, a very nice couple who helped us search for flight information on the Internet for Judy when we returned there on September 14.

On September 11, my route went through Warrington, which is east of Liverpool. The A49 has good walking paths, although the A559 lacks them at times. Traffic was not heavy on the A559, however. I was on my own for lunch and ate at a McDonald's (for speed, not quality).

A few minutes after 2 p.m. (9 a.m. in New York) I was walking north of Warrington when I received a call from Bonny on the cell phone. She said, "This is not a joke," and then the line went dead. What was not a joke? I could tell from the intensity in her voice that she was serious. Could somebody in our family be sick or hurt? If so, I would have received the news first because I had the cell phone. The only person it could be was Judy. Had she looked left instead of right while crossing the street? A surge of fear went through me.

I received another call from Bonny. Again she said, "This is not a joke" and the line went dead. Finally, after several tries she called me and didn't get disconnected. She told me that planes in the US had been hijacked and crashed, and that President Bush had declared war. Against whom, I asked. Maybe Palestine. It wasn't clear.

We agreed to meet at a tourist office at Wigan Pier, near Wigan. By the way, there is no significant water at Wigan Pier. In a daze I walked to Wigan Pier, but couldn't find the tourist office. I went into a police station. An officer gave me a map of Wigan and showed me where the Charles Dickens Hotel was. Bonny had booked a room there for the night.

I walked to the hotel and was given a room on an upper floor. I went upstairs to the room and turned on the telly. The BBC was showing continuous coverage of the devastation. Over and over I saw the flames engulf the World Trade Center buildings and the second plane hit the South Tower. As I watched in horror, the buildings collapsed. I also saw the damage to the Pentagon, which the English pronounce with an accent on the first syllable but not the third, and heard about the crash of the fourth plane.

Bonny and Judy were at the Public Record Office in Preston, north of Wigan, at 2 p.m. As they arrived, one of the employees was on a phone call to a friend in the US, receiving a blow-by-blow account of the planes crashing into the New York World Trade Center. The employee repeated what he heard out loud. Bonny's immediate thought was to call me, but her hands were shaking so much that she could barely press the buttons. She reached me for a few seconds, only to be disconnected because she hadn't put enough money in the payphone. Finally, an employee helped her use one of the office phones and she told me what she knew.

Bonny and Judy got caught in heavy traffic and didn't reach the hotel until a couple of hours after I did. We received a call from our son, Andy, who told about the problems he and his wife, Melissa, had encountered getting home to Virginia from their jobs in Washington, D.C. He heard the plane that crashed into the Pentagon as it flew overhead. All of our relatives seemed to be okay. When we could drag ourselves away from the TV screen we had dinner and discussed our options. Commercial airlines were already grounded so there was no point in trying to get home. People were stacking up at London's Heathrow Airport and the hotels near there were doubling their rates.

We felt safe where we were so we decided to stay away from London and continue with our vacation plan. Judy's flight home on Saturday, September 15 was cancelled. At one point during the following days, while he was trying to get Judy another flight home, Phil, Judy's husband (and my brother), told us on the phone that he was incredibly sad that Judy couldn't leave England. We felt the same way. Phil finally got Judy a flight home on Sunday, with the help of our cousin, Beth, who is a travel agent. Over the next several days we received phone calls from Bonny's English cousins, expressing their sadness at what had happened, and their support. Other people we met were very sympathetic to the US. Many had relatives or friends living there.

One comment about the Charles Dickens hotel: Noel Blackham, the man whose route I followed on the End-to-End and the author of *One Man and His Dog Go Walkies*, stayed at this hotel, but I'm afraid I can't applaud his choice in this instance. Judy's room was small and claustrophobic. We all slept in one room, partly for this reason and partly because it was not a good night to sleep alone. In addition to questionable rooms, the hotel had a rowdy bar on the ground floor.

Wed., Sept. 12; Wigan to south of Garstang, on A49 and A6—26 miles. I couldn't stand the thought of sitting in front of the telly and watching the World Trade Center buildings collapse hundreds of more times so I continued my walk. I walked through Preston, a good-sized city, and on to an Esso gas station several miles south of Garstang. On my own for lunch, I ate at a Burger King, which I rated slightly higher than the McDonald's.

Rain started to fall about noon and continued most of the afternoon, sometimes hard. My hooded North Face protected the top half of me just fine, but I was not wearing my rain pants, and my legs became soaked. Bonny and Judy finally rescued me at the Esso station before I got hypothermia, and drove me back to our hotel in Preston, where I warmed up in the shower.

We ate at a nice Italian restaurant, featuring background music that was all Dean Martin, all the time. We were forcibly reminded that Dino had recorded hundreds of songs in addition to "That's Amore" and "Memories are Made of This." Bonny and I had eaten at another "all Dean Martin" restaurant two years before in Balloch, at the south end of Loch Lomond.

Fri., Sept. 14; south of Garstang to north of Carnforth on A6, B6430, A6 and A6070—27 miles. I took a day off from walking on September 13 because the weather forecast was so bad—heavy rain and strong winds—that even I had second thoughts. Usually, I regard giving in to the weather as a sign of weakness. The hotel owner let us send e-mails from her computer, allowing us to keep in touch with family. We spent much of the day at the Preston Public Record Office, where Bonny and Judy did genealogy research while I read a mystery written by Bill Shoemaker (that's right—the jockey). It wasn't bad. We stayed at our hotel B & B for a second night and ate at the same Italian restaurant, listening to the same Dean Martin songs.

On September 14 I walked from my Esso station north on the A6, then the B6430, to Garstang, returning to the A6 to go through Lancaster and Carnforth. I jogged right on the A6070 and continued on to the intersection with the road to Yealand. The English walk much faster than typical Americans, and I was sometimes passed as I walked through cities where pedestrian traffic was heavy. When this happened I had an urge to ask the person passing me if he could keep up his pace for 25 miles. On my own for lunch, I ate a "chickwich" at a pub in Lancaster. It was slightly better than Burger King and McDonald's.

The weather was cool and pleasant in the morning, cool and cloudy in the afternoon. There are footpaths until the A6070, but traffic on the A6070 was light. It also featured many warning signs concerning Foot and Mouth Disease, urging people to keep out of farms and off side roads. Many rural footpaths were closed.

Sun., Sept. 16; north of Carnforth to near Shap on A6070, A65 and A6—24 miles. On Saturday, September 15, Bonny, Judy and I went sightseeing in the walled city of Chester. Then we took Judy to the Holiday Inn at the Manchester Airport so she could catch a flight home on Sunday. We said goodbye to her and drove north to a hotel in Lancaster.

At dinner in the dining area of the hotel we sat next to Kieran and Diane Moran, who lived in Northern Ireland. They had just taken their daughter to a university in Birmingham, where she was starting a masters program. Kieran, who was a policeman (called a constable), assured us that we would be safe in Belfast and the surrounding area if we wanted to visit there. He bought us a round of drinks and we reciprocated, although after my one "pint" I stuck to water.

On September 16, I walked north on the A6070, which changes to the A65 south of Crooklands (the change was not shown on my map). At Kendal I picked up the A6 again. Bonny and I ate lunch in a cafeteria at a Kendal supermarket. North of Kendal the road rises to about 1,400 feet, east of the Cumbrian Mountains. I stopped beyond the peak of the hill near Shap.

Walking paths were scarce on the A6070 and the A65, but traffic was light on these roads. The weather was ideal for walking—cool, with scattered clouds. It is photo-op country, with rolling green hills dotted with white sheep and black-and-white cows. At one point government employees stopped all vehicles heading south on the A6 and sprayed them with acetic acid (vinegar) for Foot and Mouth Disease. In some places blankets had been placed across the road so that vehicles had to drive over them. The blankets were saturated with acetic acid. We stayed at the Greyhound Hotel in Shap, built about 1600, where we ate the best meal of the trip.

<u>Mon., Sept. 17; near Shap to south of Carlisle on A6—27 miles</u>. I walked through the metropolises of Shap, Hackthorpe and Penrith. Penrith is larger than the other two and actually has a Safeway, where we ate lunch. The A6 and the M6 (one of the main north-south motorways) twine around each other like snakes, south of Penrith. I went on to the intersection with the road that goes to the village of Cotehill, near entrance number 42 to the M6. It had cooled off to the point where I wore the hood to my North Face all day and my rain gloves (for warmth) part of the time. There were walking paths some of the way. The A6 follows an old Roman road for a while. Roman roads, as I have said, tend to be straight and well engineered. This one was no exception. We stayed at the Terracotta Restaurant and Lodge, south of Carlisle, which had recently been renovated. The food was good here. We were on a roll, gastronomically speaking.

<u>Tue., Sept. 18; south of Carlisle to Ecclefechan on A6, A7, A74 and B7076—24 miles</u>. The A6 goes to the city of Carlisle. From there I took the A7 north and then went northwest on the A74. The A74 becomes a motorway, designated the A74(M). I got off where the motorway started (at Gretna, which is also the Scottish border) and continued on B7076, which conveniently hugs the A74(M), to Ecclefechan.

This route differs from the route Noel Blackham walked in *One Man and His Dog Go Walkies* in 1988. He walked on the A74 north of Gretna, but that was before it became a motorway. In addition, I don't think B7076 existed then. It isn't shown on older maps. Noel complained about the heavy traffic on the A74 and the proximity of the big trucks to where he had to walk, so I am glad the B7076, which has almost no traffic, has been built.

The A74 is a dual carriageway. I walked on the left, riding on the slipstreams of the trucks, as long as the shoulder was ten feet wide, but when it narrowed to three feet I switched to the right side and bucked the slipstreams, holding onto my hat to keep it from being blown off my head.

I entered Scotland at the village of Gretna, and we ate lunch in nearby Gretna Green, at a place called the Old Blacksmith Shop. Blacksmiths could marry couples and the law apparently used to permit marriages at a younger age in Scotland than England, so teenagers would elope to Gretna Green. A comic painting on the wall commemorates this.

I walked 282 miles in 11 days (not consecutive) on this trip, maintaining my 25 miles-per-day average. In the first three segments of my End-to-End walk I covered 771 miles. We had no trouble flying home on September 23, after a short stay in Wales and a visit to several of Bonny's long-lost cousins in Sheffield, England. Planes were flying on regular schedules by then.

CHAPTER 43 UK End-to-End—Southern Scotland

I finished my End-to-End walk in May and June 2002. After visiting Bonny's long-lost cousins in southern England for the second time, we headed north. We stopped near Oxford and toured Blenheim Palace, where Winston Churchill was born. John Churchill, the first Duke of Marlborough, built the palace in the early 1700s. He was a general who never lost a battle, so Winston was the second historical figure in the family. The grounds cover 12,000 acres.

<u>Wed., May 29; Ecclefachan north to past Johnstonebridge on B7076—14 miles</u>. I only walked in the afternoon because in the morning we drove to Scotland from Sheffield, England, where we visited Bonny's other cousins again. Ecclefachan is 76 miles south of Glasgow, according to a sign on the A74(M), which runs parallel to B7076 (or vice versa). Traffic was very light on my B road because all the through traffic was on the motorway. The route is that of an old Roman road. I walked on a bike path with almost no bikes.

It rained, sometimes heavily, and the wind was gusty, but part of the time it pushed me, for which I was grateful. I walked past Lockerbie, the site of the crash of Pan Am 103 on December 21, 1988. Bonny and I stayed the night at a bed and breakfast in Lockerbie and visited the Garden of Remembrance, which is in a cemetery. It is a memorial to the 270 people killed in the plane crash. The names of all the victims are engraved on a wall and there are also some individual markers, placed by relatives.

Thu., May 30; near Johnstonebridge to Crawford on B7076 and A702—22 miles. We were in the valley of the River Clyde, which the road follows closely in places. In addition to the river, my B road paralleled the motorway and a rail line. Most of the trains were Virgin passenger trains, part of the Richard Branson empire. The road makes its way up into hills, some covered with pine trees, others green but treeless. When the rain came, the wind, which had been pushing me, turned on me and blew the cold rain into my face. My rain pants got soaked and so did my legs. The combination of wind, rain and cold did me in. Bonny hadn't seen me so disheartened in a long time and worried about my resolution to continue. We stayed at a B&B in Crawford.

Fri., May 31; Crawford to Ferniegair on A702 and B7078—27 miles. The weather improved and so did my spirits, but I still wore four layers on top and three on the bottom to blunt the effects of the headwind. The rain held off and the sun came out, playing hide-and-seek with fluffy clouds. I actually took off my North Face rain top in the afternoon. The route climbed to ever-higher valleys. The wind stream from a large truck blew my University of Michigan baseball cap off my head and it flew over a wire fence. Not wanting to lose it, I climbed over the fence to retrieve it, after checking for bulls. Bonny made friends with some cows, who crowded around her. The ubiquitous sheep hadn't been shorn yet, but they had lots of babies. We stayed at a B&B in Larkhall.

Sat., June 1; Crawford to Old Kilpatrick on A72, A724, A749, Loch Lomond Bike Path and A814—24 miles. I walked through Hamilton and then into the city of Glasgow. Bonny and I coordinated very closely on our approach to Glasgow so as not to lose the route or each other, as we did in Bristol two years before. Fortunately, we had detailed street maps, including the *Ordnance Survey Motoring Atlas.* I carried a color copy of the map page I was on in a plastic holder.

Within Glasgow, I followed the north bank of the River Clyde. I walked through the grounds of the Scottish Exhibition and Conference Center and then picked up the Loch Lomond bike path, which paralleled A814. Coming out of Glasgow the A814 didn't appear to have any kind of a shoulder, anyway, and it would have been almost impossible to walk on.

Sheltering trees often lined both sides of the bike path, creating a sense of isolation, and it is laid out so that it crosses few streets. Some bicyclists, dog walkers and children from nearby high-rise apartment buildings played on the path. Usually, I am not allowed to walk off-road, but since Bonny and I had agreed to meet in Old Kilpatrick I could pick my route to get there. I switched to the A814 at Clydebank and followed it to Old Kilpatrick, which is almost literally underneath the high-arching Erskine Bridge. After mid-afternoon it was T-shirt weather.

Meanwhile, Bonny had befriended the woman manager of an ice cream and sundry store in Old Kilpatrick, who invited her to have a drink and use the store telephone to call me on my cell phone and tell me where she was. We stayed at the Ibis Hotel in Glasgow.

<u>Sun., June 2; Old Kilpatrick to Balloch on A814, A82, A813 and A811—9 miles</u>. I walked on a lot of roads for only nine miles. I reached Balloch, at the south end of Loch Lomond, and finished the End-to-End at 11:30 a.m. It drizzled a little but never really rained. There were several routes I could have taken. I chose the one that went through Dumbarton and Bonhill, with a final short jog west to Balloch. I had previously reached Balloch on July 13, 1999, walking south from Northern Scotland. Appropriately, a McDonald's Restaurant had been built at my exact finish location in the intervening three years.

Bonny took the required pictures. We ate lunch in Balloch and I drank a celebratory beer, something I almost never do during the day. We strolled around the village, where we had been twice before (once with Andy and Ellen). We calculated that I walked 96 miles on this phase and 867 miles altogether. I walked for a total of 34.5 days, maintaining an average of 25 miles per day.

Alan Cook

AUTUMN WALK

The briskness of the autumn air reveals
the winds of winter following on its heels,
but I will walk with strong, unbroken stride
as long as you are walking by my side.

When we were young we ran and skipped and hopped
in breezes warm with love and only stopped
to sample kisses sweet with honeyed dew,
and there was no one in the world but you.

At times the road we trod was strewn with stones
of shadowy fears and boulders of unknowns,
but we marched on through mud and sucking sand,
as long as we were walking hand in hand.

It's autumn now, but we will still walk on,
from dawn to dusk, from dusk to glorious dawn.
Our love endures, our hearts will not grow old,
and we can't be frozen by the winter's cold.

ABOUT THE AUTHOR

Alan Cook has been an avid walker and traveler all his life and some of his more interesting walks and adventures are recounted in *Walking the World*. He also wrote *Walking to Denver*, a comic fictional version of his walk from Los Angeles to Denver. His two mysteries, *Thirteen Diamonds* and *Catch a Falling Knife*, feature senior-citizen sleuth Lillian Morgan, a former mathematics professor, who is smart, opinionated and skeptical of authority. He also wrote *Freedom's Light: Quotations from History's Champions of Freedom* and *The Saga of Bill the Hermit*, a narrative poem. Alan lives with his wife, Bonny, on a hill in Southern California. His website is alancook.50megs.com.